PUBLISH IT NOT...
The Middle East Cover-Up

PUBLISH IT NOT...
The Middle East Cover-Up

Michael Adams
&
Christopher Mayhew

Signal Books
Oxford

This edition published in 2006 by
Signal Books Limited
36 Minster Road
Oxford
OX4 1LY
www.signalbooks.co.uk

First published in 1975 by Longman Group Ltd
© Michael Adams and Christopher Mayhew, 1975
Foreword © Tim Llewellyn, 2006

All rights reserved. The whole of this work, including all text and illustrations, is protected by copyright. No parts of this work may be loaded, stored, manipulated, reproduced or transmitted in any form or by any means, electronic or mechanical, including photocopying and recording, or by any information, storage and retrieval system without prior written permission from the publisher, on behalf of the copyright owner.

A catalogue record for this book is available from the British Library

ISBN 1-904955-19-3 Paper

Cover Design: Baseline Arts
Cover Image: Nael Evans, CAABU
Typesetting: Donal Sheridan

Printed in England by Biddles Ltd., King's Lynn, Norfolk

To
John Reddaway

"Tell it not in Gath, publish it not in
the streets of Askelon;
lest the daughters of the Philistines rejoice . . ."
    (2 Samuel 1, xx)

CONTENTS

Foreword by Tim Llewellyn ❖ ix
Preface ❖ xxxvi
Introduction ❖ xl

PART ONE
Chapter One: A Personal Statement *by* Michael Adams ❖ 2
Chapter Two: A Personal Statement by Christopher Mayhew ❖ 17
Chapter Three: Political Pressures ❖ 29
Chapter Four: Personal Pressures ❖ 58
Chapter Five: Bias in the Media ❖ 76
Chapter Six: The Failure of the Churches ❖ 124

PART TWO
Chapter Seven; The October War and its Consequences ❖ 142
Chapter Eight: Can Israel Change Direction? ❖ 165
Chapter Nine: A New Look at the Future ❖ 194

APPENDICES
Appendix A: Article by Michael Adams in *The Guardian*,
15 June 1967 ❖ 212
Appendix B: Notices of Motion in the House of Commons,
23 March 1970 ❖ 214
Appendix C: Letter to *The Times*, 27 June 1969 ❖ 217
Appendix D: Letter to the Archbishop of Canterbury ❖ 219
Appendix E: Marion Woolfson's Testimony ❖ 221
Appendix F: Hidden Hands? By Shelby Tucker ❖ 235

Notes ❖ 241
Index ❖ 249

"All that is necessary for the triumph of evil is that good men do nothing."
    Edmund Burke

"I dislike the coercive methods of Zionists who in this country have not hesitated to use economic means to silence persons who have different views. I object to the attempts at character assassination of those who do not agree with them."
    Arthur Hays Sulzberger (*New York Times*, November 1946)

We are grateful to the following for permission to reproduce copyright material:
Author and author's agents for an extract from a talk given by Brian Magee which appeared in *The Listener* 19th March 1970. Reproduced by permission of A. D. Peters and Company; Mr. James Norris for two letters and Mr. Ian Trethowan for an extract from a letter.

FOREWORD
by Tim Llewellyn

No alien polity has so successfully penetrated the British government and British institutions during the past ninety years as the Zionist movement and its manifestation as the state of Israel. From the Balfour Declaration of November 2, 1917, in which the British Foreign Secretary said his government "view with favour the establishment in Palestine of a national home for the Jewish people," (before Britain had taken possession of Palestine from the Ottomans), through the twenty-six year history of Zionist exploitation of the British Mandate at Arab (and British) expense, to Britain's scuttle from Palestine in 1948 and the creation of Israel and the catastrophe for the Palestinians, and up to present-day connivance by the United Kingdom government with America's unremitting political and media support for Israel and its daily violation of international laws and conventions on Palestinian lands, the Zionists have manipulated British systems as expertly as maestros, here a massive major chord, there a minor refrain, the audience, for the most part, spellbound.

Some thirty-five years ago, the journalist, Michael Adams, and the Labour politician, Christopher Mayhew, made a unique and bold attempt to explain in writing this cuckoo in the nest of British politics. Both ardently supported a just solution of the Israeli-Palestinian struggle and were shrewd observers of the tactics of successive Israeli governments and their battalions of supporters to influence and suborn Britain's civil structures, including government, parliament and the press. They wrote *Publish it not...the Middle East Cover-Up* to set out for the public in graphic episodes of reportage and personal experience the restraints the Israelis and their friends and lobbyists were imposing on freedom of speech and action in this country. Both men suffered serious setbacks to their careers, a risk anyone in public life takes who dares to speak out against the machinations of the Israeli state, not only against the Palestinians it oppresses and abuses within its own borders, as well as in the occupied territories, but against any person or institution it reckons is standing in the way of Zionism's progress or interfering with the "correct" exposition of the Zionists' own very special versions of the past and the present.

When Adams and Mayhew wrote this book, in 1974 and 1975, they were in a hopeful mood, despite the litany of pressures, lies and dirty tricks they were recording and despite the almost unrestrained success with which Israel was going from strength to strength. The world, especially the West and most of all the United States, lay adoringly at its feet, supporting it at all costs, viewing it as a latter-day Sparta fighting against the odds, against the relentless hordes of the Arab and Islamic world.

The reason for the authors' optimism was that in 1973 this Israeli juggernaut had been, albeit temporarily, slowed down in what the Arabs call the October War and Israel the Yom Kippur War (the latter title having predictably caught on widely in the West). Hope seems to have stirred mightily in Michael Adams's breast as he wrote in his introduction to the book that Western public opinion had been seriously misinformed about the Middle East (which was true) and that the war—in which the Egyptians crossed the Suez Canal and the Arab Gulf states and Iran deployed the oil price weapon—"proved the critics' argument that if the Arabs were denied a just settlement in Palestine they would go to war to get one." It was the last time the Arab regimes were to deploy effectively any weapon, military or economic.

The two authors together wrote (in Chapter Nine), "Israel's capacity to survive [in the long-term] without making far-reaching concessions... seems very doubtful... Israel has established herself, and expanded her territories, on the basis of her dominant military power. But since October 1973 the balance of power has shifted significantly against Israel and the shift seems likely to continue in the same direction." Michael Adams (in Chapter Eight) thought that unless

Israel resolved the problems of occupation and second-class citizenship for Palestinians with Israeli citizenship, usually described in the West as "Israeli-Arabs", "the impression is likely to gain ground in the world that Israel in its present form is indeed a country without a future."

I take nothing from the dedication and expertise of these two men when I say that this showed how dangerous it was, and is, to indulge in wishful thinking about any early end to the inexorable progress of the state of Israel at the expense of its neighbours, no doubt, as Michael Adams seems to imply, eventually at its own expense and probable failure (but not just yet).

❖ ❖ ❖

After their book was published, Adams lived thirty more years and Mayhew twenty-two to see for themselves how misplaced that optimism was. In fact, neither writer had to wait anything like that long to see his hopeful prophesy begin to be undermined. Four years after the October War of 1973, two years after this book was published, President Sadat had made his ill-advised trip to Jerusalem—for once the overworked adjective "historic" is applicable—offering himself as an Arab hostage to Israeli fortune. Within another year, Egypt had traduced its Arab allies with the Camp David Accords, an American-supervised formula for a bilateral Egyptian peace with Israel. Against much Israeli resistance, these agreements were linked to a plan to give autonomy to the Occupied Palestinians of the West Bank, Gaza and East Jerusalem, and became in 1979 the first peace treaty between an Arab state and Israel. Israel, in return, gave Egypt back the Sinai peninsula, which it had seized in its 1967 blitzkrieg against its Arab neighbours. In other words, the Arab reward was to retrieve some of its own stolen property.

As it turned out, after much diplomatic fan-dancing and Israeli intransigence, the Palestinians got nothing.

Arab options in the confrontation with Israel were thus reduced to the diplomatic (and therefore ephemeral, given Israel's international clout), Egypt being the only Arab state that could pose any military threat of consequence; and the core of the Middle East conflict, the Palestinian problem, remained unresolved, as it does to this day.

Israel was quick to reassert itself. Three years after *Publish It Not* arrived on the book stalls, Israel invaded Lebanon and put surrogate Lebanese militiamen in control of a great swathe of the Lebanese South, with close Israeli army support. In 1982, Israel, with continued impunity, reinvested its presence in Lebanon dramatically and brutally, invading half the country, up to Beirut, killing seventeen thousand Lebanese and Palestinian civilians, and enabling a massacre by Lebanese Christian militiamen of up to a thousand undefended Palestinians and Lebanese in the Sabra-Shatila refugee camp in Beirut's southern suburbs, which Israeli forces had surrounded. Meanwhile, the Israelis continued to consolidate their hold on the occupied territories. In late 1982, they annexed Syria's Golan Heights, captured in 1967. By 1988 they had seized more than fifty per cent of West Bank and East Jerusalem lands and properties for Jewish settlements. In the late 1970s, Israel—now governed by the right-wing Likud Party, led by the former Jewish terrorist leader Menachem Begin—stepped up its interference in and intimidation of the Occupied West Bank and Gaza, alarmed by the growing popularity and power of local officials aligned with the Palestine Liberation Organisation. Operating with little or no restraint, Jewish underground gangs blew up and generally menaced democratically elected pro-PLO mayors. The Israeli occupation forces manipulated informers, quislings and Islamists to try to undermine the PLO, which was manifestly secular in those days. Israel's encouragement of Islamic groups was later to rebound with ominous consequences, both for Israelis and Palestinians. Short-term, tactical expediency has always been Israel's weakness.

The authors' optimism is the only misjudgement by Messrs Adams and Mayhew, and they are not the only ones, this author included, who have been tempted to see justice imminent. Many of us did so after the Gulf War of early 1991 and the Madrid peace conference later that year, when Israel was hauled to the conference

Foreword

tables with pro-PLO interlocutors and Syrians; again, flags were put out at the Oslo accords of 1993, when President Clinton drew Yasir Arafat and Yitzak Rabin into that awkward handshake on the White House lawn, Israel finally recognizing the Palestine Liberation Organisation and seeming to promise to make space for a viable Palestinian state on the West Bank and in Gaza and in Arab East Jerusalem in return for its own peace and security.

How we were fooled. How often we are still fooled. (How wry would have been the expressions on the faces of Michael Adams and Christopher Mayhew had they lived to see revealed, in August, 2005, that during the 1950s, British civil servants, without the knowledge of their political bosses, supplied Israel with the heavy water vital to its construction of nuclear weapons.)

So often, the Palestinians seem to make it, deals promised, just solutions dangled, their noses pressed to the window, their case made, as by the authors of this book and a thousand journalists, writers, aid workers, diplomats, United Nations officials and (some) sympathetic Western politicians. How inevitably are their aims and hopes undermined as *Realpolitik* is brought to bear in Washington, with Britain and the other Western states compliant, while the Israelis and their friends steal more land, destroy more futures and lives, and work to extinguish the Palestinian identity, even presence, in the Holy Land.

The essence of this book is to show how some of these Zionist deceptions were accomplished in the United Kingdom, how it *was* done being not so very different from how it *still is* done. Much has changed since the 1950s, 1960s and 1970s, the authors' main spells of duty. Some aspects of life with the Zionists have changed for the better, many more for the worse. Substantially, the plight of the Palestinians, the militaristic arrogance and aggression of the Israelis, their comrades and cronies, the subservience to Israel of the United States and its ever-amenable allies in the West, and the pusillanimity and weakness of the Arab states are more pronounced than ever. When Adams and Mayhew wrote there was at least the space for a Palestinian state and hints of even-handedness in the international community; the Palestinian movement was taking its place as a political force in the region;

international reporting was improving; politicians were waking up to the facts; Arab states seemed to be mobilizing.

Now, I am afraid I would have to tell the two writers were they able to hear me that the forces they so bravely resisted are stronger than ever.

❖ ❖ ❖

I first went to the Middle East, to Beirut, for the BBC in June, 1974, the year the authors started their book. Like many, perhaps most, of my generation of correspondents and other interested visitors I arrived with the lightly slung baggage of someone who had bought vaguely into the Zionist myth: that Israel was a beleaguered democracy fighting bravely to defend a social democratic system against the massed Arab regimes, all sworn to destroy the little state.

Reading *Publish it not* after a lifetime in the Middle East, I realize why in those days we swallowed all this. Israel had worked its spells well, with a lot of help from its friends: these lined the benches of parliament, wrote the news stories and editorials, framed the way we saw and heard almost everything about the Middle East on TV, radio and in the press. History, the Bible, Nazi Germany's slaughter of the Jews, Russian pogroms, the Jewish narrative relayed and parlayed through a thousand books, films, TV plays and series, radio programmes, the skills of Jewish writers, diarists, memoirists, artists and musicians, people like us and among us, all had played their part. As Christopher Mayhew writes in Chapter Five, the bias in broadcasting was (and still is) "a true reflection of our cultural prejudices, which are founded on half-remembered and inaccurate impressions of the Old Testament, the Crusades, the era of British colonialism, and most of all by our sense of guilt over the way we Europeans have behaved... towards the Jews."

Before I started reporting on the Middle East, pro-Israeli bias in British institutional life had been deep and wide, as the authors here elaborate. The Labour Party identified closely with Israel. Harold Wilson, Prime Minister from 1964 to 1970 and again in the mid-1970s, was a dedicated, uncritical Zionist. (Israel rewarded him with his own personal forest.) Soon after he left office in 1970, he delivered a speech in Israel attacking Resolution 242, the United Nations Security Council resolution of 1967, *conceived and drafted by his own British government's diplomats and ministers*, which called on Israel to relinquish the occupied territories. Two-Four-Two was and is the internationally accepted basis for any just settlement of the Arab-Israeli struggle. It is hard to imagine even Tony Blair, in or out of office, challenging Resolution 242 in front of an Israeli audience, inside Israel or anywhere else.

The Labour parliamentary back benches of the post-war years contained a claque of vociferously pro-Zionist MPs, red in tooth and claw, shouting down anyone who spoke up for the Arabs inside the House of Commons or out, a "dominating influence… in the Labour Party," writes Christopher Mayhew in Chapter Three. He tells hair-raising stories in this revealing chapter of this Labour Party tradition: how a British Defence Minister gave permission to Haganah, the illegal Jewish army in Mandatory Palestine, through the medium of a Zionist Labour MP, to blow up bridges between Palestine and Jordan; how, in 1944, the Labour Party National Executive Committee advocated officially the transfer of Palestinian Arabs from what was to become Israel: "Let the Arabs be encouraged to move out as the Jews move in," said the Party's ruling body.

Mayhew speaks of the "relentless way in which those of us who choose to speak up for the Arabs have been harassed by our opponents." This would not happen now, on either side of the House, and the fervent Zionist Labour MPs, some of them little better than bully-boys, Richard Crossman (not a Jew), Ian Mikardo, Maurice Edelman, Emmanuel "Manny" Shinwell, Sidney Silverman, Konni Zilliacus *et al*, are, mercifully, not only no longer with us but have not been replaced, not in such virulent form.

Labour now boasts a hard-working array of MPs who work for justice in the Middle East, though Parliament is not without its troubles. The Liberal-Democrats showed extraordinary cowardice in removing from their Front Bench one of their best MPs, Jenny Tonge, in 2004, when she tried to explain in personal terms how she could understand what might motivate a suicide bomber. In this twisted and fearful world of trying to deal with Israel, explanation becomes support, and analysis encouragement, or even incitement.

But the improvement in Parliament is almost irrelevant. The pro-Zionists are more polite, and the Arabs have more effective friends; the balance is better. But how much does Parliament matter? The executive behaves as it likes, independent of parliamentary influence and more and more in the clutch of the Prime Minister's cabal of advisers and cronies and therefore Washington (the Foreign Office, where real expertise lies, has largely been sidelined). Successive British governments have claimed to see and want to treat Palestine-Israel differently from the way the Americans do, but rarely if ever defy the United States in this arena. Their influence, whether unilaterally or through Europe, remains minimal, and a drag on more progressive attitudes inside the European Union, in France, Italy, Greece and Spain for example.

Not all the actions taken against anti-Zionists were verbal, written or the subtle behind-the-scenes rearrangement of diplomatic and political furniture in the Israeli interest. In Chapter Four, Christopher Mayhew describes the disgraceful personal and physical attacks on Marion Woolfson, the eminent Jewish Scottish journalist who has for so long fought against the machinations of the Israeli lobby and opposed the concept of a Jewish state; and the arson and other crippling *attentats* on a printing business in South Wales that dared to print pro-Palestinian leaflets and the respected specialist journal founded in 1971 by Michael Adams, Mayhew and Anthony Nutting (a former Foreign Office Minister and Arabist), *Middle East International*, which was until recently, when funds ran out, one of the few reliable British sources of news from the region.

It is arguable that such crude manifestations of Zionist anger are no longer necessary, though suspicions remain deep in the British-Arab community and its associates that Israel, often through its embassy, is by no means averse to more deeply played dirty tricks, putting into foul play its Intelligence arms and their close associations with western spy networks. The drugging and kidnapping of the unfortunate Mordechai Vanunu, the man who revealed in detail the scale of Israel's nuclear weapons programme, is one such case.

Michael Adams and Christopher Mayhew would be both amused and depressed to see how the Israeli lobby recycles old myths, canards about Palestinians and Arabs and explanations of the very creation of Israel that were refuted many years ago. Israel's apologists are not afraid or embarrassed to repeat untruths, despite the fact that its own historians, Avi Shlaim, Illan Pappe, Tom Segev and the Palestinian-Israeli Nur Mashala, to name but four, have torn to tatters the fabric of lies and half-truths. (It was Benny Morris who first broke new ground by revealing the truth of the origins of the Palestinian refugees, and their largely forced expulsion in 1948, but he has to be distinguished from his fellow "new historians" since his retrospective approval of ethnic cleansing by the Zionists, and his observations that the dispossession of the Arab Palestinians in 1948 had not been comprehensive enough.) One old favourite that in late 2003 I heard one of the Israeli Embassy's apparatchiks spouting to an audience of university students (who knew he was telling lies) was that in April 1948 Arab leaders, through Arabic-language radio stations, had urged Palestinians to leave Palestine. The reality is that Arab leaders urged exactly the opposite. Walid Khalidi, perhaps Palestine's most eminent historian and scholar, tapped and exposed this for the lie that it was in 1959, and the Irish writer, Erskine Childers, corroborated Professor Khalidi's findings in 1961. Both men had scoured Arabic newspapers and BBC/American radio monitoring of the time and found that not only had Arab and Palestinian leaders made no calls for the Palestinians to leave, but had urged them to stay and had, in some cases, played down Jewish forces' atrocities so as not to alarm the Arab population.

It remains absolutely imperative to the Zionists' case to this day that the Palestinians left of their own volition. In this way, their more vital case that they must never be allowed to return carries more conviction. What Adams and Mayhew, then, and I, now, are concerned about is not that the Zionists still make this case, however spurious, but that so many politicians and journalists in the West still swallow it.

Other distortions have entered the lexicon of Middle East discussion and go unchallenged by the careless or innocent who discuss the problem. In mid-2005 I heard yet again an Israeli government official tell the BBC that the Arabs attacked Israel in June 1967. He went unchallenged. As anyone who has cared to study the facts has known since the evening of June 5 1967, Israel on that morning attacked and won the war against Egypt, Syria, Jordan and the Palestinians in six fighting days. Israel can argue that it was provoked and threatened; but it was not attacked. Similarly, in October 1973, when the Egyptians crossed the Suez Canal into Sinai and the Syrians went into the Golan Heights they were not attacking Israel as such, they were trying to reclaim lands they had lost to Israel in 1967. Israel's helpers explain the invasion of Lebanon in June 1982 as a response to PLO terrorism launched across the Lebanese border, though there had been a cross-border ceasefire brokered by Saudi Arabia and the United States in place for nine months. It all goes towards presenting Israel as the aggressed, menaced, vulnerable entity in the region, a concept the West, and especially the Americans, largely accept.

It works well. Even the "right of return", the Palestinian refugees' absolute and internationally legal right to go back to their homes, is re-worked into the language of paranoid persecution, "throwing the Jews into the sea." In February 2005, a BBC news presenter, interviewing a reporter in Jerusalem, threw a question at him in this form: "And there are still plenty of people who want to see Israel wiped off the face of the earth?" The reporter replied, "There are, led by Hamas…" The language is provocative and loosely stated and while it is true that many Arabs would like to see Israel gone, most of them, including Hamas, have repeatedly shown that they know in practical terms this is not a possibility, and most of them have no urge to "throw Jews into the sea."

Were the question ever asked, "is it not the case that Israel has very nearly wiped Palestine off the face of the earth and is proceeding successfully towards that end?" the presenter might find himself the object of harsh criticism inside and outside the BBC. The lobby has not only altered our language but our innate attitudes.

Another myth constantly recycled in the face of historical evidence is that had the Arab armies not invaded Israel the day after the state was proclaimed on May 14, 1948, the Palestinians would have been able to stay safely in their homes and the UN partition plan dividing Palestine neatly into Arab-governed and Jewish-governed entities would have proceeded harmoniously. This ignores the fact that by mid-April, in fighting that had gone on between Arabs and Jews since November, 1947, up to a half the Palestinians had fled their homes, usually under the most harsh threats and physical attacks. The massacre by the members of two Jewish terrorist gangs (Irgun Zwei Leumi and the Lehi, or Stern Gang) of more than one hundred Palestinian civilians in Deir Yassin, a small and defenceless village in West Jerusalem, happened on April 9, 1948. It was hailed by such luminaries as the Irgun leader and future Israeli Prime Minister, Menachem Begin, as a prime mover in flushing the nascent Zionist state free of Arabs. In case anyone wishes to pass this off as an aberration by terrorists, an elite brigade of the nascent Israeli army, Palmach, played a part in the massacre. Indeed, terrorizing Arabs out of Palestine was, at best, or worst, depending on how one sees it, a much-needed plank in the Zionist plan for the region, whether part of a long-term plan or a bonus end-product of an upheaval that matched schooled and skilled militias and battle-hardened Jews against a badly organized and basically agricultural community; well-organized and well-armed fighters with air power against a motley of ill-trained Arab armies, all of them subject to weapons embargoes and, in the case of the only decent fighting force, the Jordanian Legion, British and Zionist manipulation.

The Palestinians and the Arabs never stood a chance; but the casual reader would never know it, thanks to the deft manipulations of the truth by Israel and its many and powerful supporters.

Michael Adams and Christopher Mayhew ask (and reveal): who perpetuates these historical misunderstandings, thus prolonging and intensifying the imbalance in the Middle East?

The answer remains, the Zionist lobby in all it devious forms. Since 1975, when the authors went into print, the official and institutional ranks of the Zionists in Britain have mounted and continue to mount campaigns of disinformation that dwarf their efforts of thirty and forty years ago. The parliamentary Zionist bullies of the Labour Party of the 1950s and 1960s have faded away, but the work goes on, less obviously but much more effectively, not just in selling the Israeli package to the ordinary British people but also in changing the nature of British Jews' perceptions of themselves and their relationship to Israel. Or, to put it another way, Israel's alleged centrality in the life of a British Jew.

Organizations such as the British Israel Communications and Research Centre (BICOM) have hundreds of thousands of pounds at their disposal, much of it coming directly from the United States, which sends a third of its whole, global foreign aid budget to Israel's six million citizens (the real figure, including loan guarantees, tax breaks for charities and defence deals, could be as high as $10,000m annually, a sum which puts well into perspective last year's USAID contribution of $8,800,000 to India's population of 1,100m. Or, well over $1,500 *per capita* for Israelis, about $8.00 for an Indian).

This great flow of funds bypasses most ordinary Israeli citizens and poor and needy Jews in Israel and elsewhere and goes straight to the projection of Zionist causes and colonialism wherever it might be needed. These funds prop up, here in the United Kingdom, not just BICOM, but organizations such as Labour Friends of Israel, close to the heart of Tony Blair, the Jewish Agency (whose *raison de vivre* is to get as many Jews as possible to go to Israel), the World Zionist Organisation, Paoli Zion, a Labour Party affiliate, and the Council of Christians and Jews, which keeps the Church of England leadership at Lambeth Palace in close self-restraint about Israel's crimes against Christians and Christian institutions.

There are many more. One is the Union of Jewish Students, which elbows and induces Zionistically inclined undergraduates towards influential positions in British public life, especially the media, the banking sector and information technology.

Perhaps the most long-standing and egregious of these organizations, dating back to the early nineteenth century, when

Zionism had still to be invented, is the Board of Deputies of British Jews. This influential lobby of the Zionist Great and Good is an important example of how Israel is working its magic here. Originally, the Board would have looked after Jews and Jewish interests. After all, it does not, as it claims, represent British Jewry; it represents Jews who attend synagogues and are members of Jewish institutions, and vote for the Board's content, which means, in effect less than half of the roughly quarter of a million Jews in the United Kingdom.

What has happened to the Board and is happening throughout Jewish institutions here is that they are more and more being identified not with the interests of their own people here, and with Jewishness and the religion of Judaism as such, but those of the Zionist movement and therefore of Israel. What has changed since *Publish it not* came out thirty years ago is that the aim of these institutions is to make Jewish interest synonymous with the Israeli interest. This happens in many ways, in parochial education, free trips to Israel, paid-for "gap" years or months with the Israeli Army for Jewish students—the emphasis is not on Judaism, it is on Zionism.

Soon after the Aqsa Intifada started in 2000, and led us, whomever we like to blame, into the gory business of a low-intensity war between Israel and the Palestinians, Israel realized quickly and rightly that its massive military assault on the Arabs, and its negation of the principles of Palestinian self-rule leading to independence, might be misconstrued in the West, and it might suffer a public relations crisis similar to that of 1982, when Ariel Sharon launched his invasion of Lebanon and the resultant slaughter. The American Israeli Public Affairs Committee, a high-powered outfit that has great, some would say a decisive, say in American arms of government, legislature and opinion, and has no such ironclad and aggressive equivalent in Britain, came to London to advise BICOM. The message was clear: be aggressive; pester and menace the media and the politicians in all their forms; go to court; never let up; let no adverse image or mention of Israel go unchallenged, however true, however perceived. In a word, the only story is our story: make sure everyone knows that.

If Adams and Mayhew had been appalled at the Zionist intrusions they suffered in the 1950s, 1960s and 1970s, they would have been paralysed by the sheer aggression of the Zionist movement here, especially concerning the media after 2000 and the success it achieved with its tactics, aided and enhanced beyond the Israeli government's wildest dreams by the combination of Palestinian ineptness, Arab governments' pusillanimity, the attack on America by Osama Bin Laden's agents in September 2001 and the invasions of Afghanistan and Iraq in the "War on Terrorism". For Israel's government and Zionist lobbies the first five years of the Millennium could have been made to order.

The Israelis and their friends fight fiercely, expertly and without quarter. Nowhere is this more true than with the press and broadcasters. Michael Adams, with deserved asperity, writes well and widely about this. When he was writing for the mainstream British press in the 1960s the dice were loaded against anyone trying to tell the truth about Israel's actions in Arab lands, particularly in the euphoric aftermath of the 1967 war. Israel had triumphed over its Arab neighbours, seizing much Arab territory, much of the most vital of which, in Syria and Palestine, it retains to this day nearly forty years later, and shows no sign of relinquishing. One of Adams's stories about Israeli excesses after the war, the destruction of three Arab villages near Jerusalem for allegedly strategic reasons (see Chapter Five), was suppressed by *The Guardian*; in the end he was left no choice but to withdraw his services from the newspaper (the editor, Alistair Hetherington, had taken the words of his pro-Israel friends in high places over those of the newspaper's own reporter). *The Guardian* was not the newspaper it is today.

The BBC was in the late 1960s and early 1970s as bad, if not worse: patronizing or just plain misreporting the Arabs in general and the Palestinians in particular, and tipping the balance in favour of pro-Israeli views and commentators, its presenters and editors in London more at fault than the reporters in the field. The BBC, then as now, was deft at defending itself with stonewall claims of "balance" and "fairness", as perceived in the corridors and boardrooms of Broadcasting House, advising those who rang or wrote to complain that their communications were most welcome and their views logged—in effect, "Thank you and good night." At the BBC, all was and is for the best in the best of all BBC worlds. It was to be many years after *Publish it not* that the Arabs and their supporters started to emulate their opponents' ability to reach inside the BBC, to know the individual programme editor or line manager or producer or board member or senior manager, his home address and home and extension numbers, a process the book's two authors set in train when they and others like-minded founded the Council for the Advancement of Arab-British Understanding (CAABU) and took the fight to the Zionists, albeit with a fraction of the funding and support

Michael Adams might have been excused in 1975 for optimism about the press and broadcasting, to whose practitioners he set such a brave example. Media attitudes were changing. When I arrived in Beirut in the mid-1970s the foreign press corps there were being forced to absorb the Palestinian story at first hand—from guerrillas and their leaders, refugees, students, academics, local newspapermen, agency reporters and photographers, editors, businessmen, financiers, and bank clerks, Arab diplomats and dissident floaters from the far shores of the Arab world. In the 1970s, as they fought for their survival in Lebanon and for a place contiguous with Israel, from where they could attack it and try to re-enter it, the Palestinians practically ran Beirut. No-one approved of everything the Palestinian movement and its members did, and many disapproved publicly of much; the press corps had its rows with the PLO and its apparatchiks; but at least it heard and took in the Palestinian narrative and communicated it to the outside world (much to Israel's distress).

In what I look back on as a Golden Age of Middle East reporting, Western news bureaux in Beirut, Cairo and Amman, with access to Baghdad and Damascus, helped the world see the Arabs' and Palestinians' situations through their own prisms, while in no way falling into the trap of blindly admiring the Arab regimes or falling for the blandishments of their politicians. The difference between those who reported the Arab world and many of those who in Adams's day sat in Jerusalem and Tel Aviv was that we were critical and challenged what we were told, often to our cost. Most of us had far more trouble from the Arab governments and even from their murderous agents than we did from the Israelis.

In Israel itself, in the years after the Mayhew-Adams book, the Western media began seriously to reshape their Middle East coverage. Many of the most influential British news organizations removed their often locally bred Zionist reporters who had done such a selective job in reporting their country from the 1950s onwards, and replaced them with outsiders. I found myself both in Israel and the Arab world among journalists of many nationalities, European, American, Commonwealth, who had arrived in the Middle East with many of the same pro-Israeli corpuscles in their veins as I had had in 1974 only to find that a few weeks in Israel, or viewing its government's or army's behaviour as it were from over the fence, turned them into horrified witnesses of the Israeli state's aggression and acquisitiveness, often to the bafflement of their less well-informed and more brainwashed producers. Many of these Western reporters were Jews from America, Canada, Britain and France; but they were not Zionists and, had they been so inclined, became rapidly less so watching Israel at first hand.

The BBC never, in all the twenty-five years I reported or commentated for them from or about the Middle East, ten of those years as Middle East staff correspondent based in the region, interfered with the gist of my analysis or the facts of my reporting. Most of my colleagues in ITV and the British print media would have acknowledged much the same forbearance. We reported vividly and honestly on such campaigns as the two Israeli invasions of Lebanon, the occupation of south Lebanon, the massacres that followed the invasion in 1982 and 1983, the first uprising, or *Intifada*, in 1987, and the dismal saga of the West Bank and Gaza, where Jewish settlers were commandeering more and more Palestinian land and water and terrorizing the inhabitants with Israeli army support, and had encircled and dominated most of Arab East Jerusalem, a process which is accelerating, widening, deepening and consolidating nearly twenty years later.

Foreword

For all this candid journalism from inside Israel and outside, few positive results accrued, or, if they did, as in the early 1980s, they were quickly reversed and negated. As the ardent Palestinian activist and author Dr. Ghada Karmi remarked so tellingly in a public meeting in London some years ago, the Palestinian narrative seems perpetually to be processed by a faulty computer. The stories of 1948, 1967, refugees, routs, assassinations and massacres, Tel al-Zaatar, Beirut 1982, Sabra-Shatila, the *Intifadas*, the breaking of bones, Jenin, Nablus and Hebron, land seizures and apartheid measures, the Separation Wall, which acquires for Israel yet more Palestinian territory and separates scores of thousands more Palestinians from their own lands and livelihood—all are told and highlighted on the screens to great acclaim and shock but then "automatically deleted". The Jewish narrative persists and is hammered home in all its aspects; the Israelis deploy history, or often "history", ancient and modern in their cause and do so relentlessly; the Holocaust is brandished as if it had somehow been a Palestinian responsibility or an excuse to defy international laws, morals and norms; money intended for Holocaust survivors is cynically diverted in the billions of dollars to furthering Zionism's aims and claims, especially *vis-à-vis* Arab lands. In contrast, the Palestinian tale limps along, disappearing from political notice if not public memory as Israel reasserts its influence or, sadly, the Palestinians fail to capitalize on their own strengths or yield to their organizational weaknesses.

In late 1990, for instance, Yasir Arafat vitiated three years of the Palestinian uprising and the truths it had revealed to the world by appearing to throw in his lot with Saddam Hussein. A few years later, with the United States putting pressure on Israel to make a proper peace, the Israelis outmanoeuvred everyone by escaping down the Oslo route to continued colonization of the Occupied Territories. Yasir Arafat was an author of this doomed process as well.

When I think of how hard so many honest journalists have worked to set the Israeli-Palestinian record straight in the fifty years since Michael Adams and Christopher Mayhew broke new ground and their own professional backs doing it, I realize how little effect it has all had on our political leaders. They meander through the thickets of the Middle East, displaying either ignorance or indecision, helpless against the power and prejudices of the United States and its subservience to Israel and Israeli interests. This phenomenon Michael Adams perceived early in his career and railed against, almost in despair, throughout his life.

Perhaps this can be written off as political reality—regrettable and short-sighted, but the way of a cruel world. This should not, however, be the case with British TV and radio, who are constitutionally bound by their charters and conditions to provide the British (and overseas) public with fair and properly balanced coverage. Both BBC and ITN (though not Channel 4 News) fail in their duties here, and the most important of these is the BBC, to which the majority of British people turn for their understanding of what is happening in world affairs.

Michael Adams was having trouble with the BBC nearly forty years ago. In Chapter Five, which present-day critics of the BBC will read with a wearying sense of *déjà vu*, Michael Adams and Christopher Mayhew record how in the 1960s research into programmes such as *The World At One* (and research into the *Today Programme* last summer and autumn reveals similar results) showed that the BBC gave far more time to pro-Israeli spokesmen and pro-Israeli views than it did to the pro-Arabs or to Arab perceptions. Mayhew makes one most telling point about bias, still true of the BBC, especially its main domestic radio and TV channels. He writes, after a meeting with the then Director-General of the BBC, Charles Curran, to discuss Middle East coverage:

> ...too little thought had been given to the distinction between conscious and unconscious bias. Most of the [BBC] company [appeared to have] the naïve belief that they or their staff would be charged with deliberate bias... they had not studied, and were not alert to, the serious problem, which was that of unconscious bias.
>
> Second, it was plain that no serious attempt had ever been made to analyse the Corporation's Middle East output from the point of view of "balance"; and no clear directive had been issued about the meaning of "balance" in this context.

Incredibly, more than thirty years on, the BBC is making yet another effort to study these problems but seems after a year or so of research to be none the wiser or better. At a recent meeting I attended with the head of BBC news, the head of radio news and the BBC's new Middle East editorial supervisor it was evident that, publicly at least, they could not see what was wrong with the corporation's coverage, its failure to report properly on the continuing misery of the Palestinians; the preponderance of pro-Israeli views and condescending if not hostile attitudes on the part of studio presenters and reporters to the Arabs; the failure to recount accurately the cycle of cause and effect in the deadly struggle between a sophisticated, high-technology state war machine and a primitively armed occupied population, between the oppressor and the oppressed; the reluctance to accept that most of the time it is Israeli actions—deliberate provocations—that shatter periods of calm; the use of lurid language to describe Palestinian attacks and atrocities as compared with the bland and anonymous language ("targeted killings", for example, "security fence", instead of "illegal assassinations" and "Separation and Enclosure Wall") deployed to portray Israel's excesses; the BBC's rarely alluding to the basic fact that the "the territories" are militarily occupied, and the lands therein continuously being expropriated from their rightful owners, which is illegal under the Fourth Geneva Convention and the UN Charter and in the eyes and judgments of all reputable and independent international bodies.

In the very phrase "Arab-Israeli dispute" organizations like the BBC continue to imply that this is some age-old quarrel over lands that goes back into the mists of time, like that of Owen Glyndwr and Edward Mortimer in the English-Welsh borderlands of the fourteenth century. In fact, the "Arab-Israeli dispute" is much simpler than that and something with which the British should be familiar: settler-colonialists stealing the lands and stamping on the rights of the indigenous people.

In effect, the mainstream media refuse to report the struggle for what it is: for Palestinian freedom, pledged by the British and the League of Nations more than eighty years ago, and against colonialism and dispossession.

I have little room for detail here. These fault lines in the BBC's and ITV's coverage have, however, been detailed in many journals and books, the best being the scientific study done by Greg Philo and Mike Berry of the Glasgow University Media Group, *Bad News From Israel* (Pluto Press, 2004), but also, *inter alia*, by researchers and writers at Arab Media Watch (www.arabmediawatch.com), by myself in various talks and newspaper articles (in *The Guardian* and *The Observer*) and in a chapter in *Tell Me Lies: Propaganda and Media Distortion in the Attack on Iraq*, edited by David Miller and also published in paperback by Pluto (2004), and by the indefatigable Paul de Rooij, to name but a few of the many who draw the BBC's misrepresentation of the Palestinian-Israeli issue to the attention of its policy-makers and editors.

The problems lie not so much in specific BBC or ITV documentaries or current affairs specials, which have on occasion acquitted themselves well, though they, with time to take care and exercise more judgment, are often as guilty as the news programmes; it is the news bulletins and daily analyses, with their continuing, seemingly endemic negative thrust as regards the Palestinians, their deference to the "authority" of Israel and its functionaries and their teams' failure to base their understanding of the story on the root cause of the conflict—the Palestinians' right to self-determination rather than Israel's security. All this does much to malign and undermine the Arab case. As Mayhew says, this is unconscious rather than conscious bias, something in the British soul creeping to the surface, out of our upbringing and our history and our view of "the other". This is also evident in insidious self-censorship, in which a reporter senses a way of pre-empting the anxiety of his bosses or the ire of the Israelis or both by crafting his story in a bland and therefore misleading manner: "Land *which the Palestinians say* is occupied..."; "disputed" instead of "occupied" territories, a phrase that still crops up on the BBC, though the circumlocution is legally and morally indefensible; the misrepresentation of the numbers of Jewish settlers on the West Bank and in Jerusalem; the failure to get into the public British consciousness the nature of the vast Separation and Enclosure Wall Israel is building around and into Palestinian territory, dividing and isolating its people and further damaging their already enfeebled economy.

This is still called by the BBC "a security barrier", conjuring up in the viewer's or listener's mind the image of a temporary structure the local police might put up to fence off a crime scene or to deter football hooligans.

This is all the more tragic because I know that British broadcasters reformed their attitudes in the twenty-five years or so between *Publish it not* and the year 2000. I can remember but one serious instance, in 1988, when the Israelis were pestering my foreign news editor to water down the BBC's coverage of a riot on the Haram al-Sharif in Jerusalem (one of Islam's holiest sites, known incorrectly as the Temple Mount). He cracked, understandably, and tried, unsuccessfully, to get me to insert an Israeli denial into the text of my story, which would have meant me contradicting my eye-witness account. What other efforts against me, if any, the Israelis deployed I never knew and, apart from a few very minor incidents, during a quarter-century reporting the Middle East I was unaware of any internal pressures. None of my BBC colleagues complained either.

What has changed since 2000 is worth examining.

With the failure of the Oslo peace process and the effective collapse of the two-state enterprise in 2000, at Camp David under the auspices of Bill Clinton, the subsequent outbreak two months later of what is now known among Palestinians as the *Aqsa Intifada*, after the Aqsa mosque on the Haram al-Sharif, where it began, and the disproportionately brutal response by Israel's armed forces, the Israelis were immediately aware that their reputation was in danger of attracting the same sort of international opprobrium it suffered during and after the 1982 Lebanon invasion and massacre at Sabra-Shatila and during the first *Intifada* of the late 1980s.

They deployed massive resources through their London embassy, using friends and lobbyists to cajole and put political and moral pressure on institutions like the BBC, it being much easier to do so now that most of the world's media had based their Middle East news offices and residences inside West (*de facto* Israeli) Jerusalem. The

Israelis there leaned hard on reporters and bureau chiefs. In London, they peppered producers and editors with pro-Israeli propaganda, complaints, suggestions for stories and schmoozing lunches, the cocktails flavoured with menace. One experienced Middle East correspondent told me that a *Today Programme* producer once rang him in the BBC Jerusalem office to get him to follow up a story-line suggested by the Israeli Embassy. There can be little doubt that such suggestions multiplied when, in late 2000, the BBC sent a new and inexperienced team of reporters to Jerusalem.

The events of September 11, 2001, the suicide bombs, the campaign against and invasion of Iraq all helped colour British broadcasters' view of the world, reinforcing their readiness to see the "savagery" of the Arabs and to recognize and exaggerate the allegedly aggressive militancy of Islam. The BBC's leaders tried hard to resist the attacks by Tony Blair and his henchmen, led by Alistair Campbell, on its Iraq war coverage in 2003, but were cruelly defeated by the whitewash of Tony Blair's spin doctors and their nefarious works in the lead-up to the invasion of Iraq war by Lord Hutton, the establishment-embraced Conservative Ulster judge, in 2004. Lord Hutton seemed to have heard only the evidence of the government's apologists, and the BBC took the blame for its reporting of Iraq and the circumstances surrounding it.

This induced new levels of nervousness in the Corporation and heightened caution in any dealings with the Middle East and Arabs. The BBC Governors and Board of Management were especially worried about licence fee levels and BBC Charter renewal. It showed in the reporting of Israel-Palestine. Dr. Karmi's faulty computer was in play again. As after Lebanon in 1982, the *Intifada* of 1987-91, the Baruch Goldstein massacre of Arab worshippers at the Mosque of Ibrahim in Hebron in 1994, the assaults against Ramallah, Hebron, Jenin, Nablus and the Occupied Territories from 2000 onwards, the Palestinian story was being deleted, or at least misrepresented. The BBC's appointment in 2005 of a Middle East Editor based in London, a new post provoked by the myriad complaints that flow daily into the Corporation about its lacklustre Middle East coverage, might help put its reporting back into proper balance; then again, it might not. Michael Adams and Christopher Mayhew would share my scepticism.

Meanwhile, we read our responses from the Corporation with the same disbelief at its obtuseness as Mayhew did when he received this, after a complaint of pro-Israeli leanings to *The World At One* in late 1973 from Jim Norris, Assistant Secretary and Head of Secretariat, the then Director-General's powerful minder and trouble-shooter: "….journalists doing an honest job in this country have to take account of the fact that Israeli or Zionist public relations are conducted with a degree of sophistication which those on the other side have rarely matched… an accurate reflection of publicly expressed attitudes on the issue may well inevitably reveal at times a preponderance of sympathy for the Israeli side." In other words, says Mayhew, "the BBC should not concern itself with striking a balance between the arguments for the Israeli viewpoint and the arguments for the Arab viewpoint, but should reflect the greater power of the Israeli lobby."

I doubt that the BBC of the early twenty-first century would be so openly crass. But the way it reports the Palestinian-Israeli struggle does just what Norris suggested, reflecting the view of the strong over the weak, the state over the non-state, the possessor over the dispossessed. Any righting of the balance, or trying also to see the story through the Palestinian viewfinder, a senior BBC executive told me in 2005, "would be to make the BBC into campaigning journalists." In other words, in the BBC's view, reporting the Palestinian story the way it is amounts to "campaigning".

In institutional broadcasting there is a climate of fear. Executives do not like to be accused of anti-Semitism, which is the ready-to-hand smear the Zionists and their friends have available if they think Israel is receiving a tough press.

Journalists and their bosses do not like to be harangued. They like a quiet life. They know how influential the lobby is and how well-placed are its agents in and around government and business and in the ranks of the good and the great. They want their institution to survive. In this noble cause the truth about a sensitive issue may have to go hang for a while. The BBC's duty to report honestly, as it did, say, in South Africa twenty years ago or Bosnia in the 1990s, is sacrificed on the altar of the Corporation's survival. The suits circle the wagons. The protection of the institution comes first, before its primary duty of honest reporting, rather as the United States armed forces deem "force protection"—safeguarding their own soldiers' lives at all costs—a higher duty than the security of those around them.

Just as Michael Adams was "disappeared" from mainstream Middle East reporting, so was I from the BBC. After a three-part series I wrote and narrated for Radio 4 and the World Service in 1998, *My Land Is Your Land*, the Israelis and their supporters launched a massive write-in at and to all levels of the BBC complaining about my interpretation of the state of Israel's creation in 1948, the accompanying catastrophe (*nakba*) of the Palestinians and the fifty years that had followed. When I put up a further programme, a BBC commissioning editor was heard to say at a meeting that I was "*parti-pris*", a libellous statement to make about a professional journalist with nearly thirty years BBC service under his belt. After I joined CAABU, the Israeli lobby put enormous pressure on the Corporation either not to use me at all as a commentator/reporter or to spell out on my every appearance the fact that I was on the board of CAABU. This made me appear as a propagandist; the awkward nomenclature was too long for presenters to cope with; gradually I slipped from the scene, my work as a TV/radio broadcaster virtually over.

I then found out in 2002 that BBC management had circulated a memorandum to all producers and editors that if I ever appeared it was never to be mentioned that I had ever been the BBC's Middle East Correspondent, in case my views were associated with those of the BBC. This, together with my growing indignation at BBC Middle East coverage and the general desuetude of public service broadcasting, softened the blow of my departure from the scene. I was luckier than Michael Adams, who was ten years younger than me when the Zionists put the fatal squeeze on him at the very height of his powers.

❖ ❖ ❖

We are back where we were before Adams and Mayhew wrote their book in 1974/5. In fact, the situation is worse; we are further back. Despite what I see as a long and healthy intervening period of honest—well, honestly attempted—coverage of the Middle East between the early 1970s and the end of the millennium, and signs that Britain's political establishment and the public were beginning to take notice of the region's realities, the Israelis have shown us their enormous powers of recovery and their extraordinary ability to exert their weight on British governance and institutions, twisting arms until our leaders cry "'nuff" and comply.

Against the odds, the years of good reporting and the continued efforts of a few serious newspapers and journals, the web, and a handful of outspoken honest politicians and others in public life, monitors, aid workers, international activists, have brought a massive shift in British public opinion to support of Palestinian freedom and a solution just to both sides. Adams and Mayhew and all of us would welcome this as a worthwhile result of our and their efforts. But it is not enough by a long shot. This shift in public opinion has made little impact on Britain's political leaders and the chiefs of its most influential institutions. They continue to bow before the Zionists as assiduously and effectively as they did forty, fifty, ninety years ago, an attitude enhanced by dutiful British subservience to Zionism's great sponsor, the United States of America. It is hard to believe that there is any longer the dewy-eyed zeal of the Arthur Balfours, Lloyd Georges and Winston Churchills for the idea of Israel, or any sense that this troublesome entity in the Middle East is actually of any strategic use to Britain, as may have once been thought. (Now, surely, it is a liability rather than an asset.)

Is it guilt? Weariness in the eye of the unrelenting storm of threats, bullying, influence-peddling and propaganda? Keeping in with the US at all costs? All of these, and more? But what?

Nowhere in *Publish it not* is this Zionist force and its captive hold on the British establishment *quite* satisfactorily explained. I cannot explain it myself. Middle East scholars to this day argue over the essential reasons for Balfour's Declaration. There are scores of reasons for it, and for Zionism's hold on the United Kingdom, but they do not seem to add up to one convincing one. As far as that goes, it does not matter to Israel. The Jewish state can congratulate itself on the fact that the best efforts of Michael Adams and Christopher Mayhew and those of us who have tried to follow their example have come to nothing.

The cover-up in the Middle East continues to this day, more obvious than ever, the Big Lie bigger, its promulgation more intense, the all-powerful United States more committed than ever to the prosecution of Israel's interests at the expense of all others, neighbours, allies, friends, enemies, even its own, American best interests.

Israel is not only guaranteed military and economic superiority over its neighbours by its hyper-power protector in Washington, it is now a full partner in the "war against terror", in the American drive to install US-style democracy across the Middle East and Central Asia, and in the Western defences against the perceived legions of Islamic extremists, inside our Western societies and at our Eastern approaches and frontiers. Thus Israel can remain assured that its crimes and misdemeanours will continue to be condoned, any strictures confined to words not actions, and the aspirations of the Palestinians to freedom and safety inside recognized borders, or to full rights as citizens inside one state of Israel/Palestine, ignored, with our nation's complicity.

Is there any change in sight that might, were Michael Adams and Christopher Mayhew alive today, seem to justify for them the misplaced—or perhaps, mistimed—optimism they displayed in 1975, when Israel seemed to be at a disadvantage?

One aspect of Britain that has changed radically since then is the advent in this country of an articulate and engaged Muslim and Arab population: Asians, Arabs, Africans born and raised here. They are beginning to join political life, to make their voices resonate in the mainstream media and to enter academic and professional life. The political leadership is having to take notice of them. Their views on the invasion of Iraq and Britain's feeble stance on Palestine have already made electoral differences, most notably in the 2005 general election. Young professional groups and people, British, hyphenated British and immigrant alike, are monitoring the politicians and the media as closely as their pro-Zionist rivals.

Their impact is inchoate as yet, but their influence is gaining strength rapidly. They are as aware of the corruption and hopelessness in many of their mother countries and cultures as they are of the biases endemic in British institutions. It is encouraging that rather than spout aged and discredited lies about their pasts, these young people are engaging with the world as it is, throughout Asia and the Middle East, in Europe and the US, not as they might wish it to have been or imagine it once was. Some, it is true, have been seduced by siren calls and subversions of the Islamist message. Terrorism has been a result. But these are not the chosen refuges of most of the Muslim and Arab citizens who are making their life in Britain and elsewhere in Europe. Were the message of *Publish it not* more firmly appreciated and accepted by Britain's ministers and editors, the likelihood of young people turning down these tracks would be much more severely constrained.

What most of them are looking for is a response to their anxieties and recognition by Britain's leaders and opinion-makers that justice in Palestine, or Iraq, or Afghanistan, or Kashmir, or Chechnya, is a safer and more productive policy than ill-thought interference and military posturing and kowtowing to a misguided superpower.

In 2006 *Publish it not* will have a whole new potential readership, a phalanx of people who were unborn at its original publication, to whom Michael Adams and Christopher Mayhew can now speak.

PREFACE

This book was first published in 1975, at a moment of relative optimism about the prospects for a settlement of the Arab-Israeli conflict. The October War of 1973 (also known as the Yom Kippur War) had exposed a lot of illusions and prompted a good deal of rethinking about the future in the Middle East.

It had made people realise that the grievances which had driven the Arabs to go to war, of which the central one was Israel's continuing occupation and colonisation of the territories seized from the Arabs in 1967, were deeply felt and genuine, and that they could not and should not be ignored. This was primarily a matter of justice and humanity, but the war and its aftermath also brought home to the politicians the need to face up to some hard political facts.

In particular, the use by the Arabs of the "oil weapon", through the imposition of restrictions on the production and export of oil, provided a sharp reminder to governments everywhere that the failure to resolve the Palestine problem entailed risks which they would be foolish to disregard.

So in 1974 there was a favourable climate for some new thinking about what had gone wrong in Palestine and what should be done about it. It was to assist this process that we sat down to write *Publish it not . . .*, with the aim, as we wrote in our introduction to the book, of "clearing away some of the myths" which had grown up around the Palestine problem. The myths were many and varied; and it was (and it remains) our contention that for the most part they had been deliberately created and propagated by supporters of Israel, in order to conceal the truth about the cruelties and injustices which the Israelis were inflicting on the Palestine people. That was what we meant when we gave our book the sub-title "the Middle East cover-up".

In this respect there has been a marked improvement in the fifteen years since the book was first published. During that time other books have been written, some of the best of them by Israelis, ★ which have reinforced our argument by exposing the falsity of many of the accepted ideas about the background to the Palestine problem.

There has also been a marked improvement in the way the Western media have come to handle the argument over Palestine. Fifteen years ago it was exceptional to find in a European newspaper or magazine—and rarer still in an American publication—an article which gave serious consideration to the claims of the Palestinians. Editors and reporters found it easier and, as far as their careers were concerned, far safer, to follow the fashion by portraying Israel as the innocent victim of Arab aggression and the Palestinians as a people irrationally dedicated to violence and revenge.

In *Publish it not . . .* , writing in 1974/75, we noted the beginning of a change in the British press, tracing it more than anything to the effects of the October War on thinking at all levels. Since then the change has gathered speed and although the tabloid newspapers—especially those published by Rupert Murdoch and Robert Maxwell—remain crudely anti-Arab, most of the serious papers are now well balanced in their handling of Arab-Israeli affairs.

Even more important, because of its wider impact on popular thinking, has been the change in television coverage, not only of day-to-day events in the Middle East, but also of those aspects of social and political development which lend themselves to documentary treatment. Here too, despite the measures taken by the Israelis to restrict the freedom of television reporting, the trend towards a more even-handed approach has been very pronounced. Scenes of the brutal assaults on Palestinians in the West Bank and Gaza have had a profound impact on British viewers.

From the evidence available to us, the picture elsewhere in Europe seems to be broadly similar, while even in the United States and Canada, where the Zionist lobby fights a constant and skilful rearguard action, there is a growing realisation on the part of newspaper editors and proprietors of the need for a more balanced approach to the conflict between Jews and Arabs over Palestine.

All this is very much to the good—and yet in practical terms, as far as the situation on the ground in the Middle East is concerned, nothing has changed. The Israelis remain in occupation of the whole of the West Bank and the Gaza Strip (as well as the Syrian area of the Golan) which they captured in 1967. The Palestinian inhabitants of these areas (and the Druze villagers in the Golan) continue to live a half life under military occupation, without rights of any kind and unprotected by any agency against the increasingly repressive Israeli regime. Since December 1987, when Palestinian resentment over twenty years of ill-treatment and injustice boiled over in a popular uprising, the *intifada*, the scale of the repression has greatly increased—but it has come no nearer than in the past to subduing the Palestinian drive for freedom and self-determination.

In our book we set out our proposal for a peaceful settlement, based on the co-existence of the two peoples, each in its own state, alongside each other in Palestine. The "two state solution" has the backing of the international community, as in resolutions of the United Nations, and of the moderates on both sides in the Middle East. It would involve a compromise, for both Israelis and Palestinians, between what in their dreams they desire and what in practical terms they can expect to get. It would mean sharing the land of Palestine, for whose possession both sides have fought so hard and in which, sooner or later, both must learn to live in peace.

How to achieve this is the task of the Politicians. What the rest of us can do is insist that the facts of which political decisions will have to be taken must be openly and honestly discussed. There must be no more readiness to suppress or distort the truth in defence to a pressure group, however influential, no willingness on the part of politicians to allow their decisions to be shaped by considerations of personal or political advantage.

This much we can achieve, if we are vigilant for any further attempt to mislead opinion by imposing a new Middle East cover-up and so to frustrate the search for an acceptable settlement in Palestine.

M.A. and C.M.
October 1989

* Noteworthy among these are *The Birth of Israel: myths and realities*, by Simba Flapan; *The birth of the Palestinian refugee problem, 1947-49*, by Benny Morris and *Israel's Fateful Decisions*, by Yehoshafat Harkabi, whose former position as head of Israeli military intelligence lends special weight to his criticisms of the policies and decisions of successive Israeli governments.

INTRODUCTION

This is a very personal book. It presents the views of two individuals who, from different angles, have observed at close quarters a very strange phenomenon. Some readers will be offended by what we write, and to these we can only quote the words of St Jerome: "If an offence come out of the truth, better it is that the offence come than that the truth be concealed." To others, what we have to say will come as no surprise, although we shall be inviting the reader to follow us into territory which is not often publicly explored.

Our contention, briefly, is this: that over the past half-century, and particularly since 1967, a deliberate and generally successful attempt has been made to cover up the truth about Palestine, with damaging consequences for the cause of peace and justice in the Middle East. We shall record instances of how this has been done, many of them drawn from our own personal experience; and we shall describe some of the obstacles encountered and the penalties paid by those who insisted on trying to publicise the truth about the Arab-Israeli struggle. Finally, we shall suggest what changes have to be made in our approach to the problem if we in the West are to help to bring an end to the long-standing conflict in the Middle East.

Israel's critics, such as ourselves, have been listened to more readily, and with far less hostility, since the war of October 1973. Why? Because the October War showed that Western opinion had been seriously misinformed about the Middle East, and because the war and its aftermath opened people's eyes to facts which they had been refusing to face for years. It proved the critics' argument that if the Arabs were denied a just settlement in Palestine they would go to war to get one. It supported their contention that, in the face of the rising power of the Arab World, it was dangerous and ultimately impossible for the Israelis to try to batter the Arabs into submission rather than to come to an accommodation with them. It reinforced their warnings that unless we in the West made a serious attempt to put right the injustice in Palestine, for which we ourselves were so greatly to blame, we could not expect to maintain without interruption our oil supplies from the Middle East.

Before the October War, arguments like these used to be dismissed as "Arab propaganda"; now they appear self-evident and find ready acceptance among all but the most die-hard supporters of Israel. It would be pleasant to think that our former opponents had been converted by the merits of the arguments and the persuasive way in which they had been presented. Unfortunately, it seems more likely that they were influenced by the improved performance of the Arabs during the war and by their subsequent use of the oil weapon. These have shown that, whether we like it or not, we have to take the Arabs seriously. They have introduced an element of realism into the Middle East equation, supplying a factor which had previously been missing: the factor of Arab power. Possibly the main reason why things in the past have gone so badly wrong in the Middle East is that the Arabs have always lacked the power to defend their own interests. Since October 1973 that lack has been supplied, and for the first time it makes sense to talk about the balance of power in the Middle East.

Before the October War the imbalance of power was so marked, with Israel apparently supreme, that there was little incentive for anyone to try to disturb the situation. To have done so in the interests of such abstractions as justice and humanity would have seemed foolhardy. Foreign policy, we were often reminded, must be formulated on the basis of national interests; and it was assumed to be of no great interest to any nation in the West that a few hundred thousand Palestinian refugees should be allowed to return to their homes, or that something should be done to meet the demands made on their behalf by a few inconsiderable Arab states. True, some of those Arab states controlled sizeable amounts of the oil on which the economies of Europe and America had come to depend; but there was thought to be no prospect of their combining effectively to exploit this weapon, and in all other respects their nuisance value was considered to be negligible. Above all, they commanded in the chancelleries of the West no influence comparable with that of the friends of Israel.

In short, the risks of accepting the *status quo* in the Middle East were reckoned to be smaller than the risks of upsetting it. So long as the oil continued to flow and Western business interests could be pursued without interruption, it was easy enough to forget about the refugees and about the Palestinians living under Israeli military occupation in Jerusalem and the other territories which the Israelis had seized in 1967. It was easy enough to vote at the United Nations for resolutions which called on the Israelis to put an end to the occupation, to stop building ugly skyscrapers in Jerusalem, to stop employing collective punishments in the occupied territories, and to allow the return of the refugees, since the fact that the Israelis took not the slightest notice could be ignored without penalty to ourselves.

It was easy; but, besides being unprincipled, it was extremely short-sighted. It meant ignoring not only the misery and resentment of the Palestinians, but also the rising strength and the incalculable economic potential of the Arab states. For Britain, it meant a renewed breach of the promise to the Palestinians in the Balfour Declaration that "nothing shall be done that may prejudice the civil and religious rights" of the indigenous Arab population. For the United States, it meant ignoring the undertaking given by every American president for the last fifteen years to uphold "the political independence and territorial integrity of every state in the area." It meant, in short, abandoning the Arabs because they appeared to be weak and helpless, and doing so just at the moment when in fact they were acquiring enormous power of an unprecedented kind.

It was a miscalculation of epic proportions, as we were all made suddenly aware when war broke out in October 1973 and we discovered that the Arabs realised what power they had in their hands and knew how to use it. It was such a tremendous miscalculation, with consequences whose full extent is still difficult to predict, that the question needs to be asked: how and why did the governments of the West show such bad judgment? Did they not realise the price they would have to pay for conniving at the injustice in the Middle East? Why did they tolerate on the part of Israel behaviour which so openly, even defiantly, ran counter to all the rules of international behaviour? What prevented them from seeing that Israel's behaviour would make a renewal of war certain, and that this would threaten the vital interests of all of us in the West?

The argument of this book is that these crucial facts were deliberately disguised or suppressed in Western countries by pro-Israeli pressure and propaganda; and that the purpose was to perpetuate the imbalance of power in the Middle East in the interest, not of peace or international harmony, and certainly not of justice, but of the one country that stood to gain from the *status quo*: Israel.

Paradoxically, Israel herself, as well as the rest of the world, is now paying a heavy penalty for the success of her propaganda and of the pressure which Zionists are able to exert in Western countries. Considerations of peace and justice required a quick and complete Israeli withdrawal after 1967, as did the interests of the man in the street in Britain and other Western countries; but above all it would have been in Israel's own interests to withdraw when her strength and reputation were at their highest. A generous, far-sighted policy of conciliation at that time could have removed the Arabs' sense of grievance and averted the October War. It would have enabled Israel to keep some of the international friendships which she subsequently lost. Above all, it would have greatly improved the prospects of Arab-Israeli co-existence in the critical decades ahead; and that, by a large margin, is Israel's most vital interest of all.

Instead, tragically, Israel adopted a hard-line strategy, seeking security by dominating her neighbours and occupying large areas of their territory; and in this she was foolishly aided and encouraged by pro-Israeli organisations and individuals in the West. The President of the World Jewish Congress, Dr Nahum Goldmann, has himself strongly criticised the part played by Jews in the diaspora in "fostering illusions of grandeur in Israel," by encouraging the belief that Israel could impose peace on the Arabs and that time was working on her side. Dr Goldmann was quoted in June 1974 as saying that "by blindly supporting the mistaken course of Israeli policy and by telling the Israelis only what they wanted to hear, Diaspora Jews had done Israel a disservice."[1]

Few can doubt today that Israel would have done better to listen less to her friends and to pay more attention to the advice of her critics.

In a striking leader on 23 December 1972, the editor of *The Times* observed that: "The selfish acquiescence in evil is a very shortsighted policy, since all social evils are both infectious and breed their own reaction." The truth of his words has never been more cogently illustrated than by the history of the Palestine problem. It was wrong, at a time when Britain was strong and the Arabs were weak, for us to allow Jewish pressure for the creation of a "national home" in Palestine to override the vital interests of the Palestinian Arabs. It was wrong, thirty years later, for the Americans to yield to Zionist pressure to transform that "national home" into a Jewish state, still against the vital interests of the Arab majority in Palestine. And it was wrong, after the war of 1967, for the West to acquiesce in further Israeli occupation and oppression in Palestine, in the annexation of Arab Jerusalem, the destruction of Arab villages and the establishment in their place of Jewish colonies. All these were plainly "social evils" which, inevitably, were to "breed their own reaction" in the shape of the Palestinian resistance movement. No one, we believe, has more publicly or more consistently rejected Arab terrorism than we have, but it is right to add that it would never have come into being if Palestine had not in the first place been handed over to alien domination, and if hundreds of thousands of its inhabitants had not been driven out to make way for the newcomers.

It is not our intention in this book to go in detail into the tragic history of Palestine or of the conflict which has arisen between Arabs and Israelis over its ownership. This ground has been covered by others, notably by Professor Maxime Rodinson in what still seems to us the clearest as well as the most objective account.[2] Our purpose is to assist a process which has already begun: the process of clearing away some of the myths by which the problem has been surrounded, not always accidentally, so that readers may understand not only the truth about the Middle East, but what restraints have been placed, and in some cases are still being placed, on the propagation of this truth. Until the Arab-Israeli conflict is discussed at every level as openly and with as little inhibition as other problems of international affairs, it will be impossible to achieve a peaceful settlement in the Middle East. And the promotion of a settlement which would bring justice and lasting peace to both sides has been and remains our overriding aim.

ABS
PART ONE

CHAPTER ONE

A Personal Statement

Michael Adams

It was a Saturday and I was half way through lunch with my family when our guest arrived. He was a young man from a television company, who had been told to do some research for a programme about the Middle East. I hadn't been able to find time to see him during the week so I had suggested that he came to my home at the weekend, where we could go over the ground at leisure.

After lunch we were sitting with a cup of coffee wondering where to begin when one of the children burst in to say that there was "something about the Arabs" on the radio. What sort of thing, we asked, and she replied that there was fighting and they had crossed the Suez Canal. "Must be some sort of raid by the Egyptians," I said to the young man from the television company, reflecting in those few words the universal disbelief that the Egyptians were capable of anything more substantial than "some sort of raid" against the positions in which the Israeli occupation forces had entrenched themselves along the east bank of the Suez Canal since the Six Day War of June 1967.

But—although it was to be some time before any of us realised it—this was an historic moment. By nightfall on that Saturday, 6 October 1973, the Middle Eastern seesaw had taken a wholly unexpected, possibly a decisive, plunge. Whatever means the Israelis might find of reversing the new trend, they would never again enjoy in all its fullness the advantage which had been theirs at daybreak. To alter the metaphor, it was as though an enormous explosion had blown sky-high the whole elaborate structure of political and military

A Personal Statement

conceptions governing the relationship between Israel and its Arab neighbours. It would be a long time before anyone could tell how the pieces would come down; but one thing was immediately plain: it would be impossible to reconstruct them in anything like the same pattern as before.

In anyone closely concerned, as I was, with the affairs of the Middle East, this new and unexpected development aroused expectancy as well as apprehension. It was bound to mean more bloodshed and a further twist to the spiral of bitterness and retaliation; but it offered also the possibility of escape from the stalemate in which the Middle East had been locked for years. The apparent stability created by Israel's overwhelming victory in 1967 in fact only masked a situation of permanent danger. Because that stability depended not on a treaty or an agreed settlement of any kind, but simply on the ascendancy of the Israeli army over the combined forces of its Arab counterparts, it seemed impossible that it could ever be the preliminary to any genuine form of co-existence. Indeed, it seemed far more likely that the tensions it contained would lead sooner or later to a renewal of violence; and there was the fearsome possibility that, when it came, the violence might embroil us all.

It was these wider aspects of the problem that we fell to discussing, the young man from the television company and I, as we drove up to London on that Saturday evening to join in a feverish and inconclusive conference about the shape of the programme which the producer thought of mounting next day. In the end he sensibly decided to wait a week and take a more considered look at events as they unfolded. The young man, by the way, was Jewish, and so conscious of being at least vicariously involved in these events. But he was interested to know from me, who was neither a Jew nor an Arab, why I felt an even stronger sense of involvement than he did; and since this is a question which, in one way or another, I have often been asked, and, indeed, asked myself, I feel it is right to try to answer it at the outset, for the answer has a good deal to do with the theme of the book we are setting out to write. Christopher Mayhew will speak for himself: what follows is the *apologia pro vita mea* which must explain, if anything can, why I have spent the better part of twenty years urging on anyone who would listen to me an interpretation of events in the Middle East which, on the face of it, are no concern of mine.

The answer, inevitably, is complex. Our attitudes in life—call them principles, prejudices or what you like—are not formed by a single event but shape themselves as the slowly emerging outcome of varied influences. So, at least, it has been in my own case; and the main elements are not difficult to isolate from the surrounding welter of confused and often unrelated experience. First, there is the influence of an upbringing against which I felt no sense of revolt, since I admired the attitudes to life of my parents and was happy to try to absorb and reproduce them. I tried to emulate the tolerance which my father showed to anyone and anything not obviously selfish or harmful, while from my mother—a far more combative character, obstinate and idealistic—I inherited an uncomfortably keen sense of justice; a sense, indeed, that justice itself was the true grail, for which one must embrace any sacrifice. Then, from the environment of my youth I emerged with the conviction that to be English was to have cause for pride; and when later experience persuaded me that this was not invariably the case, the revelation was all the more shocking to me. This was to be important when I came to examine Britain's role in the Middle East, and especially in Palestine.

Next, I had the experience of being for nearly four years a prisoner of war. Suffering little more myself than frustration and a modicum of discomfort, I saw others, notably the first Russian prisoners captured by the Germans in the bitter winter of 1941, humiliated and cowed beyond the point of endurance. The experience left me with a vivid idea of what it means to be wholly and inescapably in the power of another man: a man with a gun and without mercy.

Lastly, there came my way the experience I gained at first hand in the Middle East, initially as a newspaper correspondent and more recently as an individual directly involved in the events and their repercussions which form the background to this book. Diffidently at first, but with growing confidence as I came to realise that, of those who knew or understood more than I did of the forces at work in the Middle East, few were prepared, for one reason or another, to speak openly about the direction events were taking, I found this experience organising itself into a conscious point of view, one which was to lead me before long into an area of controversy where I was startled to find myself the target for venomous and often unscrupulous attacks. Perhaps because I had a fair share of my mother's obstinacy as well as her idealism, this last experience stiffened my resistance. Like a dog that has been drawn by an unaccustomed scent to the brink of some urgent discovery, I would not be put off but growled a little at those who sought to divert my attention; and I pursued my enquiries.

Here there are two points which I think it right to emphasise. The first is that, when I went out to the Middle East at the beginning of 1956, I had no preconceived ideas about the rights and wrongs of the Arab-Israeli question.

I was a dilettante, interested in many things, specialised in none, intent primarily on broadening my own base of experience and seldom if ever asking myself what use I might make of this experience, or whether there was not some useful role I might play in the world. Fortunate to have received a good education and fortified by the knowledge that, as a prisoner, I had developed a certain capacity for endurance, I was careless of material considerations, more eager to live life to the full than to earn from it any substantial reward. Above all, after that long confinement, I wanted to travel, and having since the war roamed about quite extensively in Europe and as far afield as Turkey, then spent a year exploring the United States on a travelling fellowship, I leaped at the opportunity that was unexpectedly presented to me of going as correspondent for *The Manchester Guardian* to the Middle East. But I had one anxiety. I knew little of *The Guardian* or of the newspaper world in general, but surely a newspaper of such repute would require in its correspondent some special knowledge of the area in which he was to work, an academic background perhaps, or at least an acquaintance with the language? Could it be that in offering me the post the editor of *The Guardian* had made a mistake? Had I known the paper better in this, the final phase of its glorious and unworldly Manchester existence, I should have felt certain that he had. My name, after all, was a common one, and it was possible, it was even likely, that somewhere there existed a Michael Adams who was steeped in the history and the politics of the Middle East. I speculated much on the personality and the accomplishments of this mythical namesake of mine; of only one thing could I be certain—that I was not he.

In the end, deciding to take the bull by the horns, I carried my doubts and laid them before the foreign editor in Manchester. I had for my part no reservation about accepting the appointment, I told him, nor did I think my qualifications worthless; but I wanted it to be clear between us that I had not much more knowledge than the next man of the Middle East, its peoples, its languages, its history or its culture. If some regrettable confusion had persuaded him that I had, let us dissolve the partnership before it had been consummated and go our separate ways. I was surprised as well as relieved to hear his reply. "That's all right," he said with a smile. "We just wanted someone with an open mind."

An open mind: how fortunate that this should be the essential qualification for the job, for it was the only relevant one I possessed. But I possessed it in abundance. My mind—though I did not labour the point to the foreign editor—was more than just open, it was virtually empty where the Middle East was concerned. Looking back, for instance, I am astounded now to think that, although this interview was taking place only seven years after the first Arab-Israeli war which accompanied the birth in 1948 of the State of Israel, I was almost entirely ignorant of the circumstances in which that war had been fought. During its course I had been teaching in Finland, unable to read the local newspapers or to understand the radio, so that events which were in later years to provide my chief preoccupation passed at the time without my even hearing of them.

In only one respect was my mind preconditioned for the human conflict in which I was to become embroiled in the Middle East. I had grown up in a liberal atmosphere in the England of the late 1930s and, as the youngest of a politically conscious family, I had developed a pretty sharp awareness of what it was that we were presently going to have to fight against: the whole sordid apparatus of fascist repression and racialism. The diaries I kept as a schoolboy and, in the last year before the war, as an undergraduate, sometimes make me wince, if I look at them now, to see how sure I was, without the benefit of experience or the curb of responsibility, about matters which caused our leaders at the time such agonies of indecision. But at least, looking back, I was sure about the right things: about Spain and Czechoslovakia and Munich and the Jews, and if I went out with my friends to tip off a few policemen's helmets in the Cornmarket, it was in protest against the shilly-shallying of our pre-war government, which so unaccountably (to us) prevaricated instead of unfurling the standard which we were ready to follow against these forces of evil. I knew what I was doing when the moment came. By chance it was in the company of a Jewish friend that I put on my first ill-fitting uniform (his was worse, I remember pointing out with shouts of laughter) and we embarked on our particular wartime Odyssey, to stay together until he broke his back some months later, just as we were learning to fly.

So the open mind with which I eventually went to the Middle East was clouded only by a deeply-felt awareness of the fate of the Jews in contemporary Europe. I cannot honestly say, at this distance in time, whether I felt that this gave the Jews—Zionists was at the time a term which I hardly understood—the right to a home or a state in Palestine. All I can be sure of is that I would have listened with sympathy to anyone who tried to persuade me that this was so. Of the Palestinians, on the other hand, I knew precisely nothing.

The second point I think worth making, while we are thus clearing the ground, is this. When I got to the Middle East and threw myself into the absorbing work of a foreign correspondent, I found myself not infrequently in conflict with authority. Middle Eastern governments are not conspicuous for the tolerance with which they accept criticism; nor, many people would retort, are journalists noted for their reluctance to offer it. The argument is an endless one, but the point is that, wherever the boundary line between fair comment and unfair criticism should be drawn, an honest correspondent, a correspondent who tells it as he sees it, will get himself into trouble now and then; it is one of the hazards of the game. How should he deal with the problem?

One way, obviously, is to stop being critical—or never to start in the first place; but the foreign correspondent who chose that solution would have done better to stay at home. But there really is no other way except to be critical when criticism seems justified, being very careful to make sure that it is both justified and fair, and to face the consequences. That, at least, is the formula which I tried to adopt; and if the consequence was that I found myself at one time or another banned or blacklisted, and once or twice physically deported, from almost all of the countries whose affairs it was my business to report—though fortunately not from all of them at the same time—I am neither proud of this nor am I ashamed of it, except that I remember at least one instance when I knew that I was at fault for failing to temper my criticism with good sense or good manners. Generally speaking, I established my *bona fides* as a correspondent with a mind of his own, who would not be deflected from speaking his mind by the fear of official reprisals; and this was later to stand me in good stead. The governments whose actions I sometimes found myself criticising were Arab governments. At this stage I could and did visit Israel only clandestinely, using a second passport and making use of Cyprus as a necessary political decompression chamber. Later on, when my criticisms were more often directed against the government of Israel, those who wished to discredit me as a biased witness found it harder to do so in the light of my published record as an equally forthright critic of Arab policies and institutions.

As an incidental point of interest to students of Middle Eastern attitudes, these early brushes with Arab authority made me many friends in the Arab World. Arabs do not easily harbour a grudge, and often in subsequent years I have had the experience of being received with particular warmth at some Arab frontier post by the same official whose task it had been to expel me on a previous occasion; for both of us this would provide a reason to drink an extra cup of coffee together and to meditate upon the variability of human relationships.

When I described myself earlier as a dilettante, I was not seeking especially to blame and certainly not to praise my youthful self. I wanted only to emphasise the point that I did not start out in the Middle East as any kind of crusader; far from it. If, by the time I left the area, I had begun to feel that I had some sense of a vocation, this was the unexpected, and to a large extent unwelcome, result of the experience I had gained and of the study and research which that experience had prompted me to undertake. The experience itself was varied and often confusing; those years from 1956 to 1962, which saw the last convulsions of the colonial era in the Middle East, also witnessed a series of conflicts between rival theories of Arab nationalism. I did not always feel confident of my judgment in trying to identify and accurately to assess the various forces at work in the emerging pattern of Arab society. What I did see and feel was something much simpler, something that struck much nearer home for an Englishman at large in a part of the world from which the tide of British influence was now receding.

What I saw, in brief, was the fact of injustice; of an injustice which, it seemed, had been knowingly committed and was still being deliberately prolonged; an injustice—worst shock of all—which could be directly traced to a decision taken by a British government. I am speaking, of course, of the injustice done to the Palestinians, whose dispossession from the land of their ancestors was the culmination of a course of events set in motion by the publication in 1917 of the Balfour Declaration, the document by which the British Government had offered Zionism a home in Palestine, a land over which it had no rights whatever. When I first became familiar, in 1956, with the outlines of this story, I was appalled, the more so because I realised that most people were as ignorant as I had been until that moment about the Palestinian tragedy. Even so, once I had digested the facts, I believe that I could have accepted, as the world had come to accept, the argument that the harm was done, that it was no use crying over spilt milk. I could have accepted it, that is, but for two factors whose intervention now was to exercise a considerable effect on my own subsequent career.

The first of these was the realisation that the world's ignorance of what had happened and was still happening in Palestine was not accidental: that there were plenty of people about whose primary concern it was to distort and suppress the truth about Palestine without bothering their heads with any nonsense about freedom of speech. And the second factor, which happened to coincide with my initiation into the mysteries of Middle Eastern political life, was the Suez crisis, which it became my duty to observe and to report for *The Manchester Guardian*. It was a decisive experience. Following the crisis through to its conclusion in what Anthony Nutting has called "this mad, imperialist gamble" of military intervention in collusion with Israel, then hearing the Foreign Secretary deny in the House of Commons that any collusion had taken place, I found myself by the end so disillusioned about the standards of British public life that I had no difficulty in accepting what seemed on the face of it unacceptable: that the dispossession of the Palestinians had been the result of a deliberate act of policy in which British statesmen, among others, had been willing and conscious accomplices. Subsequent researches have convinced me that this was the case.[3]

What then was to be done about it? Should one accept the argument of the apologists for Israel who admitted that the creation of the Jewish state had resulted in a certain amount of injustice for the Palestinians (a nice euphemism, this, for the displacement of the better part of a million refugees), but who urged that the file was now closed and that the Palestinian refugees must grow accustomed to their fate and put up with it, as the refugees from Poland or East Prussia at the end of the Second World War had learned to put up with theirs? Certainly, it looked in the nineteen-fifties and the early sixties as though the file had been closed, as though at best some measure of compensation was all that these unfortunate people could hope for in exchange for their lost homes and broken lives. But then, in 1967, in the wake of Israel's lightning victory in the Six Day War, the file was paradoxically reopened.

A Personal Statement

Nobody can now say with certainty how much of the territory they occupied in 1967 the Israelis originally intended to keep. Myself, I had always believed, long before 1967, that if they found an opportunity to gain control of the West Bank of the Jordan, the Israelis would never willingly relinquish it. After the war, when I put this view I was told that I had no evidence to support my suspicion. All one can say now, looking back on the wasted years between 1967 and 1973, is that the Israelis went a long way to provide the evidence that had been missing. They did annex Arab Jerusalem; they did remain in occupation of all the territories they had seized in 1967; and, by establishing more than forty paramilitary settlements in these territories, they greatly strengthened the case of those, whether inside or outside the Arab World, who maintained as I did that only force or the strongest political pressure would dislodge them.

Despite the mounting evidence, it was very difficult between 1967 and 1973 to persuade Western public opinion that it was Israeli expansionism which presented the real obstacle to peace in the Middle East. For this curious myopia there were a number of reasons, which will be examined elsewhere in this book. In essence, the refusal to face the facts about Israel was the result of another form of collusion, not always as deliberate but just as carefully disguised as the collusion of Anthony Eden and Selwyn Lloyd with the Israelis at the time of Suez. This time, as in the whole drab half-century of the Palestine tragedy, the collaborators included politicians and journalists, churchmen and officials, business men and stars of the entertainment world, who found, from motives occasionally sincere but more often founded on self-interest or self-preservation, that Israel's satisfaction mattered more to them than the fate of the Palestinian refugees. There was in fact a kind of Watergate in action, to some extent before 1967 and much more obviously after it, to protect those who made it their business to defend Israel and to subject to an insidious form of discrimination those who sought to expose the true aims of Israeli policy. Such non-conformists were subtly made aware that their jobs might be at risk, their books unpublishable, their preferment out of the question, their public reputations vulnerable, if they did not renounce the heresy of anti-Zionism. And for the most part, the merest flourish of such secret weapons was enough to reduce them to silence.

There were, however, the exceptions, those in whom this kind of intimidation produced the opposite effect. Partly out of simple conviction and partly because they were drawn to each other by their common experience of being, in one way or another, blackballed because of the views they held, these individualists came together to form a modest counterpart to the Zionist lobby in Britain. They established the Council for the Advancement of Arab-British Understanding, and set out, shortly after the Six Day War in 1967, to awaken public opinion not only to the injustice that had taken place in the Middle East but also to the dangers that were likely to overtake Britain and her Western allies if that injustice was not checked and, if possible, reversed. Their common denominator was their knowledge of the Middle East, the fact that in a wide variety of capacities they had acquired at first hand experience of a situation which was making life intolerable for the peoples of the area and whose continuation posed an evident threat to the interests and indeed the peace of the rest of the world.

Because of my interest in the Middle East and the experience I had gained as *The Guardian's* correspondent, I found myself among the founder-members of this organisation. Putting our heads together, we tried to devise the best means of correcting what appeared to us the dangerous imbalance of opinion in Britain where the Middle East was concerned; and it was then that we became aware of something that most of us had long suspected but of which only those of us who had been active in public life had until that moment any direct experience. We became aware that the imbalance of public opinion, in this deeply contentious area of foreign politics, was deliberately contrived and painstakingly maintained; and that those who were intent on maintaining it were not above resorting to some very dirty tricks against those who tried, as we were trying, to disturb it.

I was to learn this lesson myself the hard way, and there was a time when I found myself under attack from many directions, experiencing a sudden difficulty in getting my work published and receiving at the same time a stream of anonymous and often obscene letters. I cannot say I enjoyed the experience; I had no ambition to be a martyr, nor did I wish to jeopardise my own future or the prospects of my family. At the same time, the underhand nature of the attack angered me, as did the persistence of the injustice in the Middle East, which had indeed been greatly aggravated by the war of 1967 and by Israel's refusal to allow the return of a fresh wave of refugees.

Through the Council I became involved on the second front of the Arab-Israeli conflict: in the war of the lobbies, who skirmished with each other in parliament, in the press and at various levels of public life, engaged in a running fight to win public opinion and, if possible, to influence the course of British policy towards the Middle East. In the early days after 1967 it was a depressing and often frustrating campaign, but it had also, from the outset, some splendid compensations. If now, willy-nilly, I had become some sort of crusader, well, it seemed a thoroughly worthwhile crusade, aimed as it was against prejudice and injustice; and if the cause of the Arabs looked after 1967 like a lost cause, why, there is something to be said, as the Arabs themselves learned, for being in a position so bad that it can only grow better. For one thing, you find yourself in congenial company, for no one who put his own interests first would have dreamed of getting himself mixed up with anything as unrewarding as the cause of the Arabs between 1967 and 1973.

Since 1973, of course, things have looked remarkably different. The Arabs' star is in the ascendant and the governments of the West, especially the Americans, who previously had so antagonised and humiliated the Arabs, have found it expedient to court their favour. All sorts of people who in the past felt able to ignore the Arab cause on its merits now find it compelling: because it is backed by the power of the oil weapon. Today it is commonplace to hear politicians and leader-writers assuring each other that there can be no peace in the Middle East without "a just solution to the problem of the Palestinians." How few of them said so before the October War, or tried to give any practical recognition to the rights of the Palestinians when the Arabs were weak and the Israelis, thanks to the constant backing of the American government, were very strong! It is mortifying to reflect that peace could have been achieved, on the same terms as are available today, at any time between 1967 and 1973. Everything that happened during those lost years—the violence, the reprisals, the growing confrontation between the Arabs and those whom they had no option but to regard as their enemies—all this and the October War as well, with its further toll in lives and precious resources, could have been avoided had the world taken a firmer stand against Israeli expansionism. But the world stood by while the Israelis, out of greed for what was not theirs, and the Americans, because their politicians were afraid of the Zionist lobby in the United States, drove the Arabs to seek by violence what they were denied by any other means.

Nor is this said only with the wisdom of hindsight. In an article published in *The Guardian* a few days after the end of the Six Day War, I pointed out that whereas, at the start of the war, the Israeli prime minister had said that Israel had no wish to annex "even one foot" of Arab territory, General Dayan a week later was already talking casually of absorbing the Gaza Strip, the Old City of Jerusalem, the West Bank and the Golan Heights. I had no wish, I wrote, to argue about these claims; I wanted only "to state as forcefully as I can that they will destroy any chance of creating in the Middle East an environment in which Israel will be able to live at peace." If Israel now seized the first opportunity since 1949 to extend its boundaries, it would confirm the suspicion of the Arabs that territorial expansion remained the true aim of Israeli policy; and it would persuade the Arabs "that not merely their best hope, but their only one, lies in rebuilding their shattered strength and waiting for the next round—when perhaps it will be they who will adopt the Pearl Harbor technique, with what may be deadlier weapons and in a suicidal mood of disregard for the consequences to themselves or to the rest of the world."

I urged the Israelis to consider, before victory went to their heads, not only what the Arabs had lost, but what remained to give them hope for the future:

A Personal Statement

> "A physical presence in all the Arab lands that surround Israel, a rapidly growing population unversed in, but no longer wholly ignorant of, modern techniques and practices; tremendous economic resources in the shape of three quarters of the world's oil reserves; the backing of the whole Eastern bloc, so long as Israel tries to impose a settlement by force rather than seek one by international agreement; and, most potent and incalculable of all, the terrible frustration of a people that feels itself victimised, humiliated, ground down."

Surely the Jews, I wrote, should understand this? Nor should they, or anyone else anywhere in the world, be in any doubt that, rather than accept General Dayan's demand for surrender, the Arabs would start

> "to work and plan, with Russian help, for the next round in a battle which, on the time scale of history, has only just begun . . . It will condemn them to instability and extremism, to sufferings as pointless as those of an earlier generation of Jews, to revolutions and a recurrence of the bitter internal rivalries which have distracted them ever since the original Palestine tragedy. We in the West, and Israel too, and possibly the whole world, will live in the shadow of these consequences—and it is at least conceivable that out of them will emerge a people as tempered by adversity, as hard and determined as the present generation of Israelis."[4]

It saddens me to see how many of my forebodings came true, especially the decline into violence and extremism which has been such a marked feature of these last years in the Middle East and the shadow of whose consequences has certainly fallen across all our lives. So accustomed have we become to the phenomenon of terrorism in the Middle East and elsewhere that it is easy to forget how recently it has become a part of the Palestinian armoury. Before 1967 the reproach that one could most justly make to the Palestinians was that they had been too inactive, too softly acquiescent in their own fate. Towards the end of 1969, after one of the first incidents in which foreign civilians had been injured in a guerrilla attack, I recall taking advantage of the occasion of a large public meeting, which I had been invited to address in Amman, to criticise this action and to tell my audience of Jordanians and Palestinians that, much as I hoped to see them defeat the Zionists, I hoped it would not be at the price of becoming like the Zionists themselves. Even as late as September 1970, after the multiple hijack operation in which three airliners were diverted to Dawson's Field in Jordan and a fourth blown up at Cairo airport, I remember the care with which the guerrillas of the Popular Front protected their hostages in the fighting which presently broke out between the Jordan army and the resistance movement, and the respect, amounting in some cases almost to affection, with which the hostages, after their release, spoke of their captors. That some sections of the Palestinian resistance movement should subsequently have gone so far down the path of terrorism originally charted by the Irgun and the Stern Gang in the 1940s was a grave disappointment to those, such as Christopher Mayhew and myself and our colleagues in CAABU, who publicly deplored such acts and intervened when we could to try to prevent them. But neither we nor anyone else could be surprised that, where restraint had produced for them so little result, the Palestinians, "tempered by adversity", should have shown themselves "as hard and determined" as the Israelis had always been in the pursuit of their ambitions in Palestine.

Saddest of all was the fact that, despite all the warnings, and the obvious danger signals, it should have taken one more war in the Middle East to persuade the world to make a serious effort to put an end to the conflict. Immediately after the October War and the imposition by the Arabs of the oil boycott, such an effort was at last made, with the Americans, who had done most to prevent it from being made earlier, taking the lead. The question of why it had proved so difficult earlier to persuade public opinion to give a hearing to the Arab case is one that we shall examine from several angles in this book. What I hope I have made clear here are my own reasons for becoming involved in what has now become, at last, a matter of such universal concern.

CHAPTER TWO

A Personal Statement

Christopher Mayhew

When and why did I first form a view about the Arab-Israeli conflict? Searching the records, I find that as long ago as 1948—on 11 July, to be precise, in the House of Commons—I was speaking in an Adjournment Debate about the recognition of the State of Israel. The debate had been initiated by an engaging, loquacious young Labour backbencher, Mr Harold Lever,[5] and I was winding up for the Government, as Ernest Bevin's Under-Secretary at the Foreign Office. With an importunity typical of Zionists at that time, Mr Lever had started the debate at eight o'clock in the morning, after an all-night sitting, and my reply sounds appropriately tired and irritated.

> "I had hoped that my Honourable Friend would yield to my requests that we might be spared a debate on this subject at this moment. It is a bad time politically, diplomatically, psychologically, and, might I add, physically, to discuss the question of Palestine . . . Quite clearly a change of policy here would in fact discourage the Arabs and encourage the Jews. I do not deny that. Why for that reason is it right, just, and necessarily expedient? . . . Has my Honourable Friend ever heard that there is an Arab point of view? . . . The trouble with my Honourable Friend, as the whole of his speech shows, is that he is not sufficiently in touch with the Arab point of view on the Palestine problem."[6]

Even at this distance of time, I find it easy to imagine the scene.

The floor and the benches of the House would be littered with discarded order papers. Facing me, on the deserted Opposition benches, would be a single lonely figure, the duty Opposition Whip. In the Officials' Gallery, over to my left, my Private Secretary, perhaps my sole supporter present, would be silently praying that I would stick to my brief. And behind me, wide-awake, well-informed, passionate, articulate and aggressive, would be a group of twenty or thirty pro-Israeli Labour members. Most of them would be Jewish. Sydney Silverman, Maurice Edelman and Ian Mikardo would surely be among them, even at eight o'clock in the morning; and also Israel's most brilliant non-Jewish supporter, Dick Crossman.

And I can easily imagine how I myself would be feeling, sitting alone on the Government Front Bench, thumbing the stiff blue official paper on which my careful speech would have been typed. My mind would not have been on Palestine. I had never been there and had no real grasp yet of the issues. I would have been feeling friendless, nervous, and extremely tired, but sustained by a belief that Bevin was more likely to be right than the emotional, partisan people behind me, and angered by the manifest unfairness of the situation: that there should be so many powerful pro-Israeli spokesmen in the House and no one at all to speak up for the Arabs.

Ernest Bevin felt this injustice deeply too. I remember how, at the end of a particularly tense Question Time, when he had been mercilessly harried by Jewish MPs supporting Israel, he had finally burst out, "We must also remember the Arab side of the case—there are, after all, no Arabs in the House." This remark provoked an uproar, and I reproved him for it afterwards—mistakenly, I now think—on the grounds that by singling out the Jewish as against the non-Jewish supporters of Zionism he was making it easier for his enemies to suggest that he was anti-Semitic. But Bevin was unrepentant, protesting that the Zionists were "even now paralleling the Nazis in Palestine," and that they were creatures of violence and war—"What can you expect when people are brought up from the cradle on the Old Testament?" I did not then share Bevin's emotional commitment on Palestine, but I remember clearly his dislike of

Zionist methods and tactics, and, indeed, of the Zionist philosophy itself. He was passionately and unshakeably anti-Zionist. He held that Zionism was basically racialist, that it was inevitably wedded to violence and terror, that it demanded far more from the Arabs than they could or should be expected to accept peacefully, that its success would condemn the Middle East to decades of hatred and violence, and above all—this was his immediate concern—that by turning the Arabs against Britain and the Western countries, it would open a highroad for Stalin into the Middle East.

On all these points events proved him right; but in the immediate postwar years, so soon after the truth about the Nazis' treatment of the Jews had become widely known, his plain speaking struck many people as prejudiced and harsh, and enabled the Zionists to misrepresent him with some success as an anti-Semite, which he was not.

Then, as now, there was much confusion between anti-Zionism and anti-Semitism. Zionism—the idea that Jewish people everywhere should gather together in a state in Palestine—is a political concept which can and should be freely debated, one which has wide support but which many tolerant civilised people, including many Jews, strenuously oppose. But in the 1940s, and indeed until quite recently, many people confused Zionism with Judaism, the religion of the Jews, so that criticising Zionism sounded like criticising somebody's religion. Others confused Zionism with the Jewish people itself, and so made the mistake of thinking that if one were anti-Zionist one must be anti-Jewish as well. Regrettably, this last confusion was deliberately fostered by some extreme Zionists,[7] who discouraged potential opponents by making them afraid of being thought racialists.

Even today Zionism is a subject on which it is hard to speak frankly in Western countries without giving offence. Statements to the effect that communism or capitalism are wicked or inhuman may provoke disagreement, but they do not give offence. But if Zionism is similarly denounced, almost everyone is shocked, and the speaker's motives are widely suspected.

In 1947 and 1948 it was the political pressure on the Labour

Cabinet from American Zionists, exerted through the United States government, which angered Bevin most, and I shared his feelings about this to the full. At that time, Britain was dependent on American goodwill for her economic survival; and President Truman, as he later explained frankly in his memoirs, was equally dependent on Zionist goodwill for his presidential campaign funds. As a consequence, the British government was subjected to ruthless pressure from Washington to get the Arabs to accept the Zionists' demands. It was a disgraceful abuse of power. On one occasion I was exposed to the full brunt of it myself. In Bevin's absence, I had to receive the US Ambassador, Mr Lou Douglas, "with a message from the President about Palestine." Mr Douglas explained that he had been asked to repeat the President's urgent request to the British government to admit a hundred thousand Jewish refugees into Palestine immediately. In line with Bevin's views, and with the support of the Permanent Under-Secretary, Sir Orme Sargent, I objected that this was simply a prescription for war. The Ambassador then replied, carefully and deliberately, that the President wished it to be known that if we could help him over this it would enable our friends in Washington to get our Marshall Aid appropriation through Congress. In other words, we must do as the Zionists wished—or starve. Bevin surrendered—he had to—but he was understandably bitter and angry. He felt it outrageous that the United States, which had no responsibility for law and order in Palestine (and no intention of permitting massive Jewish immigration into the United States), should, from very questionable motives, impose an impossibly burdensome and dangerous task on Britain.

    I was myself comparatively slow to understand the Palestine problem and formulate my own views about it. For one thing—hard as it is to believe this now—the Foreign Office was struggling at that time with a number of world issues of even greater importance. India and Pakistan had to be given freedom. The Marshall Aid plan had to be pushed forward. Institutions had to be created for a divided Germany. NATO had to be formed. At that time, inevitably, Palestine seemed a sideshow.

A Personal Statement

My first personal brush with Zionism occurred in the strangest manner. I had been in the Foreign Office only a few weeks when the following absurd-sounding letter was placed on my desk, dated 5 December 1946, postmarked Lisbon:

"Mr Mayhew, Under Secretary, Foreign Affairs, London. Remember the very words of the great Stephen S. Wise "We are going to get a Jewish state soon in Palestine' and we fighters from Lahome Herut Israel, add 'Also against the decision of the British Foreign Office'.

Don't forget that the Jewry defeated with your British assistance the bloody and damned Nazis i.e. the first Germanic nation, and don't forget too that its now your turn as the second arrogant Germanic nation to kiss our feet.

We are determined this time to squash you British sons of a bitch and we declare war to the finish against the British.

For every Jew you stinking British pigs kill in Palestine you will pay a thousandfold in fetid English blood.

The L H I has passed sentence of death on the British pig Mayhew.

The execution will soon take place by silent and new means.

Signed Lahome Herut Israel."[8]

I asked my secretary why he bothered me with such nonsense. He replied that the Home Office considered the assassination threat genuine and had already telephoned my home to warn my friends and relations against opening suspicious parcels. And sure enough, by coincidence or otherwise, explosive packets soon began arriving through the post for people supposed (sometimes quite wrongly) to be anti-Zionist. One arrived at Sir Anthony Eden's home. I have been told that he actually stuffed it unopened into his pocket, and carried it around with him for some time before the security services relieved him of it. Another explosive packet was sent to Roy Farran, an avowed opponent of Zionism, and killed his brother, who opened it in error. To the best of my knowledge, however, no Jewish terrorist actually sent me an explosive packet, or tried to assassinate me in any other way, though we had several false alarms.

I remember vividly several meetings with Zionist deputations at this time. Usually, they came to protest against harsh measures aimed at preventing illegal immigration into Palestine. On short-term human grounds, the case for unrestricted immigration was overwhelmingly strong. Scores of thousands of desperate Jewish people, fleeing from the scene of their wartime nightmare in Europe, were being channelled by Zionist organisations towards Palestine. Most of them were destitute and many were physically or mentally crippled. How could any civilised government, let alone a British Labour government, fail to admit them? How could we use the Navy to board their ships and force them back towards Europe? Never before or since have I known a more distressing task than that of defending the government's immigration policy to outraged deputations of Zionists. These deputations were almost always well-informed, articulate, demanding, passionate and ruthless. The most formidable of their spokesmen, without question, was Mr Sydney Silverman; he would attack me personally in the most merciless fashion, placing on my own shoulders the responsibility for the deaths and suicides of immigrants whom we had turned back.

But in spite of everything, were we wrong? Was Ernest Bevin mistaken in thinking, as he said so often, that the Jews were asking for more than the Arabs could ever accept peacefully—*more than it was in the Jews' own long-term interest to demand*? I do not think so. I thought then, and I still think, that the scale of the Zionist demands and the ruthlessness with which they were pursuing them were bound to prove in the long term to be self-defeating.

But where, at Westminster or in Whitehall, was the counter-pressure from the Arabs whose land, homes and property these Jewish immigrants would soon be seizing? It did not exist: not because the Arabs did not feel strongly about what was going on in Palestine, but because they possessed at the time virtually no political influence at all. Very few Arab states had even achieved genuine independence before 1948, and there was no one who could command a hearing on their behalf. Consequently, the British government received virtually no support during these critical times from the people whose vital

A Personal Statement

interests it was trying, however ineffectually, to protect.

Partly as a result, I still had at this time only the vaguest, most detached understanding of the Arab case. Frankly, my strongest feeling about the whole tragic conflict was a pronounced distaste for Zionist methods of pressure and propaganda. This feeling was if anything increased a year or two later when, to my surprise, a determined and skilful attempt was made to include me on the pro-Israeli payroll.

It happened in 1951. I had temporarily lost my seat in Parliament, and was earning a living as a journalist and television commentator. I was indeed at that time Britain's only regular television commentator on world affairs. I was acquainted with the political director of the World Jewish Congress, Mr A. L. Easterman, and after some pressure, accepted an invitation from him to call at his office in Cavendish Square. There, in the most tactful and persuasive manner, he invited me to become an adviser to the World Jewish Congress. Whenever I was asked for, and gave, advice, I would be paid a substantial honorarium, and he assured me that the appointment would be a purely personal arrangement between the two of us, and that nothing would be set down about it in writing. His proposition was perfectly legal and was put to me so delicately that I found it hard to take offence. But it would, of course, have prejudiced my freedom of speech—and broadcasting—where Israel was concerned.

In fairness to Mr Easterman, it should be recorded that he has denied my version of his offer. Some years later, after the 1967 war, he gave his own version as follows:

> "We needed and sought help from people who had the knowledge and experience of how to formulate presentation of our ideas and proposals in such a way and by such channels as would secure consideration and effective results in official quarters. The policies and actions of Israel were not our province, other than to give support and encouragement to the people of the Jewish state ...
>
> "At no point of our talk did I offer Mr Mayhew, directly or indirectly, 'to become a political adviser' and it is nothing short of

preposterous that I offered him 'a very large salary' which, in any case, was not and is not now within the financial means of the World Jewish Congress, a far from wealthy organisation. All I did say to him about finance was that, naturally, we would reimburse him for any expenditure he might incur on our behalf."[9]

The reader must judge for himself. Was the work which I was offered to be unpaid, as Mr Easterman recollects, or paid, as I recollect myself? I had no doubts about it at all at the time and naturally asked myself whether I was the only broadcaster and journalist to be made an offer of this kind, and whether, if others had been made the offer, they had all turned it down as I had. This seemed most unlikely.

I was not as yet fully committed on the Arab-Israeli question, of which I still had little first-hand experience. It was not until 1953, when I made my first visit to an Arab refugee camp, that the Palestinian tragedy became real for me for the first time. I was visiting Jordan, as a member of a parliamentary delegation. We had been sent out by the Foreign Office to show support for King Hussein, who was at that time—as so often before and afterwards!—in danger of being overthrown. The camp was near Amman. It was very crowded and I soon found myself separated from my parliamentary colleagues in a large, mud-floored hut, filled with ragged, thin-faced refugees, including many children. There were no windows, and the only light came through an open doorway. One or two of the refugees began asking me questions, translating the answers for the rest of the audience. What was the British government going to do for the refugees? I explained what we had done to initiate and support the relief and rehabilitation work of the United Nations. I hoped this answer would be well received, since Britain's record had been a good one, compared at least with that of other countries. But to my dismay my reply only made the refugees more angry and suspicious. What was Britain doing to get their land back? I explained that we supported their right to choose between returning to their homes in Israel or being compensated and resettled. But what were we *doing* apart from talking? Did I not realise that it was we who were responsible for the Jews taking their land? What crime had they and their children committed, that they should be driven from their homes and robbed of all their possessions?

The intensity of their bitterness, anger and despair dismayed and alarmed me. But I felt that there was a great deal of justice in what they were saying. Listening to their stories, it seemed impossible to believe, as the Israelis insisted, and as nearly everyone at home agreed, that they had left their homes voluntarily. And even if they had left voluntarily, why were they not allowed to return? If the Israelis had really been willing to let the refugees stay, why had they slammed the door behind them so quickly after they had left?

This myth that the refugees in the 1948 war fled voluntarily was finally destroyed when the refugees in the 1967 war behaved in the same way and suffered the same fate. Although the Arab governments indisputably urged them to stay, they left their homes in panic before the advancing Israeli armies, and were then prevented by the Israelis from returning. The pattern was the same in both wars, except that in 1967 there were no calculated acts of terror, such as the massacre of Deir Yassin, to encourage frightened Palestinian families to leave their homes and take to their heels.

Before 1967, the myth that the 1948 refugees had fled voluntarily, in response to broadcast appeals from Arab countries, was almost universally believed in Western countries. It helped the Israelis to defend their refusal to let them return, and also the subsequent expropriation, without compensation, of their land, houses, property and personal effects. But there is now ample evidence to support the charge that in 1948 the Palestinians were deliberately driven from their land and homes, and prevented from returning, in order to make room for newcomers of a different race, and to ensure the Jewish characteristics of the new state.[10]

The Palestinians themselves, of course, have always known this, and part of their intense feelings of frustration and bitterness undoubtedly comes from the brilliant success of Israeli propaganda in suppressing the truth about their exodus and in representing the Palestinians not as victims of Zionism but of their own foolish and intemperate behaviour. In addition, they have always been exasperated that the United Nations should repeatedly assert their right to repatriation, or to compensation and resettlement elsewhere, and yet at the same time should do nothing effective to make the choice a real one. They had also seen their strongest champion, Count Folke Bernadotte, whose report on the refugee problem to the UN Secretary General had led to the UN's recognition of their rights,[11] assassinated by Israeli terrorists.

It was during this visit to Jordan in 1953 that I saw the refugee camps not merely as relics of a past war, but as seedbeds of future vengeance. I saw proud, innocent people being subjected to intolerable humiliation and misery, and felt that few would escape without deep, life-long emotional scars. I wish I could record that in consequence, on my return, I began actively campaigning for these refugees. I ought to have done so, but, apart from a brief period in 1956, when I spoke, wrote and broadcast many times against British and Israeli actions in the Suez War, I allowed other work to divert my attention from the Middle East. It was not until ten years after my visit to Jordan that I found my ideas about the Arab-Israeli conflict crystallising into an active personal commitment. This resulted, paradoxically, from a meeting with Mrs Golda Meir and other Israeli leaders, during a visit to Jerusalem.

I was a member of an official Labour Party delegation, and we had arrived in Israel after an extensive tour of Arab countries, meeting many Arabs of distinction and visiting several refugee camps. Confident, friendly and sophisticated, our Israeli hosts welcomed us at the frontier at the Mandelbaum Gate in Jerusalem, as though we were returning home from exile in some alien barbarous land. They did not argue with us about the Arabs or attempt to persuade us: they simply assumed from the start that we were on their side: that we were bound to see that the refugee camps were an artificial problem, kept alive for political purposes by the Arab states; that the Palestinians had left their homes of their own free will, and could and should now resettle elsewhere in the Arab World; that the Arabs had brought their miseries on themselves and had no claims on Israel; that most of them were anti-Semitic, though fortunately too divided and incompetent to present a serious threat; that in due course they would face realities and recognise the State of Israel; and that when that time came the Israelis, who were an advanced and generous people, would be willing to extend a helping hand to them and work with them in raising their living standards.

I was, of course, already familiar with this line of talk, but the bland assumption that I necessarily agreed with it was surprising and irritating. And why did these Israeli leaders assume that they knew the Arabs better than we did? How many of them had ever met an Arab leader or visited an Arab refugee camp? And that mocking, patronising tone of voice in which they spoke about the Arabs—where had one heard it before?

Part of the answer came to me, at a dinner which Mrs Golda Meir gave for our delegation. I suddenly realised that these Israelis, who were so confident that they "knew how to handle the Arabs", were indeed constantly meeting Arabs. They were meeting the Arabs who had stayed behind in Israel in 1948, as second-class citizens in humble jobs, as gardeners, cleaners, domestic servants and taxi drivers. That was why they felt they knew the Arabs and that was why they misjudged them so dangerously. It explained too the tone of voice in which they talked about Arabs. I remembered now where I had heard it before: at parties given by British settlers in Kenya and Tanganyika before those countries gained their independence. It was the tone in which it would be explained to visitors like myself that the African was scatterbrained but essentially a "good chap", loyal (meaning loyal to his white masters) but easily led astray by trouble makers (meaning those of his fellow-Africans who aspired to self-rule).

I was once asked by an Arab taxi driver in Jerusalem, who knew and trusted me, what he should say to Israeli clients who asked him for his views on the Arab-Israeli situation. "When I tell them what I really think, I get a smaller tip," he said. "What do you think I ought to say ...?"

It was during this visit to the Middle East that I began to feel actively committed where the Palestine question was concerned. I was shocked by the Israeli leaders' self-righteous indifference to the sufferings of the Palestinian refugees, and found myself speaking up warmly for the Arabs in their presence. This gave offence, and led to unfortunate consequences for myself. Shortly after our delegation had left Israel, two senior members of the Labour Party, Mr George Thomson, MP, and Mr Fred Mulley, MP, were invited to Israel for further talks and returned with a report for the Party Leader, Mr Harold Wilson, which included complaints about my attitude from the Israeli leaders. I wrote rather anxiously to Mr Wilson ("you may like to have a meeting about this . . . or would you like me to write you a note about it?"), but was given no chance of defending myself.

A year later, when Mr Wilson was forming his government, although I had been for some time the Opposition's Deputy Spokesman on Foreign Affairs, I was not appointed Deputy Foreign Minister. A senior Cabinet Minister, himself surprised, informed me that my unpopularity in Israel had told against me.[12] Mr Wilson denied this when I taxed him with it; but if it was in fact the Israelis who had managed to clip my wings, I could hardly blame them. I was by now firmly convinced of the justice of the Arabs' case over Palestine, and was determined to support it in any way I could.

CHAPTER THREE

Political Pressures

Christopher Mayhew

In September 1970 a dinner was held in London to mark the fiftieth anniversary of the affiliation of a Zionist organisation, Paole Zion, to the British Labour Party. The dinner was attended by two hundred guests, including the Prime Minister, Mr Harold Wilson, and several Labour MPs and peers, and was presided over by the Acting Chairman of the Labour Party, Mr Ian Mikardo, MP, himself a member of Paole Zion.

In an arrogant speech, Mr Mikardo abused those who had tried to stand in the way of the Zionist advance, attacking in particular Mr Ernest Bevin, the British Diplomatic Service, and the Arabs. Mr Bevin, he said, had been "not only an anti-Zionist, but, as I know from personal experience, an anti-Semite." Foreign Office officials were "public school boys who share with the Arabs a common tendency towards homosexuality, romanticism and enthusiasm for horses."[13]

This dinner and the Chairman's speech, though not important in themselves, are colourful examples of the dominating influence of Zionism in the British Labour Party. They may also mark the zenith of this influence. It is true that for a few more years the party's attitudes towards the Middle East continued to be strongly Zionist-orientated, but from 1970 onwards resistance to the domination of its Middle Eastern policies by its Zionist members grew steadily. Significantly, a group of Labour MPs wrote to the National Executive Committee after this Paole Zion anniversary dinner, protesting against Mr Mikardo's remarks. No reply was received (Mr Mikardo was himself Chairman of the Committee), but this minor initiative was unprecedented, and reflected a growing sense of unease among party members. Although strongly pro-Israeli and anti-Arab speeches continued to be made by party leaders up until the October War and the imposition of the oil blockade, the Zionist lobby was put increasingly on the defensive during this period.

The capture of the British Labour Party by Zionism had been a remarkable phenomenon. By tradition and principle the party was strongly opposed to territorial expansion, colonialism, racialism and military government; yet the Zionist lobby succeeded in committing it to a uniquely close friendship with a foreign government which was occupying large areas of its neighbours' territory, was exercising, through measures of military government, colonial rule over a million subjects, and was openly practising racial discrimination in its immigration and housing policies.

Nor, of course, was it only in the Labour Party that the Zionist lobby was successful. For more than sixty years, its influence had been persistent, intimate and effective in British political life generally. Its success owed much to the contrasting failure of the Arabs, at least until recent times, to exert any effective counter-pressure.

The secret of the Zionists' success has lain in the existence of a large, lively and influential Jewish community in Britain, to which there is no Arab equivalent. This factor made its impact at the very beginning of the controversy. During the negotiations before and immediately after the publication of the Balfour Declaration in 1917, the contrast between the Zionist and Arab lobbies in Westminster and Whitehall was as stark as it could possibly have been. Supporters of Zionism, whether Jewish or non-Jewish, tended to be highly articulate and sophisticated, and if they were not in positions of power themselves, they usually had easy access to those who were. The Arabs on the other hand were far removed from the scene of decision-making and were seriously handicapped by the gulf between their cultural and political traditions and those of Whitehall and Westminster.

At a time when crucial decisions had to be taken, decisions which affected the entire future of the inhabitants of Palestine, these same

Palestinians were virtually unrepresented in London, while the Zionist spokesmen were strongly entrenched in the corridors of power and made astute use of their influence. The first drafts of the Balfour Declaration, indeed, were actually written by Zionists on Balfour's invitation. The Foreign Secretary minuted:

> "I have asked Lord Rothschild and Professor Weizmann to submit a formula."[14]

So great was the influence of the Jewish community in Whitehall that the Cabinet actually paid more attention to expressions of opposition to Zionism when they came from Jews than when they came from Arabs. One decision of the War Cabinet read as follows:

> "Before coming to a decision they should hear the views of representative Zionists as well as of those who held the opposite opinion, and that meanwhile the declaration, as read by Lord Milner, should be submitted confidentially to a) President Wilson, b) leaders of the Zionist Movement, c) representative persons in Anglo-Jewry opposed to Zionism."[15]

No one appears to have suggested that any Arabs should be consulted in any way, despite the fact that the territory whose future was under discussion had a population of whom more than 90 per cent were Arabs.

On 31 October 1917, the War Cabinet finally approved the Balfour Declaration. The minutes of the meeting are revealing about Balfour's own attitude:

> "The Secretary of State for Foreign Affairs stated that . . . the vast majority of Jews in Russia and America as, indeed, all over the world, now appeared to be favourable to Zionism. If we could make a declaration favourable to such an ideal, we should be able to carry on extremely useful propaganda both in Russia and America." [16]

Immediately after the publication of the Declaration, the government took a number of steps which further increased the power of the Zionist lobby. A special branch for Jewish propaganda was established in the Foreign Office under the control of a Zionist, Mr A. Hyamson, whose propaganda material was distributed to Jewish communities all over the world.[17] In addition, a Zionist commission was dispatched to Palestine. Its object was "to carry out, subject to General Allenby's authority, any steps required to give effect to the government's declaration in favour of the establishment in Palestine of a national home for the Jewish people." The leader of the commission was Dr Weizmann, and its members included distinguished Zionists of other nationalities. It scarcely needs saying that no similar commission was established to give effect to the other undertaking contained in the Balfour Declaration: the undertaking that "nothing shall be done that may prejudice the civil and religious rights" of the Arab community in Palestine.

Unlike the Arabs, Weizmann had easy access to Balfour at all times. The manner in which he exerted his influence can be judged from a letter to Balfour, dated 30 May 1918, about British administration in Palestine:

> "The Arabs, who are superficially clever and quick-witted, worship one thing, and one thing only—power and success . . . The British authorities . . . knowing as they do the treacherous nature of the Arab, they have to watch carefully and constantly that nothing should happen which might give the Arabs the slightest grievance or ground of complaint. In other words, the Arabs have to be 'nursed' lest they should stab the army in the back. The Arab, quick as he is to gauge such a situation, tries to make the most of it. He screams as often as he can and blackmails as much as he can. . . . The fairer the English regime tries to be the more arrogant the Arab becomes. It must also be taken into consideration that the Arab official knows the language, habits and ways of the country, is a 'roué' and therefore has a great advantage over the fair and clean-minded English official, who is not

conversant with the subtleties and subterfuges of the oriental mind. So the English are 'run' by the Arabs."[18]

Though Conservative and Liberal leaders were always accessible to the Zionist lobby and susceptible to its arguments, it was the Labour Party which welcomed Zionists most warmly to its ranks and gave the most consistent support to their aims. When the second minority Labour Government was formed in 1929, the post of Colonial Secretary went to Sidney Webb (who in the same year became Lord Passfield), who thus found himself responsible for the affairs of Palestine at a critical turning-point in the evolution of the Zionist national home.

In August 1929, only weeks after the formation of the new government, serious rioting broke out in Jerusalem as a result of a religious dispute over the Wailing Wall. It spread quickly to other parts of Palestine, and among both Jews and Arabs more than two hundred and forty people were killed and nearly six hundred injured before order was restored. Webb was at once subjected to intense pressure from the Zionists; his wife Beatrice wrote in her diary on 2 September 1929:

"Roused by the tragic happenings in Palestine there have buzzed around him Jews and admirers of Jews, great and small, in a state of violent grief and agitation demanding revenge and compensation. It is noteworthy that no representative of the Arabs—not even a casual admirer of the Arabs—has appeared on the scene."[19]

Sidney Webb's Under-Secretary of State, Sir Drummond Shiels, wrote that "there was never any relief or escape" from Palestine, and that

"the representatives of the Zionists in London were constant in their requests for interviews with the Secretary of State, with myself, or with the Head of the Palestine Division. . . . Vigorous Zionist propaganda was being carried out in the press and in Parliament.

There was no Arab agency in London at that time and there was no popular public statement of the Arab case ... Only the Zionist side of the Palestine question was heard and pressure was constantly being applied to the Colonial Office by MPs and others ... It can be imagined that Sidney Webb found this subject difficult. It was one in which reasoned argument was often in abeyance."[20]

A special commission appointed by the British Government to investigate the riots found that the underlying cause was Arab opposition to Jewish immigration and to the whole policy of establishing in Palestine a Jewish 'national home'.[21] There was nothing new about this; the opposition of the Palestinian Arabs was well known and, as we can see now, perfectly justified, since the policy to which they were objecting was indeed, as they feared, to lead to their own dispossession from their homeland. But up to this point the Zionists had always been able to use their influence to see that Arab objections were overruled.

In 1929, however, it looked as though the rioting in Jerusalem might persuade the government to think again about a policy which aroused such heartfelt opposition. The government showed itself sufficiently concerned to institute a further enquiry into the whole question of Jewish immigration, which evidently lay at the root of the trouble. This enquiry, carried out in 1930 by Sir John Hope Simpson, revealed something that the British administrators in Palestine knew to be the case, but to which ministers in London (under constant pressure from the Zionists) had so far turned a blind eye: the fact that Jewish colonisation was causing the displacement of many Palestinian Arabs, who were being evicted from any lands bought by the Zionists. It was a point of cardinal importance, and it impressed the fair-minded Sidney Webb and prompted the Labour Government to issue in October 1930 the important declaration of policy known as the Passfield White Paper. This reasserted a principle that was in danger of being forgotten: the principle that in Palestine

"... a double undertaking is involved, to the Jewish people on the one hand, and the non-Jewish population of Palestine on the other," adding that "Any hasty decision in regard to more unrestricted Jewish immigration is to be strongly deprecated ..."

All that the White Paper did was to remind all parties that Britain's support for Jewish immigration and the national home was not unconditional; it was qualified by the guarantee, contained in the Balfour Declaration, that the rights of the indigenous Palestinians were to be safeguarded. Yet this simple reassertion of a principle which should never have been in doubt threw the Zionists into consternation. The success of their undertaking depended precisely on persuading the British Government to throw overboard its promise to protect the Palestinians. Faced with what they rightly saw as a crisis in their fortunes, the Zionists mounted a characteristically vigorous and thorough counter-attack. Demonstrations against the White Paper were mounted outside British consulates as far apart as Warsaw and Chicago. A massive press campaign was launched in Britain and Members of Parliament were energetically canvassed. All the sympathisers of Zionism rallied: Lloyd George, General Smuts, Baldwin, Chamberlain; and Weizmann obtained an introduction to the Prime Minister, Ramsay MacDonald (through Lady Astor), and set to work to win him also to the Zionist point of view.

The upshot was the same as it had been on previous occasions. Ramsay MacDonald beat a hasty retreat, taking control of Palestine affairs out of the hands of Sidney Webb and handing it over to a Cabinet committee, which was authorised to discuss the question with a committee from the Jewish Agency. Between them these two committees drafted a long letter to Weizmann which MacDonald signed in February 1931 and which amounted to a complete repudiation of the White Paper. Weizmann in his autobiography emphasises the importance of MacDonald's surrender:

"... it was under MacDonald's letter to me that the change came about in the Government's attitude, and in the attitude of the

Palestine administration, which enabled us to make the magnificent gains of the ensuing years. It was under MacDonald's letter that Jewish immigration into Palestine was permitted to reach figures like forty thousand for 1934 and sixty-two thousand for 1935, figures undreamed of in 1930."[22]

The Zionist lobby often included distinguished and influential non-Jewish supporters. In the 1930s, the most active of them was probably Arthur Balfour's niece, Mrs Blanche Dugdale. Her diaries give a clear picture of the intimacy of the Zionist lobby's contacts with the Cabinet. This, for example is the entry for 3 September 1936:

"Yesterday in London (Cabinet) considered Palestine. I went in morning to Zionist Office. At 1.15 Walter[23] rang me up to say that the subject had only just been reached on (Cabinet) agenda, and they would go on after lunch. So Lewis[24] and I lunched with Chaim[25] at Carlton Grill, rather cheered because Walter said discussion beginning well. Returned to Roland Gardens to pack, and then again to Zionist Office to wait. About 4.30 Walter rang up to say all was *well*. No departure from Billy's[26] statement in House last July that violence must cease before negotiations. I went into Chaim's room, where he, Lewis, Ben Gurion and Arthur Lourie, and told them on condition news should go no further, not even to Shertok.[27] A moment of great emotion and thankfulness and then we began discussing the next steps . . ."[28]

What is extraordinary about this extract—and many others in Mrs Dugdale's revealing diaries—is that she is describing without apology (quite the contrary) a pattern of behaviour which would normally be considered scandalous, if not positively treasonable. A member of the British government was communicating Cabinet secrets to a private individual acting on behalf of a group of foreign nationals—a group, moreover, which represented one party to a dispute closely involving theinterests and the reputation of the British people.

The Zionists also enjoyed easy access to ministers in Mr Attlee's postwar Labour government. A striking example is given in Professor

Hugh Thomas's biography of Mr John Strachey,[29] who was at this time Under-Secretary of State for Air:

> "Only on Palestine did Strachey have any serious dispute with the government. One day, Crossman,[30] now in the House of Commons, came to see Strachey. The former was devoting his efforts to the Zionist cause. He had heard from his friends in the Jewish Agency that they were contemplating an act of sabotage, not only for its own purpose but to demonstrate to the world their capacities. Should this be done, or should it not? Few would be killed. But would it help the Jews? Crossman asked Strachey for his advice, and Strachey, a member of the Defence Committee of the Cabinet, undertook to find out. The next day in the Smoking Room at the House of Commons, Strachey gave his approval to Crossman. The Haganah went ahead and blew up all the bridges over the Jordan. No one was killed, but the British Army in Palestine were cut off from their lines of supply with Jordan."

Here the implications are even more startling. At a time when the hard-pressed British army in Palestine is struggling to uphold the policy of the British (Labour) Government against attacks mounted by Zionist terrorists, a (Labour) Member of Parliament who supports the Zionists feels free to approach a Minister and ask him whether to encourage a specific terrorist action *against the British army in Palestine*. Most astonishing of all is the fact that the Minister, who is actually a member of the government's Defence Committee, gives his "approval" for the action, which mercifully (and against the expectations of those who had planned it, and presumably of the MP and the Minister as well) caused no loss of life, but which did aggravate the difficult and dangerous situation of the British army in Palestine.

Such behaviour by supposedly responsible members of the Labour Party and Government would be inconceivable in any context other than that of Zionism.

Over the years, Zionists have been much more active and influential inside the Labour Party than inside the Conservative or

Liberal parties. The Liberal Party is perhaps the most deeply committed to Israel of all the parties, but it has never had organised bodies of Zionist activists within its own ranks, as has the Labour Party. There have been Jewish Socialist groups in Britain since 1902, and in 1920 Paole Zion, the British section of the International Organisation of Socialist Zionists, was affiliated to the Labour Party, and from then on campaigned actively for Zionism within the party. It regularly presented resolutions to the annual conference, and organised a range of "front" organisations, of which the most important was, and still is, the Labour Friends of Israel.

Before the affiliation of Paole Zion there is no record of any Labour MP raising the subject of Palestine in Parliament; but after 1920 a steady stream of pro-Zionist questions began. The first speech on Palestine from the Labour benches was made in 1922 by Mr Josiah Wedgwood, MP for Newcastle-under-Lyme, who argued that Zionism was welcomed by the Arab common people and opposed only by feudal landlords. This line of propaganda became a familiar Zionist theme in subsequent years; it was, of course, completely fraudulent, as later became apparent, but it greatly influenced generations of credulous Labour Party members. Ironically, the Zionist trade union movement in Palestine, the Histadrut, which was warmly supported by Labour Party members, was ensuring at this time that jobs created by Jewish capital went to Jews only and that where land was bought from Arab landlords, the Palestinian Arabs working on it should be evicted and replaced by immigrant Jews. Discrimination of this kind, in matters directly affecting the welfare and indeed the livelihood of the poorer Arabs, greatly increased their resentment towards the Zionists and was repeatedly cited by British officials during the 1920s and '30s as the cause of the growing unrest in Palestine. Unfortunately the Zionists were able to use their influence in Britain to play down these dangerous realities, of which the public had little idea.

In the 1930s and '40s the Zionists consolidated their grip on the Labour Party and came completely to control its policy on the Middle East. Occasional attempts were made at party conferences, usually by left-wing members, to draw attention to the rights of the Palestinians, but these lacked organisation and secured little or no support in the votes. The extent of Zionist influence in the party can be measured by the following passage in the National Executive Committee's report for 1944, which was officially adopted by the party's annual conference:

> "Palestine surely is a case, on human grounds and to promote a stable settlement, for a transfer of population. *Let the Arabs be encouraged to move out, as the Jews move in.*[31] Let them be compensated handsomely for their land and let their settlement elsewhere be carefully organised and generously financed. The Arabs have very wide territories of their own; they must not claim to exclude the Jews from this small part of Palestine, less than the size of Wales. Indeed we should examine also the possibility of extending the present Palestinian boundaries by agreement with Egypt, Syria or Transjordan."[32]

This statement of policy was so extreme that it embarrassed even the Zionists themselves, who were more sensitive than some of their supporters to the effect it might have on liberal opinion. Looking back at the episode in his autobiography, Weizmann wrote:

> "I remember that my Labour friends were, like myself, greatly concerned about this proposal. We have never contemplated the removal of the Arabs, and the British Labourites, in their pro-Zionist enthusiasm, went far beyond our intentions."[33]

In the event, of course, the birth of the Jewish state was to cause the dispossession of some three-quarters of a million Palestinian Arabs. The Israelis, whether or not they provoked the Arab exodus, certainly profited by it; but, as Weizmann said, they never officially advocated the removal of the Palestinians, and the Israelis to this day deny that they ever intended it.[34] (Their protestations are seriously weakened by the fact that, whether they meant to get rid of the Palestinians or not, they have adamantly refused ever since to allow them back.) Thus the

Labour Party, which took on itself the role of a kind of Zionist fifth column in 1944, is probably the only political party in the world to have openly advocated that the Palestinians should be exiled from their home-land to make way for the future Israelis. Certainly nobody else has suggested, as the Labour Party did in 1944, the possibility of extending the boundaries of the Jewish state (which at that time did not even exist) at the expense of Egypt, Syria and Transjordan. It is not surprising that today Arabs with any knowledge of history feel deeply suspicious of the intentions of the British Labour Party where Palestine is concerned.

After the war, with the election of a Labour government, the Zionist campaign within the Labour movement became particularly intense. Much of the new effort was concentrated on the Parliamentary Labour Party,[35] but the pressure was also fully maintained inside the National Executive Committee, whose chairman for 1945/6 was Professor Harold Laski, an active pro-Zionist, who declared that he was trying to organise "an internal opposition to fight the Attlee-Bevin betrayal of the Jews."[36] During 1947 he had an "angry and futile" correspondence with Attlee and "bitter recriminations" with Bevin, of whom Laski said: "E.B. has got to a stage of anti-Semitism that is fantastic."

In his allegations of anti-Semitism against Ernest Bevin Laski was joined by Kingsley Martin, who was also a Zionist. In his book on Laski, Kingsley Martin wrote of Bevin:

> "The Foreign Secretary's hatred of the Jews was not hidden, it was only too terribly apparent in New York. It gave colour to the view that Ernest Bevin wanted to see the Jews crushed."

If, however, Martin had had any evidence that Bevin was anti-Jewish and not merely passionately anti-Zionist, he would surely have quoted it. The fact that he did not do so suggests that the aim of this passage was simply to discredit Bevin. It was the technique which the Zionists were to employ throughout their struggle: the technique of promoting damaging personal attacks on those who stood in their way, rather than trying to counter their arguments.

Since the Second World War, Zionist pressure on Labour governments has been exerted less through the National Executive Committee than through the Parliamentary Labour Party. According to the *Jewish Chronicle*,[37] forty-six Jewish MPs were elected in the general election in October 1974, and all except one or two of them were dedicated supporters of Israel. Jewish MPs who are pro-Israeli tend to be much more active and persistent lobbyists than MPs who are friendly to the Arabs, for whom good relations with the Arabs is simply one good cause among many. Pro-Arab MPs may be sincere and courageous but since they are not themselves Arabs they do not feel the consuming emotional commitment of the pro-Israeli Jewish MP. Consequently they tend to be less militant and vociferous.

It is hard to convey the bitterness with which Labour MPs who spoke up for the Arabs between 1967 and 1973 were treated by their Zionist colleagues in the Parliamentary Labour Party. One of the first victims was the late Will Griffiths, MP for Manchester Exchange, who made a brave speech in the House of Commons on 31 May 1967, to the accompaniment of almost continuous barracking. Hansard records that he gave way to seven interventions and that there were no less than twenty-three other interruptions and attempts to shout him down.[38]

The Guardian recorded a similar experience of my own at this time, when I tried to address a meeting of the Labour Party's Foreign Affairs Group, which had been called to discuss the Middle East.

> "Bitterness came to the surface when Mr Mayhew began to speak . . . The interruptions began when he argued that it was wrong to talk in terms of racial extermination by the Arab forces in their war against Israel . . . He was almost shouted down when he went on to claim that the existence of the Palestinian refugees was the root of the crisis."[39]

I remember that meeting very well. From the moment I stood up, Zionist MPs did not stop shouting abuse at me. I was given no protection by the Chair, and after struggling on for about five minutes, gave up. I know of no other instance of a member of the Parliamentary Labour Party who had been called upon to speak by the Chairman not being allowed a hearing.

In later years, as the case against Israel became more widely accepted, it became difficult to get the Middle East discussed at all in the Parliamentary Labour Party. After the October War, an attempt to raise the question was successfully stifled by the pro-Israelis, and at the time of writing there has been no discussion of the Middle East at a Parliamentary Labour Party meeting for several years.

So uneven was the balance of forces in the Parliamentary Labour Party that an initiative by pro-Arabs was likely to provoke a formidable and emotional counter-offensive. A typical example occurred in 1970, when a number of Labour MPs put down an Early Day Motion about arms deliveries to the Middle East. Within a few days, the Order Paper had been flooded with amendments from pro-Israeli MPs.[40]

Until October 1973, a major asset to the Zionists in the Labour movement was, of course, the antipathy towards the Arabs and the deep personal commitment to Israel of the Party leader, Mr Harold Wilson. Towards the end of 1972 the *Jewish Chronicle* reported a typical speech of his:

> "Mr. Wilson said that the Labour Party had proved both in and out of government that they had given the strongest support to Israel at moments of greatest danger. 'This is not in doubt and what I say has been supported on public occasions by every leader in Israel,' he declared. Mr and Mrs Wilson are going to Israel next month when they will visit their son Giles, who is working on a kibbutz . . . 'I do not see that there will be a permanent solution at the moment,' he declared. The Arabs, he said, want Israel to move back to the boundaries that existed before the Six Day War. 'It is utterly unreal to talk of withdrawal,' Mr Wilson told his audience. '. . . Israel's reaction is natural and proper in refusing to accept the Palestinians as a nation. It is not recognised as a nation by the world.' "[41]

Attempts have been made[42] to list the names of the influential Jewish supporters of Israel who enjoyed easy access to Mr Wilson during his political career, not only as members of the Parliamentary Labour Party, the Labour Friends of Israel, the Jewish Board of Deputies and Paole Zion, but as his ministers, legal advisers, publishers, employers, press officers and personal friends. There can be little doubt that as Prime Minister he was far more accessible to Zionists and pro-Zionists, and—at least until October 1973—far less accessible to Arabs and pro-Arabs than any previous British statesman, including even Mr Balfour.

The one-sidedness of Mr Wilson's contacts naturally caused considerable concern, especially among those who were responsible for promoting British exports to the Arab World. In April 1970, it was decided to form a high-level deputation of such people, and to ask the Prime Minister for an interview. The deputation included the Chairmen of three concerns of outstanding importance to British interests in the Middle East: the Mitchell Cotts Group, the Inchcape Group, and the British Bank of the Middle East. Two other members were Sir Maurice Bridgman (now Lord Bridgman) and Sir Charles Duke, President and Director-General respectively of the Middle East Association, which represents British firms with business interests in the Middle East. Remarkably, Mr Wilson declined to see the deputation. Surprised by the discourtesy, its members subsequently wrote to him as follows:

> "We are naturally anxious that those who are concerned for good relations between this country and the Middle East as a whole, and for the promotion of the immensely important British commercial and financial interests in the Arab World, should enjoy the same access to yourself as is obtained by organisations representing Zionist and Jewish opinion in this country, such as the Jewish Board of Deputies. We feel very strongly the need, in the interests of this country, to ensure that all points of view on the Middle East should be seen to be fully taken into account when British policy is being considered. This was the reason for our seeking a meeting with you. From our

contacts in the Arab World we are convinced that there is a widespread impression among the Arabs, rightly or wrongly, of bias in this country in favour of Israel and that this is most prejudicial to British interests. We would urge that whatever is possible should be done to counteract it."[43]

The one-sidedness of Mr Wilson's contacts with the Middle East may help to explain his remarkable speeches on the Arab-Israeli conflict during the period up to and including the October War. On 27 December 1972, for example, speaking in Jerusalem, he attacked the nearly unanimous resolution of the United Nations General Assembly of 8 December, comparing the British Government's support for it with support for the Munich Settlement, and declaring that it could endanger Israel's integrity and even its existence.[44] This resolution was supported by eighty-six member states and opposed by only seven. It invited Israel to declare its adherence to the principle of non-annexation of territory by force; affirmed that respect for the rights of the Palestinians was an inseparable element in the establishment of a just and lasting peace in the Middle East; and called upon Israel to desist from policies and practices affecting the demographic structure and physical character of the occupied Arab territories.

Support for such objectives would be normal for a social democratic party, and was indeed forthcoming from almost all the social democratic parties of the world. Possibly the British Labour Party, in view of its strong Zionist orientation, might have been expected to take a compromise position, neither supporting nor opposing the resolution. But in fact, astonishingly, Mr Wilson committed the party to outright opposition, thereby aligning Her Majesty's Opposition with Costa Rica, the Dominican Republic, El Salvador, Haiti, Nicaragua, Uruguay and Israel herself against virtually the whole of Africa, Asia, Western Europe, and the Communist World. Not even the United States government (whose representative abstained in the voting) ventured to go so far in support of Israel as Mr Wilson did, on behalf of the British Labour Party.

The *Jewish Observer* of 29 December 1972, under the headline *Pilgrim Harold*, reported:

> "Tidings of comfort and joy were brought to Israel's political leaders this week by Harold Wilson. The Opposition Leader told members of the Knesset Foreign Affairs and Security Committee that the British Labour Party supported in principle Israel's views on the Middle East."

Two days earlier, Mr Wilson had celebrated Christmas Day in Jerusalem by making a public personal attack on Mr Andrew Faulds, MP, and myself. The *Jewish Chronicle*[45] reported:

> "Speaking in Jerusalem on Monday, Mr Wilson indicated that the Parliamentary Labour Party in Britain will soon 'deal with' the speeches made by Mr Christopher Mayhew and Mr Andrew Faulds in the Foreign Affairs Debate in the House of Commons before the House rose for the Christmas recess.
>
> "While referring to the close links between the British and Israeli Labour movements, Mr Wilson said that he recognised that there were 'a couple of mavericks in our (the British Labour Party's) ranks ... who made extraordinary speeches in the last debate (in the Commons) which the Party would deal with.'"

There can be little question that Mr Wilson's speeches were very widely welcomed in Israel and had a powerful effect, reinforcing the position of those Israeli leaders, such as Mrs Golda Meir and Mr Moshe Dayan, who held that there was no prospect of a renewal of war, that Israel could best achieve its ends by holding on to Arab territory, and that therefore there was no need for the Israelis to pay attention to the resolutions of the UN calling on Israel to withdraw from the occupied territories and to respect the rights of the Palestinians.

Today it is widely recognised that the policies to whose support Mr Wilson committed himself and the British Labour Party were gravely mistaken and that they were the principal cause of the fresh outbreak of war in the Middle East in October 1973.

❖ ❖ ❖

Compared with the pervasiveness and power of the Zionist lobby, Arab pressure on British governments up to October 1973 was virtually negligible. This was particularly true of the years immediately before and after the publication of the Balfour Declaration. True, petitions were sent to London from time to time by various groups of Arab notables in Palestine. One of these at the time of the Versailles Peace Conference read:

> "No sooner were we delivered from the yoke of the Turks, than we heard the rumours disseminated by the Zionists to the effect that our country would be a national home for them ... The principles of justice and equity cannot admit of the crushing of a nation by an influx of a greater number of another foreign nation that will assimilate her ... The country is ours and has been so of old. We have lived in it longer than they did, worked in it more than they did. Our historical and religious relations with it, we Moslems and Christians, far exceed those of the Jews ...
>
> "The number of Jews in Palestine does not exceed at the highest estimate one eighth of the number of the natives, and their land possessions are not more than three per cent. Does justice then allow of the violation of the rights of the majority? The native Jews of Palestine have been and still are our brethren in pleasure and sorrow.
>
> We can live with them peacefully and happily, and enjoy the same individual freedom ..."

An official of the Foreign Office coolly minuted on this petition:

> "The associated governments are all so wedded to Zionism that the appeal is foredoomed to failure. I suppose we should send on the petition addressed to President Wilson, through the US Embassy."[46]

In 1920, a letter was sent to the Chief Administrator in Jerusalem from "a number of persons of Nazareth and district":

"In view of the declaration of the decision of the peace conference regarding the establishment of a Jewish national home in Palestine, we hereby beg to declare that we are the owners of this country and the land is our national home . . ."

Another letter, from "Beduin chiefs of Transjordan", read:

"We the undersigned Sheikhs of the Tribes and Heads of the Clans are of the opinion to put before your eyes the following facts. 1) Palestine is dear to us therefore we can never accept that the newcomers should rob it from our hands. 2) Palestine is sacred to us, consequently we can never forget the danger surrounding it. 3) The Zionist danger which threatens Palestine at present shall soon menace us and the Arab nation at large . . . It is not just therefore that you should give no heed whatever to our request . . ."[47]

Appeals of this kind from Palestine, artless, moving and prescient, were brushed aside, and it was not until several years after the Balfour Declaration that the Arabs actually came to London to present their point of view. Then, in August 1921, an Arab delegation arrived consisting of both Muslims and Christians. It was typical of the manner in which the dice were loaded against them that they should have been preceded by patronising reports on their personalities from the Palestine High Commissioner, Herbert Samuel, who was a leading Jewish supporter of Zionism. Their visit, though protracted, was a failure. The pro-Zionist Colonial Secretary, Mr Winston Churchill, treated them with little courtesy, and when they at last left he declined to bid them farewell in person.

But even if the Arabs had enjoyed the same access to the decision-makers as the Jews, and had been as persistent and persuasive as they were, it would have availed them little. For, as Mr Balfour himself explained, with remarkable frankness:

". . . in Palestine we do not propose even to go through the form of consulting the wishes of the present inhabitants of the country, though the American Commission has been going through the form of asking what they are.

"The four Great Powers are committed to Zionism. And Zionism, be it right or wrong, good or bad, is rooted in age-long traditions, in present needs, in future hopes, of far profounder import than the desires and prejudices of the 700,000 Arabs who now inhabit that ancient land . . .

"Whatever deference should be paid to the views of those living there, the Powers in their selection of a Mandatory do not propose, as I understand the matter, to consult them. In short, so far as Palestine is concerned, the Powers have made no statement of fact which is not admittedly wrong, and no declaration of policy, which, at least in the letter, they have not always intended to violate."[48]

However, the delegation found some support in Parliament, especially in the House of Lords. On 21 June 1922 the following motion was moved by Lord Islington:

"That the mandate for Palestine in its present form is unacceptable to this House, because it directly violates the pledges made by His Majesty's Government to the people of Palestine in the declaration of October 1915, and again in the declaration of November 1918, and is, as at present framed, opposed to the sentiments and wishes of a great majority of the people of Palestine; that, therefore, its acceptance by the Council of the League of Nations should be postponed until such modifications have therein been effected as will comply with pledges given by His Majesty's Government."

Remarkably, this motion was carried, by 60 votes to 29, and the Government was defeated. Immediately afterwards, however, the decision was overwhelmingly reversed in the House of Commons, and the Colonial Secretary was able to telegraph to the administration in Palestine:

"Last night House of Commons by a majority of 292 to 35 rejected motion criticising Palestine Mandate . . . I stated that special significance attached to the vote by reason of adverse vote recently recorded in House of Lords . . . No doubt is left by vote in House of Commons that in their Palestine policy His Majesty's Government have support of country . . ."[49]

During the 1920s there were one or two Labour Members of Parliament who spoke up in the House of Commons for the Arabs. Mr T. S. B. Williams, MP for Lambeth, and Mr F. Seymour-Cox, MP for the Broxted Division of Nottinghamshire, bravely argued that Labour support for Zionism contradicted the principles of self-determination and was bitterly opposed by the overwhelming majority of the inhabitants of Palestine. Seymour-Cox waged a long, though unsuccessful, campaign to get the Hussein-MacMahon correspondence of 1915-18 published, and persistently pointed out that the pledges which Britain had given to the Arabs two years before the Balfour Declaration were totally inconsistent with Zionist claims. He was supported by Mr Fenner (later Lord) Brockway, MP for Leyton East, and by the Reverend Gordon Lang (Oldham) and Mr J. J. McShane (Walsall).

All these attempts to explain the Arabs' point of view were the spontaneous initiatives of a few courageous individuals. It was not until much later—after the 1967 war—that MPs who were friendly to the Arabs began to organise themselves, for much-needed mutual aid and encouragement. In January 1969 twenty-nine Labour MPs, drawn from the right, left and centre of the party, established the Labour Middle East Council, and elected the present writer as Chairman. The Council's objectives, as defined in its constitution, are:

"In furtherance of the aims of the Labour Party, to work for peace and justice in the Middle East and for the implementation of the United Nations resolutions to that effect by promoting inside the Labour movement a constructive and balanced view of the Arab-Israeli conflict."

At the Council's first annual meeting, a unanimous decision was taken to affiliate to the Labour Party. But the application was rejected by the National Executive Committee, on the sole ground that the objects of the Council "differ only in emphasis from those of the party nationally . . . It was felt that the present constitution and rules adequately cover the objects as set out by your Council . . ."

Thus the Council's application for affiliation was rejected on the grounds that its aims and objects agreed with those of the Labour Party. But this is true, of course, of all affiliated organisations: if their aims conflicted fundamentally with those of the party they would not be affiliated.[50] The NEC refused even to receive a deputation from the Labour Middle East Council, and also refused to include any reference to its decision in its report to the Annual Conference of the Labour Party, so that the decision could not be debated there.

LMEC renewed its application to affiliate in 1971 and again in 1972. On each occasion the application was rejected, and without further explanation.

In 1973, however, following some lively criticism in the party of Mr Harold Wilson's speeches in Israel, there appeared to be a slight change of mood on the NEC. The Labour Middle East Council was invited to submit its views to the International Committee. A memorandum was submitted, and the NEC's subsequent draft foreign policy document contained one or two significant changes. It emphasised "the necessity of involving the Palestinian community fully in any settlement which has a chance of working" and also, in a passage dealing with terrorism, referred to terrorist attacks as "the symptoms of what is wrong rather than the root cause, which is the failure to find a fair and humane solution to the problems of the Palestine community."

When the October War broke out, Mr Wilson, as expected, gave the party a strong pro-Israeli lead. Speaking in the House of Commons on 18 October 1973, he exonerated Israel from all blame for the failure to reach a settlement, named the Arabs as aggressors and put forward a formula for British arms delivery which would in practice have permitted arms supplies to Israel but not to the Arab countries. He specifically rejected a policy of neutrality for Britain:

> "I doubt that there will be in this case much of a role for the professional neutral. The role of mediation is most likely to rest upon those who have won the confidence not of both sides ... but upon those who have won the confidence of one side ...
>
> "It (peace) will come, I believe, through the wisdom and patience of the duellists' seconds, of the duellists' friends, not from those who may have tried to avoid any commitment in this situation."

But on this occasion Mr Wilson notably failed to carry the party with him. An attempt by Mr Robert Mellish, MP, himself a strong supporter of Israel, to impose a three-line whip aroused strong resistance. More than eighty Labour MPs made it clear that they would oppose the imposition of such a whip; and the Shadow Cabinet finally took the unusual decision that, while they themselves would vote against the Government and in favour of a more pro-Israeli policy, the rest of the party would have a free vote. In the subsequent division, no less than ninety Labour MPs failed to vote with their leaders, and fifteen of them actually voted with the Government. Shortly afterwards, criticism of Mr Wilson's line was expressed at a meeting of the Shadow Cabinet, and two senior members of the Shadow Cabinet informed leading Arab ambassadors that Mr Wilson's speeches did not represent official Labour Party policy. This partial emancipation from the tyranny of the Zionist lobby was especially noteworthy in view of the exceptional steps taken by the Israeli Embassy to influence the outcome of the debate.[51]

After this set-back, it seems doubtful whether the Zionist lobby in the Labour movement will ever again exercise the same easy domination over party policy in the Middle East. As has already been noted, its success in converting to Zionism and to the support of Israel an organisation with such strong anti-colonialist and anti-racialist traditions was an extraordinary feat of political propaganda and pressure. It meant, inevitably, that the Labour Party had to apply double standards in the starkest manner in its dealings with Israel and with the rest of the world. This can perhaps be seen most clearly when we compare the party's differing attitudes to Israel and to South Africa. Its support for the former has been as strong as its opposition to the latter; yet to the unprejudiced eye there are remarkable similarities between the two countries. Both treat the United Nations with contempt and repeatedly violate its charter and resolutions. Both are in violent conflict with left-wing liberation movements. Both present themselves to the West as bulwarks against communism—although both, in practice, are a blessing to the communists in their regions. In addition, both countries are colonialist and rule over large numbers of subject people in conquered territories. Neither has any legal or moral right to its colonial possessions, where each bases its stand openly on *force majeure*. South Africa's claim to Namibia and Israel's claim to East Jerusalem are both groundless. The Israeli claim, in particular, has been rejected unanimously both by the General Assembly and by the Security Council of the United Nations.

There are of course differences between the two countries in their treatment of their colonial populations. Police methods in East Jerusalem, though bad, are much less brutal than in Johannesburg, and the Arabs inside Israel (as opposed to those in the occupied territories) undoubtedly have more civil rights than the Africans in South Africa. But in other ways Zionism actually appears to bear harder on the subject race than apartheid. While apartheid removes non-whites from their homes, Zionism removes non-Jews from their homes and their country. Moreover, South Africa has no parallel with Israel's "Law of Return", under which no one who is not Jewish has the right to settle in Palestine, even if he was born there and his family had lived there for centuries, whereas anyone has the right to settle in Palestine, irrespective of anything else, provided only that he is Jewish.[52]

A further interesting similarity between the two countries emerges from the arguments used by their defenders to support them. "They have performed miracles of social and economic development," it is claimed in defence of the Israeli and the South African governments. "Surrounded by hostile countries, what else can they do?" And again: "They provide better wages and social services for the natives than those natives would get in their own countries." Arguments of this kind, used by the supporters of both Israel and South Africa, are acceptable only to those who put economic and political considerations above those of simple humanity. To expose their hollowness, we only have to ask ourselves whether we would prefer economic development or improved social services *under foreign rule* to the freedom to run our own affairs in our own way.

This parallel between Israel and South Africa is fully accepted by the Jewish community in South Africa. Discussing the matter at a time when Israel was riding high after the 1967 war, the South African-Jewish publication, *Jewish Affairs*,[53] showed an admirable frankness:

> "The argument that Israel and South Africa have a basic community of interests in the Middle East and further south has more than a grain of truth. There is nothing secret or sinister about it. Strong ties between the two countries, closer than ever since the 1967 war, are inseparable from their geographical and strategic position, from their anti-Communist outlook, *and from all the realities of their national existence* . . ."[54]

It is a remarkable fact that the Labour Party leaders, although representing a movement which has always vigorously opposed racialism, colonialism, militarism and the acquisition of territory through conquest, appear never to have made any (recorded) public criticism of Israel at all. They have denounced every form of oppression of man by man except the oppression of Palestinians by Israelis. They have expressed sympathy for every other colonial liberation movement, but not for the Palestinian struggle for a national identity. They have opposed colonialism and military government in every part of the world except Palestine. They have attacked racial discrimination by Russians against Jews, but never by Jews against Palestinians.

What, then, is the secret of the astounding political success of the Zionist lobby in Britain? It is to be found mainly in the degree of commitment and dedication to Israel of many influential Jewish people, going far beyond the sympathy for Eire felt by many British citizens of Irish extraction, or the nostalgic identification with Pakistan of many Pakistani emigrés. The commitment to Israel of many Jewish people is passionate, purposeful and elaborately organised. Moreover it is encouraged and exploited for her own purposes by Israel, in a manner which the Irish and Pakistani governments wisely abjure.

Such a deep commitment to a foreign country inevitably exposes British Zionists to the charge of dual loyalties. In their defence to this, Zionist organisations have issued formal statements declaring that Jews in the Diaspora have only one political allegiance, their allegiance to the countries of their citizenship. Similarly, the state of Israel has stressed that only Israelis enjoy the rights and are subject to the obligations of citizenship in Israel; and has given formal assurances that whatever it may do through the channels open to it as a sovereign state to protect Jewish rights abroad, it does not act with any authority on behalf of the Diaspora.

Thus the formal situation is that British Jews are entitled to become citizens of Israel simply by virtue of being Jews; but that unless and until this happens, they are British citizens who acknowledge their political allegiance to the United Kingdom. Whether or not they can fairly be said to hold dual loyalties must plainly be a matter of judgment in individual cases. Among Jewish MPs in the House of Commons, for example, feeling for Israel ranges from a cool detachment at one extreme to passionate loyalty at the other.

Nevertheless, official Zionist policy statements strongly suggest that non-Israelis who are active Zionists can be fairly said to have dual loyalties, if not, indeed, a prior loyalty to Israel. Take, for example, these quotations from policy resolutions of the latest World Zionist Congress, held in Jerusalem in 1972.

> "Congress instructs the incoming Executive to ensure that all territorial Zionist organisations and individual members of the

Zionist Movement use their influence with the Jewish international, national and local organisations and associations which operate in the political, religious, youth, educational, welfare, cultural or social fields, in order to make them more and more Israel-oriented in accordance with the principle of the centrality of Israel in Jewish life . . .

"The following obligations stem from . . . membership in the Zionist organisation:

To realise his *aliya* (emigration) to Israel . . .

To study Hebrew, to give his children a Jewish education, and to bring them up towards *aliya* and Zionist self-fulfilment . . .

To contribute and to be active on behalf of the Zionist funds and to actively participate in the consolidation of Israel's economy . . .

"...The members and leaders of the Zionist Movement are called upon to use all the means at their disposal to encourage the present and future flow of *aliya* in their communities, especially through the intensification and the expansion of Jewish education.

"... As a step towards the personal fulfilment of the members of the Zionist Movement, Congress calls upon every parent to send at least one member of his family on *aliya* so that he may serve as a forerunner.

"... Zionists must make it their duty to link their own fate with that of Israel as potential *olim* (immigrants).

"...They must be ready to defend the state of Israel and the rights of the Jews wherever they may be; and contribute themselves and solicit from others contributions designed to strengthen the state of Israel and enhance absorptive capacity . . ."

Nobody who studies official Zionist pronouncements of this kind, or who examines the work of Zionist and other pro-Israeli organisations, can doubt that the question whether Zionists have or have not got dual loyalties, or even prior loyalties to Israel, is a serious and important one. Zionists themselves, however, tend to be extremely sensitive on the subject, and to try to suppress discussion of it, sometimes even suggesting that those who raise it are racialists. For example, when Mr Andrew Faulds, MP, ventured to refer to the matter in the House of Commons, in the foreign policy debates on 14 December 1972 and 18 October 1973, he was not only severely taken to task by his Party Leader, but actually deprived of his post as a Front Bench spokesman. In a letter to Mr Faulds dated 10 December 1973, Mr Harold Wilson wrote:

> "Your dropping from the Labour Front Bench had nothing to do with the 'unacceptability' of 'your Middle Eastern views'. Leading figures in the Party hold such views, and have never been criticised for this . . .
>
> "It was because of 'uncomradely behaviour'. In the Foreign Affairs Debate last December, you caused great offence by impugning the patriotism of Jewish Members of Parliament implying that they had dual loyalties. Despite the fact that this speech was publicly rebuked by me at a subsequent party meeting, you insisted on repeating the charge of dual loyalties in a Middle East Debate on the 18 October."

Mr Faulds was a member of the Executive Committee of the Labour Middle East Council, which came to his defence with a public statement in the following terms:

> "We believe many party colleagues will sympathise with Andrew Faulds. Party members should be as free to criticise Zionism and Zionists as to criticise capitalism and capitalists. Both are political doctrines which conflict at many points with the principles of democracy and socialism. One feature of Zionism, which is particularly resented by anti-Zionist Jews, is that it calls on Jewish people everywhere for acts of loyalty towards Israel. When the interests of Israel conflict with the interests of the nation to which these Jewish people belong, this inevitably creates divided loyalties. Nobody can understand the Middle East without taking account of this aspect of Zionism, and nobody should be penalised for discussing and criticising it freely."

Whether or not Zionists can be fairly said to have dual loyalties, they certainly support Israel with great vigour and often from positions of considerable influence. It is sometimes alleged that they give financial assistance to pro-Israeli political leaders and parties, but, if so, then British Zionists show much greater discretion about such transactions than their counterparts in the United States. No attempt has been made to conceal or "launder" the vast sums contributed by Jewish supporters of Israel to American political leaders such as Senator Hubert Humphrey, Senator Edmund Muskie, and Senator McGovern.[55] Referring to Mr Abraham Feinberg, then Chairman of the Board of Directors of the Israel Bond Organisation, the *Jewish Post and Opinion* of 21 May 1971 said:

"His gifts to Mr Humphrey ranged from $250,000 to $ 1 million."

This degree of commitment to Israel on the part of Jewish citizens of other countries is a source of danger as well as strength to the Jewish people as a whole. It inevitably sets them apart from their fellow-nationals and exposes them to the charge of lack of patriotism. It was a distinguished Jew—the only Jewish member of Lloyd George's cabinet at the time of the Balfour Declaration—who wrote, in a Cabinet Paper, more than fifty years ago:

"Zionism has always seemed to me to be a mischievous political creed, untenable by any patriotic citizen of the United Kingdom. If a Jewish Englishman sets his eyes on the Mount of Olives and longs for the day when he will shake British soil from his shoes and go back to agricultural pursuits in Palestine, he has always seemed to me to have acknowledged aims inconsistent with British citizenship and to have admitted that he is unfit for a share in public life in Great Britain or to be treated as an Englishman."[56]

CHAPTER FOUR

Personal Pressures

Christopher Mayhew, Michael Adams

Christopher Mayhew writes

The Arab-Israeli conflict arouses strong feelings among the supporters of both sides in Britain. Each side puts its arguments with passionate conviction; and it is right that they should. But a striking feature of the way this 'battle of the lobbies' has been fought, especially between 1967 and 1973, has been the relentless way in which those of us who choose to speak up for the Arabs have been harassed by our opponents. They seem not to be satisfied with trying to prove us wrong; they have to prove us wicked as well. Indeed, they sometimes showed themselves much less concerned to answer our arguments than to try to damage our reputations—and they can be surprisingly unscrupulous in the way they go about it.

We on our side, as we have shown in the preceding chapters, had no preconceived loyalty to one side or the other in the Middle East and stood to gain nothing—in fact, we stood to lose a good deal—by taking the unpopular side of the argument. The great majority of those who supported Israel, on the other hand, had much to gain by so doing, and were also motivated by a strong sense of kinship. In the light of the recent history of the Jews in Europe, it is easy to understand this feeling of solidarity, and indeed to sympathise with it. But it certainly could not be called an objective approach.

Perhaps it was this sense of personal involvement on their part that made our opponents so bitter against us. Perhaps it was fear that made them so anxious to deprive us of influence. But I believe the main reason was that their own devotion to Israel was so intense and unquestioning that they genuinely could not conceive that anyone would wish to criticise her except for thoroughly disreputable reasons. For them, Israel was such a splendid country, and her claims were so obviously just, that her critics must be either mad or bad; they must be left-wing crackpots, or anti-Semites, or else in the pay of the oil companies.

It followed logically that it was the duty of every right-thinking Jew to denounce these people, to expose their venality, their mendacity, their anti-Jewish prejudice, and to reveal them as being (whatever they might say to the contrary) supporters of terrorist attacks on defenceless women and children. Such people must be socially ostracised, and their influence as politicians, businessmen, writers or broadcasters neutralised as far as possible.

Feelings of this kind were at their most extreme in the period shortly after the June War of 1967, when the Israelis had achieved what looked to be a decisive advantage and their supporters made a determined effort to stifle any criticism of their policies of annexation and colonisation in Palestine. It was then that, to explain the Arab case on Palestine, and the importance to Britain of friendship with the Arabs, we formed the Council for the Advancement of Arab-British Understanding and the Labour Middle East Council.

During 1967 and 1968, and to a lesser extent right up to the October War of 1973, this meant swimming against a very strong tide of pro-Israeli opinion, a tide which was reflected in the generally pro-Israeli bias of the press and the broadcasting services and in the attitudes of the political parties. We had not expected to find our task an easy one, but we were startled by the vehemence with which, when we wrote a letter to *The Times* or spoke on public platforms, we were attacked and exposed to insult, and by the extraordinary anonymous letters which we became accustomed to receiving. In some respects these attacks were so bitter and unrestrained as to appear pathological.

Nevertheless, both organisations flourished and attracted support.

For a year the CAABU office was maintained courageously and almost single-handed by Miss Grania Birkett, with intermittent help from some of her friends. Then, in the spring of 1968, we felt the time had come to enlarge the staff, and Michael Adams was invited to become its Director. Though he would have preferred to continue his work as a writer, when he found that even the columns of *The Guardian* were no longer open to him he took office as part-time Director of the Council.

Michael Adams writes

When I took up the appointment with CAABU, I had already been under fire from the Jewish press in Britain over a series of articles I had written for *The Guardian*,[57] so I was not surprised to find myself attacked again; but even so, I was intrigued by the thoroughness with which an attempt was made to seal off all outlets for my work as a writer. For instance, a leading Jewish paper published in London reported that I had accepted the post of "public relations adviser to the Embassy of the United Arab Republic." The solicitor I consulted got the paper to publish an apology a week or two later, but the report must have prejudiced a lot of unsuspecting Jewish readers against both CAABU and myself. Soon afterwards, a paper called *Israel Today*, then published in Glasgow and today happily defunct, made an attack on me which the same solicitor said was undoubtedly libellous, although he advised against taking legal action.

The Israeli Ambassador in London, with remarkable presumption, summoned the managing director of a Jewish publishing house to account for the fact that he was employing me to edit a substantial reference book about Middle Eastern politics. Even the Director of Voluntary Service Overseas, for which I used to enjoy lecturing (and still do) to volunteers going out to work in the Middle East, received an urgent telephone call from a stranger who urged him not to make use any more of so dangerous a person as myself.

This kind of interference was to continue throughout the early years of my association with CAABU, causing me much unpleasantness and some loss of income, but I was relatively fortunate in being a freelance and so, when one outlet was closed to me, able to look for another. Several others among those who were active in the early days of CAABU found it necessary to discontinue or modify their activities with the Council in order to protect their livelihoods. And, for all their efforts, the Zionists were not always successful; often, indeed, they failed through overplaying their hand. The Director of VSO, for instance, had no hesitation in sending his anonymous caller about his business. Likewise, and more remarkably, the Jewish publisher of that reference book about Middle Eastern politics[58] stood out manfully against the pressure brought to bear on him by the Israeli Ambassador. After explaining to me his difficulty (without identifying the ambassador) and obtaining from me an assurance about the need for an objective approach, he not only published the book I edited for him but afterwards wrote a spirited defence of his action in the *Jewish Chronicle*, under the title, if my memory serves me, of "Why I stopped being a Zionist". Others found it harder to stick to their guns and it was very difficult, between 1967 and 1973, to persuade a publisher to take on a book which stated the Arab case over Palestine. The reasons for this were well known but they were seldom plainly stated. The following item in the *Evening Standard's* Londoner's Diary on 27 September 1972 was exceptional:

"*Granada drop book on the Arab problem*
"A book called *The Palestine Problem* has mysteriously disappeared from the lists of Rupert Hart Davis, a division of Granada Publishing, the chairman of which is Lord Bernstein. A detailed study of Palestine and the refugee problem, it was commissioned from Pamela Ferguson, a London journalist with wide experience of the Middle East, two years ago.

"Publication was to have been in January, as announced in the autumn edition of *The Bookseller*, and the text had been finally approved, up-dated and revised. Then Miss Ferguson discovered, when she rang up to inquire when the proofs would be ready, that the book was not to be published . . .

"Miss Ferguson suspects that the book was stopped because of political objections to it. She has been told unofficially that the objection came from high up in the Granada organisation.

"A spokesman for Granada denies that the objection is political, but declines further comment."

Nor was this the end of Miss Ferguson's problems. Six months later the *Evening Standard* took up the story again:

"Pamela Ferguson, a freelance journalist who spent two years in the Middle East, is encountering further problems in finding a publisher for her book, *The Palestine Problem*.

"The book has just been rejected, albeit reluctantly, by Tom Stacey, the publisher, on political grounds. His managing editor, Robin Wright, told Miss Ferguson's agent: 'The problem is that this excellent, level-headed and interesting book takes an anti-Zionist view, which unfortunately conflicts with a large project on which we are about to be engaged, where the panel of consulting editors are largely made up of eminent Zionists. As you will appreciate, it could make things awkward for us if this panel decided that the firm with whom they are associated was publishing a book which took a line, though not admittedly violent, against their own beliefs.' "[59]

Such an attitude was still commonplace, although publishers were beginning to resist attempts by the Zionists to browbeat them. All the same, the attempts were invariably made, often with remarkable effrontery. In 1972 I was asked by the publishers of the authoritative *Europa Year Book* to write an introductory article for their new edition of *The Middle East and North Africa*, as well as a short summary of the international issues raised by the Israelis' annexation of Arab Jerusalem. I did so, and this time it was the *Jewish Observer* which took it upon itself to tell the publishers their business, under a headline which suggested a certain lack of a sense of proportion:

"*The Amazing Rape of Europa*

"Of all the reference books about the Middle East, I have long held the *Europa Year Book* in the highest regard, especially since, a few years ago, it widened its framework to include North Africa.

"But the 19th edition, for 1972-3, has undergone a disturbing change. At the front of this remarkable compendium of hard facts we find three blatantly political articles. One is by Lord Caradon, Britain's former Ambassador to the UN, in which he spells out his 'essentials for peace'. It is all very high-minded but, unlike the facts in the rest of the book, hardly sacred. More surprising are the two other articles by Michael Adams, information director of the Council for the Advancement of Arab-British Understanding (CAABU). Even with the best will in the world, it is hard to expect him to give a balanced reading of *The Arab-Israel Confrontation 1967-1972*. Sure enough, he doesn't ... If the 20th edition of the Year Book is to merit the prestige of the first 18, it should drop Mr Adams' contribution like a hot potato."[60]

The publishers of the *Europa Year Book* were made aware of this criticism and I imagine they were grateful for the publicity. At all events, it is pleasant to record that they disregarded the advice proffered in the last sentence and in each succeeding year have asked me to expand my original articles and bring them up to date.

Even when an author was successful in getting a manuscript accepted by a publisher, and when nothing intervened to prevent its publication, there remained the problem of getting the book distributed and reviewed. A classic example here is Professor Maxime Rodinson's *Israel and the Arabs*, first published as a Penguin Special in 1969, re-published as a Pelican in 1970 and still probably the best book on the subject. Professor Rodinson's reputation as an orientalist, together with the fact that, although Jewish, he taught for seven years in Syria and the Lebanon and travelled widely through the Middle East before taking up his present post at the Sorbonne, should have ensured for his book a very warm reception. Instead it went virtually unnoticed. I have in front of me a letter from the publisher complaining that, although 220 review copies had been sent out, only one national daily or weekly paper had noticed it at all (*The Guardian*, with three column inches). It was ignored also by all the book programmes on radio and television, despite the fact that it was published a year after the June war of 1967, when the Middle East was constantly in the news.[61] The publisher's letter contrasted this reception with that given to the much inferior book on *The Six Day War* by Randolph and Winston Churchill (a joint publication by Penguin Books and Heinemann). Highly sympathetic to Israel, the Churchill book was widely reviewed and serialised in the *Sunday Telegraph*. By contrast, and allowing for the differences in subject matter and authorship, the publisher found the reception of Professor Rodinson's book "muted, to say the very least" and remarked that "even the most average Penguin Special can expect far more review coverage than *Israel and the Arabs* got."

It would be tedious to list the similar cases where a book challenging some of the widely accepted Israeli assumptions about the Middle East either failed to achieve publication or went unnoticed by the reviewers;   but it is worth singling out the remarkable *Palestine Papers 1917-1922, Seeds of Conflict*, edited by Doreen Ingrams and published in 1972 by   John Murray. Here again, an outstanding work, in this case one which threw new and important light on the origins of the Arab-Israeli conflict and provided, from the documents in the Public Record Office,   substantial justification for the claim that the Palestinians had been the victims of a deliberate injustice, went unnoticed by reviewers except in *The Times Literary Supplement* and such specialist journals as *Middle East International* and the *Journal of the Royal Central Asian Society*.

❖ ❖ ❖

Christopher Mayhew writes

Today, in the much more relaxed and open-minded atmosphere produced by the October War, when so many Israelis and their friends are themselves so critical of Israel, it is hard to recall the bitterness with which this battle for public opinion was fought in Britain and the lengths to which the Zionists were prepared to go to discourage the expression of views sympathetic to the Arabs. In my own case, I describe elsewhere in this book attempts to keep me off the air, threatening letters, an offer of a place on the pro-Israeli payroll, and some pressure to stop me from becoming Deputy Foreign Secretary. None of these moves against me disturbed me in the slightest; but I did become annoyed when the Zionists began using against me their most feared and effective weapon, the charge of anti Semitism. It is a colourful accusation, one for which you need provide no evidence to get it quickly repeated—and if it is believed it is damaging in every way: politically, professionally, socially. Above all, it is an extremely difficult accusation to disprove. So it came as a considerable relief to me when, in the summer of 1968, one of my Labour colleagues in Parliament, writing to the *Jewish Chronicle*, suggested that I was anti-Semitic in terms which enabled me to sue him. For months past, my friends had been reporting to me conversations in which this kind of allegation had been loosely thrown about: now at last—or so I thought—I could clear myself with a court action.

In the prevailing climate of opinion, merely to have proved that there was no evidence for the charge would not have helped much; and if that had been all that a High Court action could have established, I would not have issued a writ. Fortunately, however, I had a long and rather notable record of active opposition to anti-Semitism, and when I re-counted this record to my solicitor, he simply asked me to choose whether to accept a large sum of money from the defendants (which might, however, take a long time to collect) or to have them make a public apology.

I chose the latter course, and the following statement was read in open court on behalf of the *Jewish Chronicle* and my rash parliamentary colleague:

> "The Plaintiff is the Labour Member of Parliament for Woolwich East and is a former Minister of the Navy. He has for many years

sympathised with the Arabs and their misfortunes in Palestine and is an outspoken critic of Israeli policies and of many aspects of Zionism, but he is not and never has been in any sense anti-Semitic. On the contrary, he has a long and distinguished record of opposition to anti-Semitism and of support and friendship for Jewish people. Before the war he took part in the East End demonstrations in support of Jewish residents against the British Union of Fascists, and in the post-war years as a member of the Intergovernmental Committee for Refugees and of the International Refugee Organisation, he assisted the re-settlement of victims of Nazism including many Jews. In his writings and broadcasts he has shown sympathy and understanding of Jewish questions, and a television film he made about Judaism was widely acclaimed by Jewish people in Britain.

"The Plaintiff has attended many meetings and functions of Jewish organisations and has rendered assistance to the Jewish community in his own constituency, for example by helping them to acquire a site for a new synagogue. He has visited Israel on several occasions where he has been the guest of the Chief Rabbi in Jerusalem and of the Prime Minister and Foreign Secretary. . . . The Defendants offer their sincere apologies to the Plaintiff . . . they wish to pay tribute to his record as a person of liberal opinions, an enemy of intolerance and a man who has on many occasions manifested friendship to Jews."

This, I thought, was handsome enough,[62] especially coming from the leading Jewish newspaper, and since it was published fairly widely and prominently, I hoped that this would see the end of suggestions that I was anti-Semitic. But this was not to be. Shortly afterwards, the *Sunday Times* published a reference to me by a Mr Frederic Raphael as "a Judophobe—a significant mutation of the old-style anti-Semite." And at about the same time a strong suggestion that I was anti-Jewish was made publicly by Mr Sidney Goldberg, then General Secretary of the Labour Friends of Israel. He was speaking in Jerusalem on behalf of a visiting mission which included five Labour MPs, two of them Junior Ministers. The *Jerusalem Post* (18 January 1970) reported him as follows:

"Mr Goldberg noted that Mr Mayhew had a twenty-five-year-old record of violent anti-Israel activities. As Under-Secretary to Foreign Secretary Ernest Bevin he was a devoted supporter of Bevin's anti-Jewish policies . . . He added, 'Mayhew does not understand that it is impossible not to be anti-Jewish and to be anti-Israel, because those who strike at Israel are striking at the Jewish people.' "

My friends continued to report to me, albeit less frequently, conversations in which I was referred to as anti-Semitic. In 1973 a well-known Labour leader was overheard to say at a diplomatic dinner, "Chris Mayhew? A good man really. Pity he hates the Jews."

Though many people avoid criticising Israel from fear of being labelled anti-Semitic, many more hold back simply because they do not want to offend our talented, influential and sensitive Jewish community. Many Jewish people have reached high positions in our society, in politics, commerce, finance, the law, and the media; and a person who needed their goodwill would be foolish to risk offending them by criticising a country for which so many of them feel such a deep attachment. Soon after I became Chairman of MIND (The National Association for Mental Health), it was put to me by our professional fund-raiser that, to avoid offending potential Jewish subscribers, my name should not appear in any of the appeal literature we were addressing to the City. Readily I agreed. Nevertheless, it seemed so incongruous that this admirable charity should suffer in this way because of my views on Palestine that I decided, at the risk of being snubbed, to make a direct approach to the opposition. I obtained an introduction to a particularly well-known, wealthy and influential Zionist businessman, and called on him at his office. I suggested that it was surely wrong that a charitable appeal on behalf of the mentally sick and handicapped should suffer because of its Chairman's views about Palestine: would it not be a pleasant gesture, in everybody's interests, if he were to become a sponsor of the appeal? He simply replied, with obvious satisfaction, "You'll get not a penny from me and not a penny from my friends."

If it is unwise for fund-raisers to criticise Israel, the same is obviously true of businessmen, or MPs with business interests, or employees of pro-Israeli Jewish firms. Such people are unlikely to come to harm if they criticise Britain, the United States, the Soviet Union, France, or a hundred other countries: but if they criticise Israel they can pay a heavy penalty. One businessman who has suffered very severely in this way is Mr Claud Morris, formerly a South Wales newspaper proprietor and the owner and manager of an old-established printing business near Swansea with a turnover approaching £150,000.

Mr Morris's interests flourished vigorously until, in the late 1960s, he undertook, in the normal course of business, the printing of *Free Palestine* and leaflets on the Palestine problem. Soon afterwards, in June 1970, his rotary press was—according to the police reports—deliberately destroyed by arsonists, who were never identified. His newspapers also came under heavy pressure. The *Jewish Chronicle* of 22 October 1971 reported:

> "A number of Swansea and district Jewish traders reduced their advertising in *Voice* publications when it was discovered about two years ago that a pro-Arab paper, *Free Palestine*, was being printed at the same works."

Elsewhere, this report stated:

> "South Wales newspaper-publisher Mr Claud Morris, who has thrown in his lot with Mr Anthony Nutting and Mr Christopher Mayhew in *Middle East International*, a pro-Arab publication, has lost a number of his senior staff, who are starting their own giveaway newspaper in Swansea."

The leader of the staff breakaway, a Mr Vernon Thomas, who had just been appointed Mr Morris's sales director, gave political reasons for his strange action. He said he could not contemplate associating with *Middle East International*. This is a serious, widely-respected, monthly magazine, subscribed to by scores of governments (including the British Government) and by university libraries throughout the world. But Mr Thomas told the *Jewish Chronicle*, "My appointment would have involved meeting people concerned with this anti-Israel publication. I had no wish to be associated with it in any way."

Aided by people of Mr Thomas's kind, opposition from pro-Israeli Jewish people seriously crippled Mr Morris's publishing and printing interests in South Wales. Among other setbacks, it became necessary to close down his Swansea newspaper.

The reasons for Mr Morris's misfortunes are obvious enough, but known critics of Israel are often faced with nice tests of judgment when something goes wrong for them. Is it just bad luck, or is it their own fault? Or are they paying a penalty for their convictions? Not long ago, a famous firm of jewellers agreed to donate to MIND the proceeds of the sale of catalogues at one of their exhibitions. Our Royal Patron, Princess Alexandra, had agreed to open the exhibition, and had told me she was hoping to see me there. As Chairman of the Association, I made arrangements to go, but was surprised to find that by the day before the opening I had not received an invitation. This was awkward. Was it simply a mistake? Or had the firm decided that it was not necessary to invite the Chairman? Or could it be that the firm was Jewish and Zionist and determined to have nothing to do with me? It was not easy to decide. Eventually, I came to the conclusion that the last explanation was the likeliest, and decided, for once, to make a fuss. I telephoned to the head of the firm, thanked him for the firm's promised donation, and said that my invitation had not arrived. The reply came back that this was a Zionist firm and that an invitation to an anti-Zionist like myself had not therefore seemed appropriate. "But what would you think," I objected, "if our positions were reversed? What would you think of somebody who refused to have any social or business dealings with you simply because you were a Zionist?" After a pause, the jeweller, a man of character, declared that he had been wrong, and that my invitation would be sent round immediately. So I went to the exhibition, where I was warmly welcomed by the jeweller and the members of his charming family.

But I could not help asking myself, as I wandered around among the Fabergé and the diamond clusters, from how many social and professional gatherings I had been excluded, without knowing it, because of my views on the Middle East.

And there are other questions and mysteries which tantalise critics of Israel. Why, for example, between 1967 and 1971, did the Treasury persistently misinform the House of Commons and myself about the status and activities of the Jewish National Fund? Were its errors due simply to lax administration, or was there in them an element of deliberate deception prompted by sympathy for Israel? Even after studying a special confidential report on the subject commissioned by the then Prime Minister, Mr Heath, I am still not sure what the answer is.

The story is as follows. Despite the extreme weakness of sterling during this period—a £50 travel allowance was in force—the Treasury allowed the free transfer of sterling overseas for "specifically charitable purposes", and very generous sums were remitted by Jewish organisations to Israel after the 1967 war. But at least one of these organisations, the Jewish National Fund, seemed to be stretching the concept of "charity" unreasonably far. For example, one of its appeal booklets read:

> "Today the JNF tractor follows in the wake of the army tank. Areas which have been restored to Israel as a result of the Six Day War are being put under the plough. The preparation of this land is the primary task of the JNF.
>
> "All areas throughout the country where new settlements and kibbutzim are to be established are reclaimed by the JNF."

Quite apart from weakening sterling, it seemed wholly wrong that British citizens should be allowed to send money to Israel in this way to help colonise conquered Arab territories. Such colonisation was expressly forbidden by the Fourth Geneva Convention. To subsidise it would aid and encourage Israel to continue defying UN resolutions, and would conflict with the foreign policy aims of successive British governments. Moreover, such remittances would plainly not be "specifically charitable". So I was asked by my colleagues in CAABU to try to discover the facts, and if necessary to persuade the Treasury to stop an abuse of the currency regulations.

My subsequent siege of the Treasury, which lasted four and a half years, proceeded in two stages. The first stage lasted from 21 June 1967 to 28 July 1971. During this period I wrote fifteen letters to Treasury ministers, asked five parliamentary questions, and attended two ministerial meetings.

Successive ministers—Mr Niall McDermott, Mr (later Lord) Diamond, Mr Harold Lever, Mr William Rodgers—explained repeatedly that the Jewish National Fund was a registered charity; that it was particularly sensitive about preserving its charitable status; that Treasury officials had met and questioned its organisers; that they were completely satisfied that none of the sterling remitted to Israel had been spent for non-charitable purposes, or in the occupied territories.

In explanation of the JNF's publicity statements, which plainly contradicted these assurances, Mr Rodgers wrote:

> "I am aware of statements such as you mention. They were one of the reasons for the special enquiries which have been made by the Treasury of representatives of the JNF. When asked about the booklet these representatives said that, in campaigning for funds, they had constantly to look out for new and dramatic slogans which would catch the imagination and purses of potential contributors. I am however satisfied by the assurances which were given that no remittancesfrom this country have been sent for the purpose of helping to build settlements in the occupied territories."[63]

But if the organisers of the JNF had indeed mis-stated the aims of their appeal, as Mr Rodgers argued, then they plainly ought to be reported to the Charity Commissioners. So I did this; and in the process discovered, to my astonishment, that the JNF was not, and never had been, a registered charity, and that whenever the Treasury ministers had apparently been referring to the JNF in letters, and answers to parliamentary questions, they had not in fact been referring to the JNF at all but to another organisation with a similar name operating from the same address. As was explained to me on 28 July 1971 by the new Financial Secretary to the Treasury, Mr Patrick Jenkin, MP,

> "It was of course a mistake that the Treasury failed to distinguish clearly between the JNF and the JNF Charitable Trust from that time and accepted the documentation for Charitable Trust expenditures as covering both bodies. This mistake was most regrettably repeated in a series of letters to you.
>
> "As I told you in my last letter, JNF remittances are being taken out of the standing authority and will in future be permitted only on specific application and subject to appropriate examination. I felt it right to make this change in view of the grave doubts you expressed and the fact that the previous enquiries did not cover these remittances with sufficient care."

Thus the stable door was bolted, with the horse disappearing into the distance, and the first stage of my enquiry ended. But the questions remained: had the Treasury's extraordinary mistake arisen simply through slack administration or was there somewhere along the line an element of deliberate pro-Israeli deception? Was it really possible for Treasury officials to cross-examine the organisers of a charitable fund without discovering that they were not the organisers of that fund at all but of a quite different fund? And even if this were possible, how could the organisers themselves be unaware of the ridiculous mistake the Treasury officials were making? And why did they then keep silent?

I felt angry and suspicious, and I wrote to the Prime Minister, setting out the Treasury's misdeeds and asking for an independent enquiry. Mr Heath, while refusing to set up an independent enquiry, called for a full personal report from the Head of the Treasury. This report, which Mr Heath will not allow to be published, was long and painstaking and acknowledged that I had been misled; but on the main question it was entirely unhelpful and unconvincing. At this stage, however, although extremely dissatisfied, I decided that this subject had already taken too much of my time, and I dropped it. So the mystery remains.

The Zionists reserve their most bitter and relentless attacks, not for people like Michael Adams and myself, but for critics of Israel who are themselves Jewish. These brave people play a role of particular value and importance in the Arab-Israeli conflict, not least because they serve as a striking reminder to the Arabs that their enemy is not the Jewish people but a political movement, Zionism, which many courageous and thoughtful Jews strenuously oppose.

Among the most distinguished Jewish critics of Zionism is Mrs Marion Woolfson, a professional journalist, who developed her convictions after some articles she had written after a visit to Israel were rejected as "too critical" by the newspaper which had commissioned them.

Mrs Woolfson subsequently explained her standpoint as follows:

"As no British newspaper would publish what I had written on Israel, I eventually began to write letters to the papers instead. These were published in *The Times*, *The Guardian*, *The Sunday Times*, *The New Statesman*, *Tribune* and *The Spectator*, among other publications. It became more and more difficult for me to get work in journalism.

"When I offered to write an article on an Arab country for a national British newspaper for which I had worked in the past, I was told that 'I was too well-known for my pro-Arab sympathies and nothing I wrote would be believed.'

"I was bombarded with highly emotional, illogical and often threatening or obscene letters and telephone calls (mostly anonymous) from Zionists. I was called a 'Jew-baiter', a 'Nazi' and an 'anti-Semite' as well as many unprintable epithets. After a particularly bad spate of hysterical telephone calls, usually in the early hours of the morning, I was advised by the police to have my calls intercepted by the GPO. Finally, my telephone number was changed and made ex-directory.

"When I receive an invitation to dinner from someone who is not involved in the Middle East, I ask who the other guests are to be because, in the past, at dinner parties where there happened to be one or two Jewish guests, I have been so violently berated and insulted that I have had to walk out. I have been attacked in Jewish shops and told to take my custom elsewhere. I have been attacked in both the editorial and readers' letters columns of the *Jewish Chronicle*. I was referred to in one article as 'a self-hater' and 'a self-proclaimed Jewish pro-Arabist'.

"Although, now, I still receive letters from the lunatic fringe, I no longer hear from Zionist officials as I used to when my views first became known. At the beginning, I received 'reasoned' letters and telephone calls suggesting that I was an unfortunate, misguided creature who was being 'used' by the wily Arabs for propaganda purposes 'because they find your Jewish surname useful.' In 1970, a national newspaper agreed to publish something I had written on Zionist activities in Britain. A Zionist official heard about this and telephoned me, demanding that I withdraw the story. I refused and he called me 'nothing but a publicity-seeker'. He also said I would be sorry for what I had done. When I said that, despite his veiled threats, the piece would appear, he answered: 'We'll see about that.' It never appeared and, although, at the time, I was unable to get a satisfactory explanation from the newspaper, some time afterwards a member of the staff of the paper told me about the pressures to which the paper had been subjected.

"Some letter-writers have suggested that I cannot possibly be Jewish and hold the views I do and, therefore, I must be a 'goy' who married a Jew. Just for the record, I should like to state that I was born of Jewish parents. I have frequently been called 'a traitor'. One man wrote to me and said it was his duty 'to stop a Jewess from damaging the cause of Israel.'

"I have been told that I am going to be pushed in front of a bus and, after my telephone number was changed, a friend received a telephone call purporting to be from the Jewish Defence League, announcing that I was about to be killed. Once, a swastika was painted on the gate of my house."[64]

In the battle for truth about the Middle East, the real heroes and heroines are the small band of anti-Zionist Jewish people who speak up for their beliefs in western countries and, most courageously, in Israel itself—colleagues of Mrs Woolfson like Dr Elmer Berger, Dr Norton Mezvinsky, Mr Moshe Menuhin, Mr Mick Ashley, Dr Israel Shahak, Professor Maxime Rodinson and many others. But everyone who criticises Israel publicly, whether Jew or Gentile, must expect to pay some penalty, even in the more relaxed climate of today. The debate about the Middle East is not like, say, the debate about the Common Market, which has been conducted in Britain in an atmosphere of comparative politeness and tranquillity; and as subsequent chapters will show, the path of truth about the Middle East has proved too narrow and stony for large numbers of people in British public life, especially in politics, the media and the churches.

CHAPTER FIVE

Bias in the Media

Michael Adams, Christopher Mayhew

Michael Adams: *The Press*

When historians look back on the course of the Arab-Israeli conflict, I think it is safe to say that they will consider October 1973 as a watershed, before which the Israelis seemed likely to maintain their ascendancy, but after which the eventual victory of the Arabs was seen to be assured. It will be some time before we shall know whether such a judgment is well founded; but meanwhile there is no doubt that the October War marked a milestone in the outside world's understanding of the issues at stake in the Middle East.

Even before the fighting had come to an end, public opinion in Britain and in most other Western countries was showing itself ready to accept a number of ideas which previously it had resisted. People could see now that the Arabs were not prepared indefinitely to accept the Israeli occupation of large parts of their territories and that it was unreasonable to expect them to; that if the Israelis insisted on remaining where they were, there was bound to be further bloodshed and instability; that for Israel's own sake and for that of an oil-thirsty world, such instability was intolerable; and that if, as seemed suddenly plain, the whole trouble arose out of the injustice that had been done to the Palestinians by the creation of Israel, then something must be done to redress that injustice, even if this meant imposing restraints on the Israelis which hitherto they had always been able to avoid.

To many of us these were not novel or startling concepts. They constituted, in fact, the essence of the message which we had been trying to communicate to the British public, and to public opinion in Europe and the United States as well, for a number of years. We had been able to make some headway, especially with the younger generation, but on the whole it had been uphill work. This was not because people did not wish to hear about the Middle East, or because they found it difficult to understand the issues at stake when these were clearly presented to them. It was due rather to the fact that the issues very seldom were presented clearly; that, on the contrary, they were generally obscured by a great deal of special pleading which confused the man in the street and distracted his attention from the underlying realities. The press cannot escape a major part of the responsibility for his confusion; nor is it easy to dispose of the suspicion that much of the confusion was deliberately contrived.

The conviction is widely held in the Arab world that the British press—and with it our radio and television services—is to a large extent controlled by the supporters of Zionism. Put thus baldly, the idea is of course laughable; there is no single national newspaper in Britain which is controlled by Zionist interests. (It is not easy to speak so categorically where television companies are concerned.)[65] But it would be equally absurd to go to the other extreme and say that there is no Zionist influence at work in any British paper. Indeed, there are few papers in Britain which do not have in prominent positions, either on the editorial side or in their managements, or as freewheeling columnists, fervent and often highly articulate supporters of Israel: David Spanier of *The Times*, John Kimche of the *Evening Standard*, Eric Silver of *The Guardian*, and Terence Prittie, who was the paper's diplomatic correspondent during the critical period before and after the Six Day War, are names that spring to mind. There are papers which have had Zionist, not necessarily Jewish, editors: the *New Statesman* is the most obvious case in point, with a succession of vehemently pro-Israeli editors (Kingsley Martin, Paul Johnson, Richard Crossman) during almost the entire period since Israel came into existence, until Anthony Howard took office in 1972; after that,

The Economist, when Alastair Burnet was editor, took its place as the most uncritical supporter of Israel in the weekly press.

The most influential of these "gentile Zionists" in the newspaper world was the first and most distinguished of them all, as I learned soon after I had started work as the Middle East correspondent for *The Guardian* (*The Manchester Guardian*, as it still was) in 1956. I was visiting Jerusalem for the first time when I had a thoroughly disconcerting experience. I had an introduction to a distinguished Palestinian, a former mayor of the Arab city, who welcomed me with characteristic courtesy and invited me to meet a group of his friends. One of them, who was the principal of a college and a future foreign minister of Jordan, asked me which paper I had come to represent. When I told him, he said gently, "Ah, the Zionist paper." I was startled and, thinking that perhaps I was having my leg pulled, I smiled and let it pass; but as soon as I got the chance I made some enquiries and discovered what an important contribution *The Guardian* had made, under its redoubtable editor C. P. Scott, to the early successes of Zionism in Britain. It was Scott who launched Chaim Weizmann, later to be the first President of Israel, into British political society and so started the train of events which led to the Balfour Declaration; which in turn may fairly be called the foundation-stone of the modern State of Israel.

Now, for an Englishman there was nothing sinister about this; it was easy enough to understand how such a thing could have come about half century ago, in a Britain over-confident of its imperial authority, and through the agency of an eccentric genius like Scott, whose assurance seems never to have been troubled by the thought that there might be another side to this particular question. But consider how differently the story would look to a sophisticated Palestinian. It is not surprising that my new acquaintance in Jerusalem should have seen it as an early instance of what was to become in his eyes a familiar pattern: the British press, already in league with Zionism, helping to lay the fuse which, within a generation, was to destroy the Palestine he loved.

A distortion of the facts, many people will say, and the point is open to argument; but there is no disputing the facts themselves. C. P. Scott did introduce Weizmann to Lloyd George and put the authority of *The Manchester Guardian* at the disposal of the cause of Zionism; Weizmann's astute and not always scrupulous use of his opportunities[66] did culminate in the British Government's public declaration of support for the Zionist idea; and the policy symbolised by the Balfour Declaration did eventually lead, as it was bound to do if carried to its logical conclusion, to the dispossession or subjection of the native population of Palestine.

Among the least important consequences of all this was the fact that, when I arrived in Palestine forty years later, Palestinians (or at least the older generation among them) thought of *The Guardian* as "the Zionist paper". It was a cross I had to bear; and it was not long before I realised that there were others besides the Palestinians who thought they knew what to expect from *The Guardian* where the Middle East was concerned. This time it was the explosion of the Suez crisis, a few weeks after that first visit of mine to Palestine, which taught me an important lesson about the problems of maintaining a free press.

In July 1956 the American government abruptly withdrew its offer of substantial aid for the financing of a new high dam over the Nile (a smaller British offer also lapsed in consequence), and President Nasser responded angrily by nationalising the old Suez Canal Company. Sir Anthony Eden rapidly made plain his determination to make Nasser "disgorge", and to go to war if necessary to recover what he asserted to be Britain's rights. The British press, like the public, was sharply divided in its attitude; *The Guardian* from the outset opposed our own government's policy and incurred as a result a good deal of unpopularity. As the crisis developed, other newspapers gradually followed suit, but by then *The Guardian* had lost what for it was a dangerously large number of readers.

It is probable that a number of these were influenced by the same mixture of chauvinism and greed, with a strong dash of old-fashioned racialism, that habitually motivated British attitudes towards Egypt in that post-imperial phase of our history. To such people, whose choice of newspaper would normally be the *Daily Telegraph* rather than *The Guardian*, it was intolerable that a British government should be pushed around by an upstart Egyptian colonel. But in the particular case of *The Guardian's* attitude over the Suez crisis, a large proportion of those who cancelled their subscriptions, and who sometimes wrote to say that they were urging their friends to do the same, were members of the numerous and influential Jewish community in and around Manchester. Belonging as they did to a community conspicuous for its liberalism and its opposition to the fading attitudes of the old social order, such people felt no natural affinity with the brand of toryism represented by Eden, nor was it without a pang that many of them cut loose from *The Guardian*. What caused them to do so was their belief that, whether Eden or *The Guardian* had the best of the argument where Britain's interests were concerned, it was Eden whose policy was most likely to do good to Israel, and for that reason they condemned *The Guardian* for attacking him.

The episode provided an unusually clear illustration of the limits within which a free press has to work. The disgruntled readers who vowed never to let *The Guardian* darken their breakfast-tables again had a perfect right to exercise their freedom to choose whatever newspaper suited them best. The grounds on which they based their rejection of *The Guardian* were not the most admirable but they were certainly legitimate. But their defection came near to crippling *The Guardian*, whose base at that time was still in Manchester and which lost in the course of the Suez crisis some thousands of readers, though most of them returned to their old allegiance once the crisis had faded. There is no way of knowing how much advertising *The Guardian* also lost during this period, or how much stature the paper may have gained in the long run by sticking to its guns; but the experience was an uncomfortable reminder of the vulnerability of even the best of newspapers in the face of determined action on the part of an influential pressure group.

It would be unfair to ignore the fact that a modern newspaper editor must be to some extent a businessman as well. Putting it crudely, however firm his principles, he cannot afford to advocate unpopular policies to the point where he alienates his readers and his potential advertisers, and so bankrupts his newspaper. And if he shows signs of doing so, he has at his elbow a business manager whose responsibility it is to restrain him from going too far.

I doubt if there has been any matter of foreign affairs since the Second World War over which the information media in general have been subjected to such vigorous pressure as they have over the Arab-Israeli conflict. Nor is this altogether natural—although we have become so accustomed to the fact that we may think it is—since our own national interests, though certainly involved to some extent, have not as a rule been directly at stake. And when they have been, as over the closure of the Suez Canal after the war of 1967, the strongest pressure has been applied against our own national interests, rather than in defence of them. There have, of course, been pressures on both sides, but what is disturbing is that far stronger pressure has been applied on one side than on the other in a controversy in which Britain has been ostensibly neutral; that this pressure has been applied on behalf of a foreign government; and that it has had a perceptible effect in shaping British policy, generally in a direction unfavourable to British national interests.

There are those who will dispute these contentions, but you will not find among them those with any close knowledge of the subject. No editor will be found who can put his hand on his heart and deny that he has ever been under pressure from the supporters of Israel. No correspondent who has worked in the Middle East can remain unconscious of the forces at work to influence the balance of both news and comment in his newspaper. Nor is there any doubt as to which of the pressure groups, the pro-Israeli or the pro-Arab, was the stronger before October 1973. As Director of Information for the Council for the Advancement of Arab-British Understanding, it was my task and that of my colleagues during much of this period to pit our resources, David-like, against the might of the various Zionist propaganda agencies and pressure groups in this country. From a standing start in 1967, we made a substantial impression and at least introduced a new element into a situation in which, previously, the

Zionists had had things all their own way. We could hardly expect to do more against an adversary firmly entrenched for half a century before our organisation was born: one with its own large headquarters in London and its branches throughout the country, to say nothing of its agents and supporters in both houses of parliament, in Fleet Street, and in the vital world of business, from which it drew its financial strength.

There have been many criticisms in recent years, voiced most often in the *Jewish Chronicle*, of the ineffectiveness of Zionist propaganda in Britain. These criticisms seem to me to be less than fair to the propagandists, with whom I have had a good deal of contact, direct and indirect, since 1967. On the whole, they have done a remarkable job, considering the weakness of the case they have had to present. It was no small achievement to persuade a majority of the British public, as the Zionists did until recently, to give its support to a country built, as Israel was and is, on land belonging to others, with the principle of racial discrimination built into its basic law and with a government openly committed, in defiance of repeated United Nations resolutions, to territorial expansion at the expense of its neighbours. That the public finally saw through the propaganda was due to the fact that, to a broadly liberal and humane society like ours, these were principles and practices which could not command support; but the partial failure (and it is only partial so far) of Zionist propaganda was certainly not due to any lack of effort.

The effort was made at various levels and in different ways by a wide variety of individuals and organisations throughout the country. It is of course still being made, but with rather more restraint than was the case before the October War of 1973. It was made openly, and on the whole ineffectively, through such organisations as the Zionist Federation and the Jewish National Fund, with their research bureaux and their press officers. It was made more discreetly through the influential Board of Deputies of British Jews and the powerful Zionist members of the Jewish community in Britain, men like Lord Janner, Lord Shinwell, Sir Marcus Sieff, as well as many Jewish MPs, who can claim the ear of the Editor of *The Times* or the Director-General of the BBC where lesser mortals would be turned away. It was made, more crudely, through Jewish advertisers. And it was perhaps most effectively made, in the long run, by the many Zionist sympathisers, both Jewish and gentile, who were actually employed in the press or who, as freelance commentators, enjoyed a much readier access to the columns of our leading newspapers than did comparable writers whose views were critical of Israel.[67] Among these last, we must note the truly extraordinary phenomenon of the Jewish correspondents employed in Israel by almost every newspaper and by the BBC, of whom there will be more to say presently. Nor should one forget the Israeli Embassy in London, whose staff were diligent, as they had every right to be, in cultivating the press and in inviting them for highly organised tours of Israel.

It is impossible of course to quantify the results of so much industry, but no journalist concerned with Arab-Israeli affairs between the wars of 1967 and 1973 could fail to be aware of it. I remember a conversation with a journalist friend who had risen to be a diplomatic correspondent and so found himself from time to time on the receiving end of the pressure. I asked him how it worked and he told me plainly. He said that if he had written something about the Middle East which could be construed as being unfriendly to the Israelis, he could expect to find on his desk next morning a note from the Chairman of his organisation saying he would like to have, before midday, answers to three or four critical points which had been put to him about the piece, "and then," he said, "I feel a small shiver go down my spine." And he added with a smile to soften the blow: "if you make the same sort of complaint on behalf of CAABU, it doesn't worry me nearly as much."

That little parable has much to say about the situation we are considering. There emerge from it three points which deserve to be remembered. First, that anyone, no matter how strong his credentials, who writes an article for a national newspaper or a talk for the BBC which earns the displeasure of the Israeli Embassy or its friends in this country, can expect to be called to account for it at once. Second, that any complaint about it will be registered, not, as a rule, by the embassy itself, but by some individual or organisation friendly to it, at the very highest level. And third, that the person to whom the complaint is addressed, no matter how highly placed he may be, can be expected to act on it with an urgency that suggests more than a hint of sanctions in the background.

These considerations will certainly keep a journalist on his toes and that may be an excellent thing; they will also discourage him from publishing anything, however authentic he may know it to be, unless he is in a position to quote an exact and unimpeachable source for it. As I remember another senior foreign affairs writer telling me, when I asked him why he had not written about the Middle East for a long time: "When you know you're going to have to account for every bloody comma, it just isn't worth it." In fact, as any journalist knows, such limitations are likely, by discouraging the fair exercise of a specialist's expertise, to inhibit the publication of much that ought to be published. Nor would even this matter so much if the same inhibition applied to comments on both sides of the controversy; but they do not, as again anyone can testify who has had any connection with the presentation of news and views about the Middle East. To give a single salient example, allegations about the ill-treatment of Jews in Syria are repeatedly published in the press, on the strength of unsupported hearsay evidence from other Jews, despite the fact that similar stories have repeatedly been disproved in the past; while authenticated accounts of the ill-treatment of Palestinians in Israeli prisons, even when they are put forward by neutral or even Israeli sources, are almost invariably ignored by the press.[68]

Overwhelmingly then, in 1967, though a little less with every year that followed, the reading public was invited to sympathise, if not positively to identify, with the Israelis. Even the most unpromising facts, for instance that Israeli gaols were full of political prisoners and that Israel was in military occupation of territories three times its own size, were ingeniously turned to good account. This was "the most benevolent occupation in history"; and only the more tiresomely persistent reporters looked behind the facade to uncover the facts about torture and intimidation on the West Bank or the constant process of expropriation and expulsion by which the Israelis extended their control at the expense of the Palestinians. When the Palestinians, on the other hand, despairing of the justice which was promised them by repeated UN resolutions but never translated into fact, lost patience and resorted to violence, the British press was swift and fearless in its denunciations.

Strangely, this imbalance on the part of the press was at its most marked and most unanimous in the second half of 1967, when the Arabs were at their lowest ebb after their devastating defeat in the Six Day War and the Israelis were triumphant and unrelenting. At that time, and in such a situation, it might have been supposed that the press would give careful attention to any suggestion that the victors were oppressing the vanquished; or at least that the press would give as good a hearing to the vanquished as to those who held them in their grip. It is depressing to recall that exactly the opposite happened. Almost exclusively, the reports in the British press about developments both in Israel and in the occupied territories came at that time from correspondents—Moshe Brilliant for *The Times*, Walter Gross for *The Guardian*, Michael Elkins for the BBC, Francis Ofner for the *Observer*, and so on—who were not foreign correspondents in the normal sense of the term, since they were in fact at home in Israel, being themselves Jewish and in most cases actually Israeli citizens, and so subject in either case to the intense pressures of a society which expected the strictest loyalty from any Jew, and made no bones about it. Sharing the preferences and the aspirations, not to mention the prejudices, of the society on which they should by rights have been turning a critical gaze, they were in fact, and by definition, identified with it. Whatever other merits any of them might possess, their objectivity was bound to be in question.

It seems extraordinary that British editors, who would not think of employing in South Africa a South African who was a devotee of apartheid, or in Moscow a dedicated Russian communist, should see no objection to retaining in Israel Jewish correspondents whose sympathy for Zionism must call in question their objectivity. It is not even normal for a British paper to employ a Frenchman in Paris or a

German in Bonn, or even an American in Washington, presumably because there would be times when such a correspondent, even in the relatively calm atmosphere of Europe or America, could find himself faced with a choice between two conflicting loyalties, to his country and to the truth.

It is hard to think of a situation where this conflict would be more acute for a correspondent than it should have been in Jerusalem in the latter part of 1967. Here was a city which symbolised the conflict at whose heart it lay; a city of particular significance to millions of people all over the world, but especially to the two warring communities who met, as occupiers and occupied, within its walls. For the rest of us it was vital to understand, and if possible to reconcile, their rival viewpoints. Yet if we depended, as most of us inevitably did, on the press for our information about them, we could and did hear only one side of the argument.[69]

With only the rarest exceptions, the press at that time took the part of the conquering Israelis; when a dissident note was struck by individual reporters who questioned the benevolence of the Israeli occupation regime or asked how and why it was that refugees continued to flee from the occupied areas of Palestine, and from the Syrian Golan Heights, which the Israelis had also occupied in the recent war, months after the war was over, the reports were generally disregarded or else the writers were defamed as biased witnesses.

I had some experience of this myself. Invited by the BBC, six months after the Six Day War, to visit a number of Arab countries and write a series of documentary programmes about the state of Arab opinion, I turned aside to visit the occupied territories to see for myself what was happening. I had no clear idea of what I should find, for I had been away from the area for some years and there had been very little in the press to inform me. Apart from an article by David Holden in the *Sunday Times*, which contained one or two ugly indications of oppression by the Israelis, the general impression given was one of calm and resignation on the part of the Palestinians. It was difficult to believe that this was the entire story, for whole populations do not normally submit without coercion to alien occupation.

I harboured doubts about the situation in Palestine, but the resident correspondents in Jerusalem agreed so closely in the picture they presented that I was almost persuaded, like the vast majority of their readers, that the suspicions I had been feeling and expressing about the state of affairs in the occupied territories were at least exaggerated. As I left for Jerusalem, I remember saying to my wife that when I got back I might have to eat my words.

In the event, the situation I found was far worse than anything I could have expected; and this was to present me with some considerable problems. The least important of these were personal ones, of which something has been said elsewhere in these pages; they resulted from trying to swim against a tide which at that time was running very strongly in favour of Israel. But the immediate problem, and the most important one, was the problem of communication, of getting across to others a true picture of a state of affairs which was appalling, and of whose dangerous implications the world seemed oblivious. Before leaving England I had arranged with *The Guardian* that I would write a series of articles about conditions in the occupied territories. There was no specific contract between us for we knew each other well enough after an association which had lasted for twelve years; but the paper put up a small sum of money towards my expenses and otherwise left me, as usual, a free hand.

After all these years it is still difficult for me to recall that journey without emotion. Basing myself on Jerusalem, I travelled for a fortnight through the occupied areas of the West Bank and the Gaza Strip, meeting at first with blank suspicion on the part of the subject Palestinians, who had learned to keep their mouths shut in the presence of foreign journalists. They had met few, and not many of these had shown any interest in the problems of the Palestinians, being more concerned to share in the triumph of the Israelis and reflect it to an admiring world. But I had sought the advice of a Palestinian friend in Beirut, one of the many exiles from Jerusalem, whose family had played a distinguished part in the life of the city for centuries before the birth of a Jewish state, and he had armed me with a list of names and a scrap of paper bearing a few words in Arabic. With these

I found myself passed from hand to hand all through the occupied territories, amongst people who felt themselves imprisoned and had almost despaired of re-establishing contact with the world outside.

From them I learned the truth about the occupation: about the pressures on the civilian population, both physical and psychological, by which the Israelis sought to persuade them, and sometimes merely forced them, to leave their homes; about the punitive curfews, the mass arrests, the detentions without trial, the expropriations and demolitions and all the rest of the shabby machinery by which the conquerors tried to break once and for all the spirit of the Palestinians. It was a frightening and at times a heart-breaking experience, relieved only by the resilient humour with which so many of those I met endured their tribulations; and the worst aspect of all was the sense, which I gradually came to share with them, that some kind of screen had been erected between them and the rest of the world, a screen of prejudice against which even the truth seemed powerless to prevail.

For in Jerusalem I found that there were members of the large foreign community—consuls, clergymen, welfare workers, United Nations officials—who knew of the abuses which had been brought to my attention and who in some cases were as angry as I was about them; but always there seemed to be some compelling reason for their silence, at least in public. They knew, many of them, of the young men who disappeared in the night, and the women and children confined for days on end to their huts in the Gaza refugee camps; of the looting that had everywhere accompanied the Israeli victory: not even the headquarters of the United Nations in Jerusalem had been spared, though not a single British newspaper reported the fact. They knew of the road out of Ramallah which had been closed for six months while the Israelis totally destroyed three Palestinian villages and carted away the rubble and ploughed over the land where they had been. They knew, but they had their reasons for keeping silent; and in some cases, though not in all, their silence pained them. On some of them it was imposed by their status as diplomats or international civil servants; on others, so far as I could judge, by simple considerations of self-preservation (the churchmen, in particular, seemed anxious to give no offence to the new masters of Jerusalem); while there were a few whom I remember with affectionate respect, who decided to bend the rules and share their knowledge with me.

All of these attitudes I could understand. What I could not understand and what made me angriest at the time was the knowledge that some at least of the journalists in Jerusalem, the so-called "foreign" correspondents, must have known of these abuses and must have found reasons satisfactory in their own eyes for remaining silent about them. Not all of them, certainly; many found it simplest to shut their eyes and ears to the more unpleasant aspects of what was happening all around them. I did not hear of one who had penetrated to Gaza, which some people thought a dangerous place in those days. Nor indeed would there have been much point in these Jewish correspondents trying to establish contact with the Palestinians in the occupied territories, who would naturally have taken them for spies and informers. Even so, there must have been some among them who could, if they wished, have debunked the legend of the "benevolent occupation" before it got a grip on world opinion. In my mind they are bracketed with those Germans who somehow "never heard about" the Nazi concentration camps.

Years later I went to hear one of these same correspondents speaking off the record to an invited audience in London. It was in the spring of 1974, six months after the October War, when Israel was in the throes of the crisis that led to the resignation of Mrs Meir. People's eyes were beginning to be opened to the truth about Israel, but even so it came as a surprise to hear this correspondent speaking with great frankness about his adopted country, acknowledging the decline in moral standards in Israel, the loss of confidence in its leaders, the evident failure of the government's basic foreign policy. His audience, which included both supporters and critics of Israel, was startled to hear such uncharacteristic comments from a journalist whose tone, when his observations were for the public record, was so different. At the end of his talk, I congratulated him on his frankness and objectivity and remarked that some of us, when we had tried to make to a wider audience the very same points that he had been making to us, had found it hard to persuade our hearers, because there had been no voice coming out of Israel and using the same objective tones.

This was the problem at the time of that visit of mine to Jerusalem at the beginning of 1968. The reports I filed to *The Guardian* on the situation in Gaza, on the continuing flight of the Palestinians from the occupied territories, and on the state of affairs in Arab Jerusalem, which the Israelis had annexed and where they were expropriating land on which to settle Jewish immigrants inside the Arab sector—these reports painted a picture which conflicted starkly with the one which the Israeli government, thanks to the co-operation of the resident correspondents, had managed to put across to British and other foreign newspaper readers. Since almost all of the correspondents reporting for British and American newspapers were themselves Jewish, and often Israeli, it was not surprising that their readers came to see things from the Jewish angle, sharing the sense of exuberance which animated the conquering Israelis and ignoring the feelings of the Palestinians, who saw their rights and their homes being bulldozed to open a path for Zionist ambitions.

The problem was not mine alone. The editor of *The Guardian*, who published the dispatches I sent, found himself the target for much criticism and even abuse as a result. A campaign was orchestrated, in which the Israeli Embassy, the Jewish press in Britain and a number of individuals tried to discredit me, and through me the paper. The *Jewish Observer* published an "Open letter to *The Guardian*", criticising the editor's irresponsibility and suggesting that he was somehow in league with what the writer called "your Arab friends". A paper called *Israel Today*, which, happily, went out of business not long afterwards, openly accused him of publishing anti-Semitic material. The Israeli press attaché wrote a long letter denying the very precise accusations I had made about breaches of the Geneva Conventions by the Israelis in Gaza, which was published, ironically, just after I had had a meeting in Jerusalem, at my own request, with a senior representative of the Israeli Military Government, who had confirmed that the facts of the situation in Gaza were as I had represented them. These were the outward and visible signs of the pressure being exerted to silence me and, while they were not difficult to answer, I could not be surprised if the editor was disturbed by them and by the personal interventions which were being made to him.

I was enormously grateful for the confidence he had shown in me, and had written to tell him so on my return from Jerusalem, sending him at the same time a long list of the people in Jerusalem who would vouch for my facts although they were inhibited by their official positions from speaking out themselves. He had not replied to this letter, and as the controversy over my articles developed I felt his confidence in me weakening. At the height of it he wrote me a letter which gave me an idea of what I was up against. Remarking first that he had seen a letter from me in the previous day's paper replying to a Mr Lehmann, he went on to ask:

> "Have you, I wonder, seen the piece in this week's *Jewish Observer*? It seems to me to contain some more serious points. I enclose a print, in case you haven't seen it, and I've side-lined the ones that interested me.
>
> "In particular—given that treatment of the Arabs was a central part of your theme—is it true that alternative accommodation of at least comparable or better standard was made available to those turned out of their homes? This has been alleged in one or two other letters I've had, and was also put to me by Lord Sieff when I happened to see him a day or two ago.
>
> "It's certainly true that the bulk of Jewish readers here believe that the Israelis have behaved with astonishing restraint. That's perhaps why they find it difficult to accept at face value your reporting of intimidation."

Here was the difficulty I mentioned earlier: the fact that none of the resident correspondents in Jerusalem were reporting the intimidation of the Arab population there and in Gaza made it much easier for the readers of *The Guardian* to believe that I had invented it.

This I could see; and many of them may have been sincere in believing it. It was difficult for anyone in London, though less difficult for a newspaper editor than for the ordinary citizen, to check with those in Jerusalem who could easily have confirmed my allegations: the representatives of the Red Cross and of the United Nations, the Anglican Archbishop, the American Consul-General and the various neutral officials and welfare workers and private individuals whom I had listed in the letter I wrote on my return. But, without such an attempt to confirm or dispute my facts, I could see no good reason why my word, as a practised and independent reporter on the spot, should not be accepted in preference to that of Mr Lehmann, the *Jewish Observer*, Lord Sieff and "the bulk of Jewish readers", who, besides being all of them committed without reserve to the defence of Israel, were two thousand miles away into the bargain and depended for their information principally on the Jewish correspondents reporting from Jerusalem, whose limitations we have already considered.

Now that the facts I had uncovered are public knowledge and have been reiterated and confirmed and even written into the records of the United Nations, it is depressing to pursue the story to its conclusion. Matters came to a head when I submitted the last of my articles, the one, paradoxically, where the facts were least in doubt, although once again they had not previously found their way into the British press. This, it is ironical to recall, was one of the reasons the editor gave for not publishing this article, which related how the Israelis, after their victory in 1967, had obliterated the three Palestinian villages of Imwas (the biblical Emmaus), Yalu and Beit Nuba.

I could indeed understand that he found the story difficult to credit; it had about it such a terrifyingly authentic flavour of the Old Testament that I too had hesitated to believe it until I had verified it with my own eyes. The place where the three villages had stood lies between twelve and fifteen miles from Jerusalem as the crow flies, and the fact that not one of the British correspondents in Jerusalem had reported their destruction reflects badly, to say the least of it, on the journalists' sources. It made it easier for the editor to believe that, if I had not actually invented the story, I must at least have left out of account some justifying factor; it was only some months later, when he sent another correspondent, who was not Jewish, out from England that the story was confirmed and at last published in *The Guardian*.[70] By then, and as a direct result of the argument we had had over this episode, the editor had put an end to my connection with *The Guardian* by telling me that he would never again publish anything I wrote about the Middle East.[71] I was bitterly disappointed by his refusal to publish my article, for I had never written anything about which I felt so strongly; nor did I doubt that if the story had been the other way round, with the Arabs destroying three Israeli villages and driving their inhabitants into destitution, every newspaper in Britain would have carried the story on its front page.

This, I believe, is a fair comment and one which is highly relevant to the theme of one-sided coverage by the press of the Middle East conflict. It is also fair to add that no other paper maintained a more balanced approach towards the Middle East in 1967 and 1968 than *The Guardian*. As at the time of Suez, the paper ploughed a lonely and sometimes erratic furrow, in which others were to follow when the going became easier a year or two later. I doubt whether at that time any other daily paper would have published my articles about Gaza and Jerusalem. The article about the destroyed villages which *The Guardian* refused was then submitted to and accepted by *The Times*, which at once set it in type—and then, without explanation, changed its mind. I had almost concluded that the fate of those villages would never become known, when the article was accepted and eventually published in *The Sunday Times*, a paper which, a few years later, was to carry some of the most critical reports about Israel, but which in 1968 betrayed little interest in the Middle East and was taken by surprise by the volume of readers' letters which the article provoked.

Such detachment was unusual in those days. For the most part the British press, during the two years that followed the 1967 war, seemed mesmerised by the military strength and the political invulnerability which Israel had somehow acquired. Editors were curiously reluctant to criticise Israeli policies and actions, even when these conflicted with United Nations resolutions, as over Jerusalem, for instance, where Israel's annexation of the Arab sector of the city and the subsequent expropriation of hundreds of acres of Arab land were carried out in defiance of specific rulings by both the Security Council and the General Assembly, or when they damaged British interests, as over the Suez Canal, which remained closed, at great expense to British exporters and taxpayers, because of Israel's continued occupation of Sinai. On the other hand, these same editors fastened with relief on the mistakes of the Arabs, and were especially severe in their denunciations of terrorism on the part of a desperate minority of Palestinians, who now began to resort to force in an effort to break the hold of the Israelis on the occupied territories. It is important to remember that terrorism was the result, not the cause, of Israeli repression in the occupied territories. The first hijacking took place in July 1968, six months after the shocking events I had described in Gaza.

In short, it was very rare, in those years after 1967, to find in the British press any coherent statement of the Arab point of view over the Palestine question or any explanation of the origins of the Arab-Israeli conflict. The same thing was true elsewhere in the West, where opinion was influenced by the same guilt feelings towards the Jews and where Zionists were well placed to exploit these feelings by bringing pressure to bear on leading public figures and on the press. The Arabs, who enjoyed no such advantage, found themselves virtually cut off from access to Western opinion and felt frustrated over the absence of any balanced discussion of the issues at stake in the Middle East. To break through this barrier of what seemed to them deliberately manufactured incomprehension, they decided that, if they could not get space in the press in any other way, they would buy it; and so, in the summer of 1969, the Director of the Arab League's London office arranged for the publication in *The Times*, in the form of a paid advertisement, of a four page supplement on Palestine.

With the object of providing within this small compass as comprehensive a picture as possible, he invited a number of specialists to write on different aspects of the subject: its historical background, the clash of nationalisms in Palestine, the treatment of the Palestine question at the United Nations, the refugee problem, the involvement of the surrounding Arab countries in the conflict over Palestine and the effect of this on Britain's relations with the Arab World. These were important topics and they were treated with the seriousness which readers of *The Times* would expect. One article was contributed by a Palestinian employed in the Arab League office; otherwise, the writers were all Englishmen well known in the context of Middle East affairs. They included two former ministers of the Crown, one Labour and one Conservative, with another member of parliament who was shortly to achieve office; two former ambassadors who had spent most of their working lives dealing with the Middle East; and myself, as a former Middle East correspondent.

Now nobody would suggest that ministers or ambassadors are infallible, any more than foreign correspondents; but I think it is fair to say that in that four page supplement there was concentrated more detailed and accurate information about Palestine, past and present, than had been available in any previous edition of *The Times*, and a good deal of information about the background to the Arab-Israeli conflict that had never appeared in *The Times* at all, certainly not since June 1967. The writers, to be sure, had each of them a point of view to express; but, looking back at the pages of that supplement today, it is hard to fault them either on their exposition of the history of the Palestine dispute or on their analysis of its future implications for the combatants themselves and for the rest of the world.

Yet the behaviour of *The Times* in publishing the supplement was strange. By mutual agreement, the supplement was clearly described as an advertisement; the word ADVERTISEMENT in fact appeared in heavy capitals at the head of each of the four pages. For the unobservant reader a notice, also in heavy type, was printed on the first page reiterating that the supplement constituted "a political advertisement sponsored by the London Office of the League of Arab States," and making the curious assertion that *The Times* "has accepted it for publication in accordance with its traditional policy, but does not vouch for any of the facts or opinions expressed" in it. To be on the safe side, somewhat in the manner of a government organising an election in a country where the majority of the population is illiterate, *The Times* took the further precaution of reproducing alongside this notice the emblem of the Arab League, providing an English translation of the words "League of Arab States" which appeared below the emblem in Arabic script. It was further pointed out to the reader, who by this time, one might suppose, would be growing impatient to get to the substance of the supplement, unless, of course, he had been frightened off by these fearsome warnings about its contents, that "the authors of these articles have accepted the invitation of the London Office of the League of Arab States to contribute to this feature."

By this point any averagely literate reader of *The Times* must have grasped the point that the editor, who had of course agreed, unlike the authors, to accept for his paper a substantial sum of money in return for the publication of the articles, wished to dissociate himself from the views they expressed. It might even have occurred to some of his readers that he was being a shade overemphatic in disclaiming with such repetitive zeal any suggestion of complicity with the contributors. But the editor evidently felt otherwise, for in addition to all these elaborate defence mechanisms, and without any indication to the advertiser of what he intended to do, he felt constrained to publish in the same issue of the paper a leading article in which he did his best to negate the effect of the supplement by describing it as "extremely partisan" and the contributors as "people in Britain who strongly sympathise with the Arab cause," adding the final anti-climactic observation, which threw a curious light on his decision to publish it at all, that the supplement "is certainly not the sort of publication that is helpful."

It is behaviour of this kind on the part of our leading newspapers that lends colour to the suspicion widely entertained in the Arab world that the British press (and even more the American press) is dominated, if not actually controlled, by Zionist agents. When one seeks to disabuse Arabs of so naive a suspicion, the task is made a great deal harder by the sight of the editor of *The Times* going through such contortions to persuade his readers that, while he is prepared to take money from the Arabs, he would never do anything so discreditable as to give a fair hearing to their point of view. As though to emphasise his own partisanship on this occasion, the editor carried on the front page of the same edition of *The Times* a dispatch from his correspondent in Tel Aviv, himself an Israeli. As the contributors to the supplement pointed out in a letter which *The Times* subsequently published,[72] the editor felt no need to describe his own correspondent as "extremely partisan", nor had he found any difficulty in publishing, a short time before, a supplement on Israel whose contributors, though otherwise undistinguished, were all known to sympathise with the Israeli cause. He had not felt it appropriate to comment on this or to label the Israeli supplement as an advertisement or to explain to his readers whether he thought the publication of their views "helpful" or otherwise.

Even this was less outrageous than the behaviour on one occasion about this time of the editor of the *New Statesman*, Paul Johnson. Mr Johnson, an extreme supporter of Israel, had published a letter from a reader, and a diary note by himself, which could have been taken as suggesting that Christopher Mayhew was anti-Semitic; and when Mayhew wrote in to defend himself, Mr Johnson, instead of refusing to publish the letter, which would have been nothing unusual, excised its most telling points, without consultation with Mayhew, and published a mangled version. He then published a further letter the following week repeating the innuendo that Mayhew was anti-Semitic.

On this occasion Christopher Mayhew reported Mr Johnson to the Press Council and the Council upheld his complaint.[73] Mayhew's reputation had undoubtedly been damaged; Paul Johnson, by contrast, was subsequently appointed by Mr Harold Wilson to be a member of the Royal Commission on the Press.

The strange fact is that in 1969 it was still a common assumption at many levels of British public life that, whereas it was evidence of partisanship, or worse, to publish the views of Arabs or their sympathisers, the same was not true of Israelis and those who supported them, although such pro-Zionist sympathisers often expressed themselves with extraordinary intemperance. In fairness to the Editor of *The Times*, it has to be remembered that, like the Editor of *The Guardian* in the instance I quoted earlier, he was subjected in this context to pressures which at times became very difficult to resist. For the most part, of course, these pressures were exercised privately, but now and then they emerged into the open, providing an opportunity for the public to appreciate the degree of resolution required of a newspaper editor who found it necessary to criticise some aspect of Israeli policy or behaviour.

A striking example occurred a few months after *The Times* had published the Palestine supplement. On 28 October 1969 *The Times* carried a long article by the paper's foreign editor, E. C. Hodgkin, who happened to be a specialist with very long experience of the Middle East in general and of Palestine in particular. The article discussed the condition and the attitude of mind of the Palestinians in the territories which had then been under Israeli occupation for two and a half years. Mr Hodgkin recorded his conclusions that the occupation was detested by the bulk of the population of the West Bank of the Jordan, that it was maintained by severely repressive policies on the part of the Israeli military government, and that it appeared to be the prelude to outright annexation. He described various forms of repressive treatment meted out to the inhabitants, remarking that the innocent as well as the guilty suffered from these collective punishments and suggesting that they provoked rather than subdued resistance on the part of the Palestinians, who saw no alternative to force as a means of resisting absorption into the Jewish state.

The article, predictably, caused a sensation, not least because it recorded a picture which contrasted so strikingly with the picture of life in the occupied territories which the resident correspondents of *The Times* and other newspapers had been presenting to their readers. It was understandable that for that reason alone some readers of *The Times* should have found the article startling and disturbing.

Considering, however, that its author's responsibility and authority were second only to those of the editor of the paper, and considering that, while he had no commitment and owed no loyalty to either side in the Middle East, Mr Hodgkin was an expert of long standing in the affairs of the area, it might have been assumed that his word would be accepted rather than the word of those whom he appeared to contradict, and who were themselves explicitly partisan. Yet the initial response from some of the leading supporters of Israel in Britain, including members of parliament and even former ministers of the crown, was frenzied and brutal. One of them, Mr Julian Snow, MP, said in the House of Commons, in a reference to Mr Hodgkin's article: "I am personally not surprised that that newspaper, which was friendly to the Nazi Government and its sinister and terrible anti-Semitism, should now see fit to publish an article like that." When another member of the House protested at what he described as "a slanderous attack on . . . an extremely distinguished student of the Middle East and a man of great objectivity," he was in turn accused of anti-Semitism by Mr Emanuel Shinwell, MP (later to become Lord Shinwell).

When the editor of *The Times* replied to such criticisms in a leading article on 1 November 1969, his situation was a paradoxical one. As he rightly remarked at the outset of his leader, "In the great war between Israel and the Arabs, *The Times* has been basically sympathetic to Israel," and yet he found himself and his foreign editor under passionate attack on account of a single article which, while critical of Israel, was well documented and whose conclusions were presented with moderation by a journalist whose personal reputation and qualifications were unimpeachable. The episode was an instructive one in a number of ways, but most of all because it provoked the editor to explain to his readers some of the problems faced by a newspaper which tried to present the arguments of both sides to the conflict in the Middle East. Some of his comments on the response to Mr Hodgkin's article are worth quoting, since they illustrate *ex cathedra* the dilemma which faced all his colleagues at that time and from which they are by no means free today:

"There are a number of things to be said about this response. In the first place it is obviously hysterical. If a calmly argued report of the conditions of the Arab people in the occupied territories is equated with the anti-Semitism of the Nazis, then nobody except an avowed Israeli propagandist can be allowed to discuss the state of Israel at all. Mr Shinwell has always used ridiculously exaggerated and unjust language and his language as an old man is no more defamatory than was his language when he was young. But unfortunately Mr Shinwell and Mr Snow do represent a reaction which anyone has to face who publishes any grave and substantial criticisms of any part of the Israeli position.

"This does not do us much harm. *The Times*, like members of the House of Commons, is in the business of discussing public policy. We expect to be banged about from time to time and, on the whole, enjoy it rather than otherwise. We do not like being called anti-Semitic because that is the whole world away from our position. It is, however, clearly damaging to the interests of the State of Israel. It does Israel harm by pretending that she is a special kind of state which either can do no wrong or, when she does wrong, must not be criticised because of the memory of the wrongs that have been done to the Jews by other nations."

These were brave words and with most of them I agree wholeheartedly. But the editor's apparent insouciance barely covered his real anxiety. When he said that, because they were engaged in the discussion of public affairs, he and his colleagues "expect to be banged about from time to time and, on the whole, rather enjoy it than otherwise," those words "on the whole" expressed a significant qualification, whose meaning the editor underlined when he went on to say that "we do not like being called anti-Semitic . . ." There is indeed a world of difference between being "banged about" a bit in a playful way, or even quite vigorously, on account of one's views on apartheid or penal reform or the Common Market, and being savagely attacked by men of standing with the imprecise and immensely damaging accusation of anti-Semitism, because one has dared to criticise Israel. This is true even for the ordinary citizen; for the editor of a national newspaper, as for anyone prominent in public life, the damage, however unjustified the slander, can be far-reaching and permanent. It is perhaps surprising that, knowing this, anyone should make use of so brutal a weapon without being absolutely certain of its justification. It is certainly not surprising that, in order to avoid its wound, a politician or an editor, or anyone else whose life must be lived before the footlights of public life, should feel inclined to temper or to suppress altogether what he knows to be justifiable criticism of Israel.

Then again, I doubt if the editor was right in saying that the kind of attacks launched on behalf of Israel against *The Times* by Mr Snow and Mr Shinwell did little harm to the paper but much to Israel itself. On the contrary, and judging from what followed, I think it almost certain that the violent reaction to Mr Hodgkin's article helped to stifle for some time to come the sort of criticisms which he had voiced and which might have been widely echoed elsewhere (for there were plenty of people by now who knew that what Mr Hodgkin had written was true) had it not been for the chorus of vituperation directed against *The Times* on account of the publication of this one article. As for the personalities involved, Mr Shinwell and Mr Snow were presently elevated, on Mr Wilson's recommendation, to the House of Lords; and Mr Shinwell, despite his lack of experience of the area and his fanatical partisanship for Israel, continued to be regarded by the BBC, especially, as an appropriate choice when an "objective" comment on Middle Eastern affairs was required. Mr Hodgkin, on the other hand, when he ceased to be foreign editor of *The Times* a little more than a year later, disappeared from public life.

It seems all the more curious that the British press, during the year that followed the publication of Mr Hodgkin's article, should have remained for the most part silent about the continuing allegations of ill-treatment by the Israelis in the occupied territories. Curious, because during that year a number of reports were published in which neutral observers provided more and more specific and detailed confirmation of the truth of such allegations. In April 1970

Amnesty International produced a *Report on the Treatment of Prisoners under Interrogation in Israel*, which was admittedly incomplete but which put forward "*prima facie* evidence of the serious maltreatment of Arab prisoners." Shortly afterwards the London-based Jerusalem Committee sponsored the publication of a report (dated March 1970, the report appeared after that of Amnesty International) on the more specific subject of *Torture of Arabs under Israeli Rule*. And in September 1970 the International Committee of the Red Cross took the altogether exceptional step of publishing an account of its activities on behalf of "Protected Persons," meaning the civilian population in the areas under Israeli occupation.

Remarkably, none of these documents received the attention their authors might, in another context, have reasonably expected. The Amnesty International report aroused some controversy, but only because the Israeli Embassy in London reacted angrily at the manner of its publication as well as the nature of its contents. Some sections of the press reported the argument, but none gave much attention to the content of the report. The Jerusalem Committee's findings were ignored, with more excuse in that the Committee was a small and little known organisation, although its report was an unusually thorough one, compiled through painstaking and exhaustive enquiries on the spot. The case of the Red Cross report was in every way more significant and, on the face of it, inexplicable.

To begin with, in making public in this way its attempts to obtain from the Israeli authorities compliance with the provisions of the Fourth Geneva Convention, the International Committee of the Red Cross was departing from its usual practice of revealing its findings only to the governments concerned. The introduction to the report made it clear that this exceptional step had only been taken because the Red Cross had been unable to overcome Israel's refusal to admit that the Fourth Convention applied to the hundreds of thousands of civilians in the occupied territories. In consequence, as the report itself again made clear, this Convention had been repeatedly breached by the Israelis in such matters as the deportation of civilians, their detention without trial, the demolition of individual houses and, in a number of specified cases, of whole villages, and collective punishments—all these being specifically outlawed by the Fourth Convention. In general, the facts contained in the report were not challenged by the Israelis, who had in many cases themselves made them available to the Red Cross. The point at issue was the legitimacy of the repressive measures taken by the occupation authorities against the civilian population of the occupied territories.

The technical aspects of the matter can best be studied by reference to the report itself.[74] What is of interest here is the fact that, despite the gravity of the contents of the report and their implications for the welfare of many thousands of defenceless civilians living under military occupation, and despite the obvious intention of the Red Cross, by taking exceptional action to make these facts known, to give them the maximum of publicity, the report was ignored by all but one national newspaper in Britain. The exception was the *Sunday Times*, which carried on 11 October 1970 a careful account by Philip Knightley and Alan Macgregor. Under the headline "Israel Guilty of Geneva Breach, says Red Cross", their article referred to the report as "something of a landmark in Red Cross history" and explained its publication by saying that "After two years of protest, a Red Cross spokesman said last week: 'We have not been able to obtain from the Israeli Government a satisfactory response on its attitude to the Fourth Convention.'"

There can be no question at all that such a report by the Red Cross, had it referred to similar breaches of the Geneva Conventions in Vietnam or South Africa, in Syria, Greece, Turkey or Chile, or Northern Ireland, would have been treated by the British press as front page news. It would have been closely examined and there would certainly have been vehement demands for international action to back it up, or at the very least for an international enquiry to verify its allegations. Such an enquiry had been asked for by Amnesty International and was in fact set on foot by a United Nations Special Committee to Investigate Israeli Practices in the Occupied Territories. The Israeli Government refused to co-operate with this or any similar enquiry, repudiating its authority and eventually rejecting its findings, which broadly confirmed those of the International Committee of the Red Cross.

It is impossible to know now whether other newspapers would have felt able to follow the example of the *Sunday Times*, if they had not felt intimidated by the onslaught the Zionist lobby had made on *The Times* over the Hodgkin article a few months earlier. I believe it is very likely; and it is interesting that the only newspaper to give publicity to the Red Cross report should have been the *Sunday Times*, whose financial strength put it in a much stronger position to resist pressure from advertisers than its rival the *Observer* or any of the serious daily newspapers at the time.

And yet there was by this time no lack of information about these and other aspects of the Arab-Israeli conflict, and voices were being raised in various quarters calling for a less partial approach to the situation in the Middle East. First among these it is right to mention the fearless Chairman of the Israeli League for Human and Civil Rights, Dr Israel Shahak, who did more than any other person to document the facts about the Israeli occupation. Our own Council for the Advancement of Arab-British Understanding was also active in collecting such information and passing it on to those who might, if they wished, have acted upon it. In general, the information was ignored by the press, even when it came, as in the case of the Israeli League, from individuals or organisations inside Israel itself with no possible ulterior motive for its dissemination. There were also more influential voices raised in Britain in protest against the bias and the suppression of facts which at that time characterised so much of the press coverage of the Middle East. Two days before his death in February 1970, Bertrand Russell had addressed a message to an International Conference of Parliamentarians in Cairo, in which he urged them to put an end to Israeli expansionism, and stated:

> "The tragedy of the people of Palestine is that their country was 'given' by a foreign Power to another people for the creation of a new State. The result was that many hundreds of thousands of innocent people were made permanently homeless. With every new conflict

their numbers have increased. How much longer is the world willing to allow this spectacle of wanton cruelty?"

In much the same terms Professor Arnold Toynbee observed, in the introduction to a recent book about the Palestine question: [75]

"The present generation of mankind is sensitive, in general, to human suffering anywhere in the world—in Nigeria, for instance, and in Vietnam. The Arabs' sufferings have been disregarded by the world as callously as the wrongs by which the sufferings have been caused. Yet there is no reason why the Arabs' cause should be ignored or why the Israelis' conduct should be condoned. Right and wrong are the same in Palestine as anywhere else. What is peculiar about the Palestine conflict is that the world has listened to the party that committed the offence and has turned a deaf ear to the victims."

The advent to power of a Conservative government in Britain in 1970, which marked something of a watershed as far as British attitudes towards the Middle East were concerned, raised a small corner of the curtain of incomprehension behind which the facts about the Arab-Israeli conflict remained hidden from the general public. Those who had expected from the Conservatives a Middle East policy bitterly flavoured by the after-taste of Suez were surprised when the new Foreign Secretary, Sir Alec Douglas-Home, made to an obscure party gathering in Yorkshire what was later to become famous, and to Zionist sympathisers notorious, as the "Harrogate speech". The speech, with its insistence on a political settlement in the Middle East which would take fair account of the interests of the Palestinians, in fact said nothing that had not previously been stated by British ministers. What lent it importance was the fact that Sir Alec restated a position from which the preceding Labour administration had gradually retreated in deference to Israeli objections. The fact was noted, with annoyance by the Zionist lobby inside and outside parliament, with hesitant approval by those sections of the press which had by now begun to be conscious of the extent to which they had been used by pro-Israeli propagandists.

There had of course always been exceptions to the general rule of support for Israel. The *Observer*, with an editorial policy which teetered uncertainly between one side and the other, had been well served by its diplomatic correspondent, Robert Stephens, who provided the paper with the most consistently balanced analysis of Middle Eastern affairs throughout this difficult period. The *Financial Times*, apart from the excellent coverage it provided of the economic affairs of the region, had shown more scepticism than most about Israeli claims and pretensions and had kept its correspondence columns notably open to the expression of divergent views. The *Sunday Times*, while it had remained uninvolved to the point where it appeared to ignore the Middle East altogether for months at a time, had, as on the various occasions we have noted, published material which the rest of the press seemed to find too hot to handle. Later, the *Insight* team was to become still more adventurous, as in its exposure of Israeli terrorism as the precursor of the hijackings and murder raids with which the Palestinians were associated in the early 1970s. *Tribune*, with less space at its disposal, had regularly shown a decent regard for the interests of the underdog, and had been quicker than most to understand and acknowledge who the underdog was, in the Middle East. The *Daily Mirror*, through the excellent reporting of John Pilger, had several times drawn attention to the tragic predicament of the Palestinians. *Private Eye*, with characteristic disregard for the majority view, had made no attempt to disguise its contempt for the insensitivity and the growing atmosphere of militarism which distinguished the Golda Meir period in Israeli history and which seemed unaccountably to appeal so much to the leaders of the British Labour Party.

All these had, in varying degree and not always consistently, preserved, where the Arab-Israeli conflict was concerned, something of the reputation of the British press for independence of mind and freedom of comment. With the exception of *Tribune* and *Private Eye*, they had all of them shown a much quicker and more instinctive interest in the Israelis and in Jewish causes in general, than in the

Palestinians or in the wider Arab cause. There had been times when all of them, with the same two exceptions, had seemed to succumb to the mesmerism of the Israelis, or else to the pressures exerted by their supporters. It had consistently been much more difficult, throughout this period from 1967 to the end of 1970, to place with any national newspaper an article presenting an Arab, let alone a Palestinian, viewpoint, than it had been to place such an article if it put forward an Israeli or a broadly Jewish viewpoint. But the papers I have mentioned, including *The Guardian* and, less convincingly, *The Times*, had tried at least intermittently to look at both sides of the conflict in the Middle East.

After 1970, their willingness to do so and their lack of inhibition gradually, and most unevenly, increased. *The Times* at last began to use Eric Marsden, a non-Jewish Englishman, as its correspondent in Jerusalem. No other paper, however, followed its example; *The Guardian* and the *Observer*, indeed, moved in the opposite direction, replacing the Jewish but non-Zionist Walter Schwartz with Eric Silver, former London correspondent of the *Jerusalem Post* and a notably enthusiastic admirer of Israel and all its works. The BBC, despite repeated criticisms, retained Michael Elkins.

Gradually, in the light of the Israeli government's resolute defiance of world opinion over Jerusalem,[76] where its politically-motivated building programme alienated even many of its leading supporters, and of the growing evidence that Israel intended to keep much or all of the occupied territories, where more and more settlements were planted as symbols of the Meir-Dayan policy of "creeping annexation", it became increasingly difficult for pro-Israeli leader-writers to resist the conclusion that it was Israeli intransigence which was preventing a tolerable settlement in the Middle East. When the war of October 1973 shattered the basis of all their calculations about the balance of power between themselves and the Arabs, it came as a further shock to the Israelis to find how deeply the sympathy they had once commanded in the West had been eroded.

Even their staunchest supporters now began to voice their reservations. Papers like the *Daily Telegraph*, the *Sunday Telegraph*, the

Daily Mail, which had seldom if ever committed themselves to any serious editorial criticism of Israeli actions or policies, or given any serious consideration to the rights of the Palestinians,[77] now began to point out the weaknesses in official Israeli thinking. At first they were hesitant and one could almost hear the grinding of gears in the *Daily Mail* office before a leader-writer could bring himself to say, on the third day of the October War that ". . . we have never found it more difficult to voice unequivocal condemnation of Arab aggression," or that "one day when they feel at their cockiest and feel capable of biffing every Arab in sight, the Jews (sic) will have to take a gamble on trading territory for Arab recognition . . ."[78] And the *Daily Telegraph*, after supporting through thick and thin Israel's refusal to strike a fair bargain with her opponents, preferred to let an unidentified "Special Correspondent" demolish the whole of its past editorial policy towards the Middle East in half a dozen lines by writing: "The military balance is still slightly in Israel's favour, and the Arabs are willing to make peace. If the Israelis wait until it tilts in the Arabs' favour, they may no longer have a choice of peace . . . There is no such thing as absolute military security, and its continued pursuit will be the ruin of their nation."[79]

In thus paraphrasing what I had written in *The Guardian* in June 1967,[80] I suppose the *Telegraph*'s correspondent was paying both the paper and myself an unwitting compliment. But during the intervening years a terrible amount of harm had been done by the uncritical support which the editorial writers of the *Telegraph*, as much as anyone, had given to Israel. For the sufferings of the Palestinians during those years, and for the carnage of the October War, which need never have been fought had Israel been brought earlier to reason, the responsibility must be shared by those newspaper publishers, editors and leader writers who had encouraged the Israelis to persist in policies which were ultimately self-defeating. The fact that those policies were incidentally extremely damaging to British interests, and led us all directly into the energy crisis and its attendant complications, hardly strengthens the case for those in the British press who encouraged them.

But then, as Arnold Toynbee has again pointed out,

"There is a nemesis for condoning wrongs, as well as for committing them. The world has condoned the wrong that has been done to the Palestinian Arabs by Zionism. The Palestinian Arabs have been despoiled and evicted by force, and the force by which they have been coerced was first British, before the Israelis built up the military strength to do their own fighting—with American supplies of arms and American economic and political support. The responsibility for the wrong done to the Palestinians is widespread: now nations and individuals alike must assume the imperative task of informing themselves of the nature of the conflict in the Middle East."[81]

Christopher Mayhew: Radio and Television

The pro-Israeli bias in British broadcasting has been for the most part inbuilt and unconscious, a true reflection of our cultural prejudices, which are founded on half-remembered and inaccurate impressions of the Old Testament, the Crusades, the era of British colonialism, and most of all on our sense of guilt over the way we Europeans have behaved in the past towards the Jews in our midst. But the bias has also come—often without deliberate intent—from the influence of sympathisers with Israel inside and outside the broadcasting organisations.

My first direct experience of this was in 1967, just before the June War. At my own suggestion, I had gone to Cairo for the BBC to try to obtain a television interview with Nasser, something which every film and television company in the world was trying to get at that time. I thought I was a jump ahead of my rivals, since Nasser had promised some months earlier to record an interview for me. Before leaving, knowing Nasser's suspicions of Zionist influence in the Corporation (which I partly shared), I asked for permission to tell him that the interview would be broadcast in full. I also asked that it should be screened immediately I got back. Both undertakings were readily given by the BBC.

All went well in Cairo. I recorded a unique forty-minute interview which gave considerable insight into Nasser's personality, ideas and intentions, and landed at Heathrow, clutching my priceless cans of film, on the morning of 3 June, a full day ahead of my nearest competitors and two days before the outbreak of war. The rushes were taken immediately to Lime Grove and seen by the responsible BBC producer, Paul Fox.

An hour or two later, Paul Fox rang me up to say that my questioning of Nasser had been very "soft" and that he did not propose to show the film that evening. I protested that my questioning had been extremely tough, and that his decision was a breach of our agreement. He stuck to his guns, and later also refused to screen the interview on the following Sunday night. On the Monday morning the war broke out, and he decided to show the interview in *Panorama* that evening, cut to ten minutes, and balanced by an interview with Mr Abba Eban. I again protested, but without effect. The two films were duly shown that evening, and the briefest examination of the transcript of the programme shows that the questioning of Nasser was far tougher than the questioning of Eban.

I am quite sure that Paul Fox had no intention of being unfair and bear him no ill will whatever; I recognise too that he was placed in an extremely difficult position by the fact that he was himself Jewish. But his decisions were demonstrably wrong. They were a breach of faith, since they disregarded the explicit undertakings we had given to Nasser. The BBC would never have dreamed of treating Israeli leaders in the same way. Beyond this, they showed a characteristic failure to grasp the validity and the importance of Nasser's arguments; and it was also characteristic that the BBC felt bound to "balance" them with an interview with Eban, although there had been dozens of occasions when the BBC, and ITV as well, had put out an interview with an Israeli leader with no balancing interview with a spokesman for the Arabs.

In fairness to the BBC and ITV, I had many opportunities at the time of the 1967 war to state my views on radio and television. I took what would now be considered a virtually neutral line, criticising both

Israel and the Arabs, arguing that Britain should not intervene except as a member of the UN, and insisting that Israel had a right to live in peace within her own frontiers. Nevertheless, the climate of opinion was so fiercely and uncritically pro-Israeli at that time that pressure soon built up among the pro-Israelis to get me off the air. A "round robin" was launched inside the Parliamentary Labour Party demanding that an announcement should be made before each of my broadcast appearances that my views were unrepresentative of Labour policy. No similar demand was ever made of Labour MPs whose views were at least equally unrepresentative in the opposite direction. The "round robin", signed by twenty-six of my fellow Labour MPs, was sent to Mr John Silkin, the Chief Government Whip. Mr Silkin, a strong supporter of Israel, issued a public statement declaring his official support for the petition, which he forwarded to the BBC. He did this without consulting me, and without either having seen the particular programme complained of or having read a transcript of it. Whether his intervention diminished the number of my appearances I cannot say, but I was heartened by a private assurance from the BBC that they considered that his approach to them had been improper.

An unusual and amusing example of unintentional bias occurred about this time in a BBC television programme called *Your Witness*. This programme took the form of a legal action conducted before a jury of young lawyers by Mr Jo Grimond, MP, as "Counsel" for Israel, and by myself as "Counsel" for the Arabs. We were both allowed to call witnesses and to present documentary and other evidence, and meticulous care was taken to ensure that the available time was divided equally between us, and that in every other way both sides were fairly treated. Unfortunately, however, one factor vital to the dispensing of justice had been overlooked: the selection of an unbiased jury. Information sent to me after the programme by a member of the BBC staff showed that, out of the panel of 110 young lawyers from whom the jury of twenty-four was to be selected, twenty-two were avowed Jewish sympathisers with Israel, and that these young people were not only allowed to serve as jurors but could put themselves forward for jury service for this particular programme, knowing in advance the subject for debate. Consequently, when I rose to open my case for the Palestinian Arabs, before an audience of about ten million viewers, I saw before me in the jury box so many apparently Jewish people that I felt I must be the victim of some macabre practical joke. In the event, the jury's verdict was a predictable triumph for Israel; and my "fan mail" after the programme included no less than sixty letters specifically commiserating with me on a "packed" jury.

In this case, I doubt whether anyone had deliberately tried to rig the verdict. As far as the BBC was concerned, the injustice done to the Palestinians and their friends was obviously accidental. But the incident illustrated the way in which a natural pro-Israeli bias is built into our broadcasting simply because our society includes a talented and influential Jewish minority.

Some members of this minority occupy powerful positions in the commercial television establishment, sometimes as a chairman, or a managing director, or a programme organiser. No one need doubt their wish that ITV's output on the Middle East should be fair and balanced, but a description which one tycoon once gave me of a projected television series on the life of Moses was far from reassuring. "How will the Egyptians come out of it?" I asked. He had not given the question much thought. "How do you mean?" "Well, will you show them as goodies or baddies?" I asked. He saw danger ahead and pondered. But then the safe, sensible answer came to him. "As it is in the Bible," he said. "That's fair, isn't it? Just as it is in the Bible."

Sadly I calculated that what seemed fair to him would also seem fair to the viewers and to the Independent Broadcasting Authority. Scene after scene of the proposed television epic filled my mind's eye. I heard the cries of a helpless Jewish baby in the bulrushes. I saw a hand-some young Moses confronting an ugly old Pharaoh. I watched as the waters of the Red Sea parted, and the heroic Children of Israel escaped from their well-armed, anti-Semitic pursuers. Above all, I saw the trailer to the series, repeated over and over again at peak hours, with Palestine being promised by God to Abraham, and Abraham being portrayed not, as the Old Testament in fact presents him, as the ancestor of both the Jews and the Arabs of Palestine, but exclusively—and inaccurately—as the forefather of the Children of Israel.

"And why not?" it will be objected. "Should not all points of view, however controversial, be presented on TV?" But how different things might be if the chairman of one independent television company happened to be of Arab descent. In that case viewers might have the same historical events presented from, say, the Canaanite point of view. They might then see peace-loving Canaanite families tilling the soil of Palestine, as they had done for centuries past, until set upon by a murderous horde of Israelites and slaughtered to the last man, woman and child. They might be reminded that the Canaanite society which the Israelites upset, and from which they gradually acquired some of the aspects of civilisation, was far more advanced than that of the invaders. They might learn that the short-lived dominion of the biblical Israelites in Palestine, just like that of the modern Israelis, was founded on the naked use of force by a people solely preoccupied by their own selfish ambitions. A distorted picture? Perhaps; but no more distorted than the one usually presented of the historical background to events in Palestine.

Complementing the bias, sometimes unconscious, of sympathisers with Israel inside the broadcasting organisations has been the external influence on the broadcasting authorities of the pro-Israeli lobby. Since there is no Arab equivalent to the Jewish community in Britain, the pro-Israelis can operate on a far bigger scale in terms of deputations, letters and personal contacts than the pro-Arabs. This disparity in the size and power of the two lobbies undoubtedly has an influence on the broadcasting authorities, and sometimes leads them to make wrong decisions.

Take, for example, this letter from Mr James Norris, the BBC's Head of Secretariat. He is defending the Corporation against a charge of bias in the radio programme *The World at One*.

Dear Michael,
As promised on 8th January I am now replying to your letter of 10th December, which arrived just before I started some sick leave.

The main target of your criticism continues to be "The World at One", which is of course a 30-minute sequence comprising a 10-minute news bulletin and 20 minutes of current affairs interviewing and discussion—all of it a good deal closer to the news than some other current affairs programmes. "The World at One" prides itself on making the second part of the programme really "newsy". Its items are quite frequently changed to accommodate new material while the programme is on the air. So it is not surprising that it does not have the same leisured air as some other programmes. Yet it is under the same obligation as them to observe all the canons of current affairs broadcasting. Though strict balance within a single programme or programme item is most often impossible, if not undesirable, every current affairs programme aims at balance over a reasonable period. Your view of what that balance may be or what is reasonable is not necessarily the same as theirs, but they certainly go all out to attain it. They have no interest in being anything but fair to all parties to a controversy. The same can be said of "P.M. Reports"—a sister programme of "The World at One"—on which Musa Mazzawi, Sir Colin Crowe, Elizabeth Collard and the Egyptian Ambassador all appeared during the period in question.

Your inclusion of General Herzog in your list of pro-Israeli contributors illustrates the danger of making your kind of tally. General Herzog was used because he had something of unique value to offer to the audience as an informed commentator on the military position. In a perfectly symmetrical situation there would have been a similar character on the Arab side—perhaps in Cairo—but alas there was not. Since we valued what General Herzog had to offer we had to make the best of what we could glean from correspondents on the other side of the line to be as fair as we could be in assessing the situation.

It may be that a strictly statistical approach to anything so fleeting as the coverage of an international crisis is inappropriate. There are so many factors in the equation that one concentrates on just one of them at one's peril. Take Philip Short's eye witness account of an Israeli air raid on Damascus, for example. It was brief, yet it spoke volumes. Comment was superfluous. Meanwhile one must acknowledge that journalists doing an honest job in this country have to take account of the fact that Israeli or Zionist public relations activities are conducted with a degree of sophistication which those on the other side have rarely matched, and that supporters of Israel in this country represent a much more vocal and powerful minority than supporters of the Arab cause. In other words, an accurate reflection of publicly expressed attitudes on the issue may well inevitably reveal at times a preponderance of sympathy for the Israeli side. If it exists it will be reflected, however hard one tries to be neutral and fair. Indeed we would be open to justified censure if we, so to speak, cooked the books and pretended that the situation was different.

One could go on in this vein for a long time. I do not propose to do so, but I will make sure that our correspondence is seen by one or two senior colleagues. If they have anything to add to or subtract from what I have said or think that there would be any value in a meeting of the kind you suggest I will let you know.

Yours ever,
Jim Norris
Assistant Secretary &
Head of Secretariat[82]

What this seems to be saying is that the BBC should not concern itself with striking a balance between the arguments for the Israeli viewpoint and the arguments for the Arab viewpoint, but should reflect the greater power of the Israeli lobby. It is a curious argument, and it shows once again how the existence of a large and influential Jewish minority, and the absence of an Arab equivalent, help to produce a pro-Israeli bias in broadcasting.

Incidentally, the complaint to which Mr Norris was referring was based on a monitoring report by CAABU members covering all the *World at One* programmes during the fortnight following the outbreak of the October War in the Middle East. The count of pro-Israeli and pro-Arab speakers was as follows:

Date	Pro-Israeli	Pro-Arab
October 7th	Israeli Ambassador	Dennis Walters, MP
	A Jewish businessman	
	General Herzog	
	Philip Windsor	
8th		Elizabeth Collard
9th	General Herzog	
10th	Israeli Ambassador	
	J. Biggs-Davison, MP	
15th	Rt. Hon. Hugh Fraser, MP	
	General Herzog	
	Michael Stewart	
16th	General Herzog	Dennis Walters, MP
	Gerald Kaufman, MP	Richard Luce, MP
18th	Israeli Ambassador	
	General Herzog	
	Philip Goodhart, MP	
Total	15	4

Fortunately, the *World at One* programmes were not typical of the BBC's output, and in general the coverage of the October War by the BBC and the IBA was far more balanced and objective than it had been during the 1967 war. Apart from *The World at One*, the only seriously unbalanced programme was *Any Questions*, which is chaired by a dedicated Zionist, Mr David Jacobs. By common consent, *Any Questions* had been one of the most biased of all programmes in 1967, and CAABU members therefore specially monitored the edition which followed the outbreak of the October War. In addition, Michael Adams asked the BBC in advance to remind Mr Jacobs of the need to keep a balance. In spite of this, however, the programme exceeded everyone's worst expectations. Replying to the subsequent complaint from CAABU, Mr Norris wrote:

15th October 1973.
Dear Michael,
Thank you for telephoning the Duty Room staff yesterday with your complaint about the remarks made by Lady Stocks in "Any Questions?". Your call was duly logged and I received a copy of it this morning. As you know, I took some action yesterday afternoon without waiting until I received a copy of the Duty Room's note.

Your complaint has been considered at a high level within the BBC. I personally listened to the second repeat of that edition of "Any Questions?" with some of my colleagues this morning. There is no doubt at all there that you had made a valid point. Lady Stocks had expressed an extreme opinion in objectionable terms from which the sting was only fractionally removed by the context (of praise for the great Arab contribution to civilisation in the past) in which she used them. It is interesting to note that there was some muttering in the audience when she made her first remark about the Syrians, and that her final comment was greeted with what might fairly be called an embarrassed silence.

"Any Questions?" is of course a live programme, and the contributors are on a fairly loose rein. From time to time one of them may make an exaggerated or highly coloured statement on a controversial matter in the hope, perhaps, of getting a laugh or a round of applause. Only in the last resort does a producer contemplate editing the recording of the live discussion before allowing the programme to be repeated. For instance, if one of the contributors said something which was patently actionable it would be folly to allow it to be repeated, for the fact that it had been repeated would tell against the BBC in any subsequent libel action. Even that is not as easy as it sounds. The libel laws are not so clear-cut that one can always identify an actionable statement immediately after it has been made. It is even more difficult to draw a line between the repeatable and the unrepeatable outside the area of manifest libels.

There has to be a "safety valve", and "Any Answers?" provides it. It exists to give listeners an early opportunity to take issue with a panellist who has said something outrageous, silly or open to

challenge on some other score. I do hope that you have written and posted your own letter to "Any Answers?". I have a feeling that it will not have been the only letter provoked by Lady Stocks' words.
Yours ever,
Jim Norris
Assistant Secretary &
Head of Secretariat[83]

Similarly, the Director-General, Sir Charles Curran, wrote to me on 12 November 1973:

"I am bound to admit that *Any Questions* on Friday, 12 October, was unbalanced in its attitude to the Middle East war . . ."

Despite these admissions, however, the programme was twice repeated in full, including Lady Stocks' racialist remarks, from which Mr Jacobs had made no attempt to dissociate himself or the BBC.

In general, the correspondents of both the BBC and the independent television companies working in Arab countries usually manage to report objectively, even though the facilities available to them in these countries are often inadequate. The correspondents in Israel, however, make little pretence of objectivity. Mr Michael Elkins, the BBC's resident correspondent in Jerusalem, is an American citizen of Jewish origin who has been living in Israel since 1963. So far as we know, he has not formally acquired Israeli citizenship, although under Israel's Law of Return he is automatically eligible for it unless he chooses positively to reject it. He is the author of a book, *Forged in Fury*, written from an extreme Zionist viewpoint, in which he gives a very sympathetic account of a Jewish organisation whose purpose is to hunt down and murder, without trial, anyone suspected of having taken part in the anti-Jewish crimes of the Nazis thirty years ago. In his foreword, Mr Elkins expresses his full approval of this system of summary justice. Mr Elkins is also named on the title page as author of *Images in a Crystal Ball*, a Zionist fund-raising pamphlet published in 1969.

Mr Elkins' broadcasts from Jerusalem have been strongly criticised for the pro-Israeli bias they reflect, and representations have frequently been made to the BBC urging that he should not continue to be employed there. There has been more than one disagreement at production level within the BBC about using Elkins' one-sided dispatches at moments of particular tension, and it is reasonable to ask whether it can ever be right to appoint a broadcaster of Zionist views as a BBC correspondent in Jerusalem. The BBC argues firmly that it can. Writing about another BBC reporter on Middle East affairs who is pro-Israeli and Jewish, Sir Charles Curran specifically declares:

> "X, who is one of a great many BBC people sent to the Middle East during the recent war, says he is not a Zionist. *Whether he is or not is unimportant* if he does what professional people are enjoined to do, and operates objectively."[84]

This statement cannot be objected to in principle, but it is no defence of the BBC's record in practice. In the first place, the Corporation has applied Sir Charles' principle only to pro-Israelis. It has appointed a Zionist of Jewish origin as its correspondent in Jerusalem, but has never appointed an anti-Zionist of Arab origin as its correspondent in an Arab capital or, for that matter, a communist of Russian origin as its correspondent in Moscow. In the second place, the Corporation surely ought to deploy its broadcasters so as to help rather than hinder objectivity. No doubt anti-Zionists, if they were given the chance, *could* report objectively from Cairo, and Zionists *could* report objectively from Jerusalem, but they would probably both do better in posts where they were less emotionally committed, and perhaps less exposed to moral blackmail from colleagues, friends and relations.

The defence of Michael Elkins put forward by the BBC takes the form of indignant denials unsupported by evidence. In reply to one protest from CAABU, Mr Ian Trethowan, Managing Director of BBC Radio, wrote:

"With regard to Michael Elkins I simply cannot accept your strictures on him. He has worked for us for a number of years and if he were indeed 'unquestionably a biased witness' I think you must accept that we would by now have spotted it. We would after all have nothing to gain by ignoring such a situation: it would in fact be a grave embarrassment."[85]

Similarly, on 20 June 1972, Mr Walter Wallich, Senior Producer, General Current Affairs, BBC Radio, wrote:

". . . I know from long experience Mr Elkins has proved a most accurate and reliable commentator on events in Israel and the Middle East."

In May 1974, following a prolonged correspondence about the BBC's coverage of the Middle East, Sir Charles Curran invited me to lunch at Broadcasting House with himself and senior colleagues to present my criticisms. What impact, if any, my presentation made I cannot say; but the discussion seemed to me to reveal two weaknesses in the Corporation's position.

First, too little thought had been given to the distinction between conscious and unconscious bias. Most of the company appeared to have come to the lunch in the naive belief thay they or their staff would be charged with deliberate bias; and evidently felt that if they could prove their innocence on this point, they had cleared themselves. Whereas, of course, this belief of theirs only confirmed one's fears that they had not studied, and were not alert to, the serious problem, which was that of unconscious bias.

Second, it was plain that no serious attempt had ever been made to analyse the Corporation's Middle East output from the point of view of "balance"; and no clear directive had been issued about the meaning of "balance" in this context.

The attitude within the Corporation is further illustrated by an incident which occurred during the preparation of this book. In March 1974, Michael Adams had written to the BBC to point out that, in a series of six programmes on six girls living in foreign countries,[86] a film about an Israeli girl had been used as the vehicle for a whole series of stock propaganda clichés. He added that he wondered once again how long it would be before an unusually adventurous producer entertained the idea of making a similar film about any of the Arab countries.

In reply, Michael Adams received from the Executive Producer concerned, Mr Anthony Isaacs, a letter which was endorsed in a bland covering note from the Controller of BBC2, Mr Robin Scott. When we asked for permission to quote from the letter in this book, Mr Isaacs wrote to say that he had consulted his senior colleagues, including his Head of Department and the Director General of the BBC, and that they agreed that he should refuse our request. He based this decision on the curious argument that the original exchange of letters had been a private correspondence—although Michael Adams had written as a Director of the Council for the Advancement of Arab-British Understanding and Mr Isaacs had replied as an official of the BBC. While Mr Isaacs was within his legal rights in refusing permission, his refusal (endorsed as it was at the highest level within the BBC) does seem significant, suggesting that on this particular topic the Corporation is peculiarly sensitive. If it were not, why should it be reluctant to allow publication of its own defence against a criticism which is manifestly of public importance?

The arguments in Mr Isaacs' letter were unconvincing and it is of interest that he suggested that a further series of programmes might later include one on a girl from one of the Arab countries. A year later, when this book went to press, no such programme had yet been shown.

The pro-Israeli bias in British broadcasting was well summarised by Mr Bryan Magee, himself an experienced broadcaster and now Labour MP for Waltham Forest, in an article in *The Listener* on 19 March 1970:

> "Unfortunately we in this country tended to look at the conflict very much from one side, the Israeli side, until quite recently. And we were

infected by the one-sidedness, the fanaticism almost. For instance, our television and newspapers reported the Six Day War of 1967 almost entirely from the Israeli point of view, without much audible protest from anyone, so far as I can remember. Yet when it was all over I presented a programme on ITV which raised the questions, how did the Arabs feel now, what are their first reactions to defeat, how do they see their immediate future, and before the programme had even finished the switchboard at Television House was jammed with telephone calls protesting about British television being given over to the Arab point of view. There were shoals of letters afterwards, the Directors of the Company received personal complaints, there was a reference to the programme in the House of Commons. When I forced people to make their complaints specific they usually fell back on saying that I had had only Arabs in the programme and I ought to have had some Israelis too. But the purpose of the programme was to find out how Arabs felt. In any case, in the previous week literally dozens of programmes had been put on embodying the Israeli point of view, with Israeli spokesmen and no Arab spokesmen, and there were no sacks of protesting mail, no criticisms in Parliament."

❖ ❖ ❖

To put this survey of past shortcomings into perspective, we should emphasise that in recent years, and especially since the October War, there has been a steady advance in the degree of objectivity shown by the press and the broadcasting services. Where television is concerned, the independent networks have drawn well ahead of the BBC. While *Panorama* has remained within the BBC a somewhat isolated island of objectivity, ITN's *First Report* and *News at Ten* now provide the widest and most balanced coverage of Middle East news. In the field of television documentaries and features, a milestone was passed in 1974 when London Weekend showed John Pilger's excellent film *Palestine is still the issue*; by the end of 1974 the BBC, with a string of highly sympathetic programmes about Israel behind it, had still attempted no comparable examination of the Palestinian case.

Bias in the Media

Turning to the radio, the BBC World Service continued to provide for listeners abroad an admirably comprehensive and non-partisan survey of Middle East news and views, which could by no means always be said of news and current affairs programmes on the home services. Of these, Radio Four's early morning programme *Today* was the only one to maintain a generally objective approach. *The World at One* and, to a lesser extent, *The World Tonight* still showed a steady though less marked preference for the Israeli side of the argument. *Analysis*, which is the only regular documentary series on current affairs to retain a place in the schedules of BBC radio, showed between 1967 and 1973 so evident a bias in favour of Israel as to excite comment even inside the BBC; during 1974, when the Middle East was constantly in the news but when there was little that could be said in Israel's favour, *Analysis* conspicuously ignored the subject altogether.

As far as the press is concerned, and with certain exceptions, of which the most notable are the *Daily Express* and the *Daily Telegraph*, the improvement has been general. There is still a constant tendency to give preference to the views of the Israelis, but almost everywhere the attempt is now made to examine the merits of the Arab, and especially the Palestinian, case. The Israelis, accustomed to having the inside track with the media of Western countries, have hastened the new tendency by the violence with which they have reacted to any criticism, however moderately it might be expressed. Western journalists, like Western politicians, have grown tired of being abused whenever their attitude towards Israel fell short of outright support. It was noticeable that when the Israelis, in November 1974, reacted with something close to hysteria to the reception given to Yasser Arafat at the United Nations, editorial writers in the press treated their outbursts with a detachment that would have been unthinkable a year or two earlier.

CHAPTER SIX

The Failure of the Churches

Michael Adams

The significance of Palestine for any Christian needs no emphasis. There were organisations of many churches in Palestine itself which did splendid work, from 1948 onwards, among the refugees, and which sent the most forthright messages requesting not only material aid but also political action from Western countries. And yet it is strange and disquieting that the Christian churches in the West have shown little interest in the fate of Palestine or of the Palestinians during their vicissitudes over the past half century. In particular, during the crucial years after the 1967 war, when Jerusalem itself was annexed by the Israelis and the rest of Palestine subjected to a military occupation, the churches accepted as meekly as anyone else a *fait accompli* for which there was no justification and which carried within it the seeds of further conflict.

One might have thought that the presence of an army of occupation would embarrass the organisers of Christian pilgrimages to Bethlehem and Jerusalem, that the Israeli soldiers with their sub-machine guns outside the Church of the Nativity or along the Via Dolorosa might strike a discordant note for those coming to celebrate Christmas or Easter in the Holy Land. Remarkably, few of the pilgrims themselves or of those who planned their itineraries showed any awareness of the desperate sense of resentment which lay behind the impassive faces of the Palestinians who watched them come and go. Few of them realised that of those Palestinians a considerable number were themselves Christians, whose resentment was blended with shame at their identification with a Christian world which seemingly had abandoned them to their conquerors.

Indeed, the ignorance of the majority of visitors from the West about the rights and wrongs of the Palestine question, or even about its basic facts, was so striking as to bring despair to the heart of even the bravest of Israel's new subjects. I remember a Dutch woman working devotedly as a nurse in Gaza, at a time when conditions there were a hideous compound of terror and repression, who told me she was appalled less by the situation itself than by the complaisant ignorance of almost all the Western tourists and pilgrims she met when she went for an occasional day off to Jerusalem. (None of these visitors of course penetrated as far as Gaza.) One of them, she said, who seemed a decent enough woman, had said when the Dutch woman told her she was working among the refugees: "Where are they refugees from?" And when she was told they were Palestinians, she had asked, "What sort of people are those?"

Again, one might have supposed that the authorities of the Christian churches would feel it their duty to combat this ignorance, just as one might have expected them vigorously to take the part of the victims of the Palestinian tragedy and to raise their voices in protest against the injustice being perpetrated all around them. Such has not been the case. The clergymen shepherding their holy tourists, like their superiors in the hierarchy, have, with few and noble exceptions, not so much ignored the injustice as collaborated in it. A few of them, sincere but befuddled, do so because they have been brainwashed into believing that the modern state of Israel is the fulfilment of biblical prophecy; and with that kind of fundamentalist belief there is no point in trying to reason.[87] Others, of whom some are also sincere and the rest merely cowardly, side with the Israelis because for a churchman, as for a politician, it is safer and less conspicuous to be on the side of the Jews. And for the rest the motivation is simply a prudent awareness that the Israelis, since they became the masters in Jerusalem in 1967, have it in their power to expropriate the properties of any individual or organisation of whose activities they disapprove; and they have made no attempt to disguise the fact that the Christian congregations in Jerusalem, whose properties are substantial, are as vulnerable to this sanction as anyone else.

And so the churches, which might have given a lead to Western opinion where the unfolding crisis in the Middle East was concerned, have for the most part kept silence; have, indeed, ignored or at best returned an evasive answer to the appeals addressed to them by those whose feelings were restrained by no such pragmatic considerations. Of these there have been plenty, although they have not achieved, nor always sought, much publicity. I have in front of me as I write one of the more remarkable documents to come out of Jerusalem at the time of the June War of 1967. In the form of an "Open Letter to the Christians of the Western World", it was written on behalf of the inhabitants of Arab Jerusalem by the American wife of a Palestinian doctor engaged in research work into malnutrition among refugee children at the Augusta Victoria Hospital in Jerusalem. Writing only two weeks after the end of the war, Mrs Nancy Nolan Abu Haydar is disturbed already by many of the circumstances to which reference has been made in this book: by the looting, the oppression, the demolitions which swiftly followed the Israeli occupation of Jerusalem; the desecration of Christian shrines and churches; the attacks on ambulances and hospitals, including the Augusta Victoria; but most of all by the fact that so little of all this was reported in the Western press because of "the reluctance of vested interests to publish or broadcast the complete and unbiased story of Jerusalem." Mrs Abu Haydar gave it as her "firm conviction" that the measures taken by the Israelis in those first days after the war combined to produce a situation "deliberately contrived as a means of forcing these people (the Arabs of Jerusalem) to leave, thereby enabling the Israeli authorities to destroy or confiscate more and more property until the demographic structure of the Old City has been completely remodelled to suit the long-term objectives of the Israeli government." She urged Christians everywhere to use their best endeavours at every level to intervene on behalf of the victims of this process and to demonstrate to them that they had not been forgotten and forsaken by the West.

Within these churches there were, of course, those who showed concern over the plight of the Palestinians and over the slow process of dispossession by which, in the course of a generation, they had been elbowed out of the land of their fathers. In August 1967 a meeting of the Central Committee of the World Council of Churches at Heraklion in Crete recorded its belief "that in supporting the establishment of the State of Israel without protecting the rights of the Palestinians, injustice has been done to Palestinian Arabs by the great powers, which should be redressed." No action followed, nor did the Central Committee's statement of a set of principles on the Middle East receive any publicity. Two years were to pass before the Central Committee returned to the subject, two years in which some hundreds of thousands of Palestinians had been added to the refugee population and in which the Israelis had embarked on their politically-motivated building programme in Jerusalem. Meeting this time in Canterbury in July 1969, the Committee restated the principles set out in its earlier statement and recommended "that the subject of biblical interpretation be studied in order to avoid the misuse of the Bible in support of partisan political views."

This was the Committee's answer to the fundamentalists. They went on to convene in the same autumn a "consultation" on the Palestine refugee problem at which to consider what measures, in addition to straightforward relief work, could be undertaken on behalf of the refugees.

The delegates to this consultative meeting, held in Cyprus in October 1969, after reiterating once again their belief that a just solution must involve "the recognition of the rights of the Palestinians, from which alone a lasting peace could come to the Middle East," took another step which showed that at least they had come to understand the nature of the problem confronting them, even if they were unable to persuade the churches they represented to do anything substantial about it. They recommended that the Churches' Commission on International Affairs should engage in further consultations about the Palestine problem, with Palestinians participating, and should "intensify regular discussions with . . . all governments concerned with influencing a political solution." And they added the significant suggestion that "the exchanges which take place should not always remain unpublished."

These last few words mask a point of the greatest importance in the context of the Palestine problem. To a remarkable extent, as we saw in considering the role of the press in the Middle East, the difficulty of resolving this problem has always stemmed from the fact that so much of the information necessary to its proper understanding has been difficult to obtain. Too often those who were in possession of the facts have withheld them, or have not been allowed to publish them, while others with a narrowly partisan viewpoint to express have enjoyed something like a monopoly of the information media. It was in order to correct this situation and, to put it more bluntly than they did, to break the stranglehold of Zionist propagandists, that the delegates to this meeting organised by the World Council of Churches adopted an important recommendation. Acknowledging the obligation on all Christian communities to disclose the facts about "the grave injustices done to the Palestinian people," the delegates sounded the following clarion call to their fellow-Christians everywhere:

> "We call upon the churches of the world, at all levels from local congregations to national and regional councils, to promote an informed Christian discussion of the Palestine question. There must be deep understanding of the inalienable nature of the fundamental rights of the Palestinian people. Our concern for justice must go forward concurrently with renewed humanitarian efforts."

But by now the myths about Palestine, so sedulously propagated in the West, were taking root. After their heady victory in 1967, a long succession of sympathetic interviews in the press and especially on television had established for the Israeli leaders an extraordinary ascendancy over Western public opinion. The first American Phantom fighter-bombers had been delivered to Israel in September 1969, and the ambitions and the presumptions of the Israeli Government were growing apace, without encountering noticeable opposition or even criticism. Indeed, the Israeli prime minister herself, in a formal interview with the *Sunday Times*, asserted that there had never been such a thing as a Palestinian people and that, *ergo*, it could not be said that the Israelis had infringed the rights of the Palestinians since "they did not exist."[88] The remark was to rebound against Mrs Meir in the end, but what was remarkable about it was, first, the degree of insensitivity and overconfidence which it revealed and, second, the fact that at the time it went virtually unchallenged. Certainly there was no audible reply from the churches in defence of those "fundamental rights of the Palestinian people," whose "inalienable nature" had been so firmly asserted in that appeal to the member-congregations of the World Council of Churches.

It is sad to record that the churches to which that appeal had been addressed—and this seems to be especially true of the Church of England —had quietly decided to ignore it and to avoid involvement in the Palestine question. Here was a situation, they must have reasoned, where all the arguments pointed to the wisdom of passing by on the other side. Pragmatism might not be the most heroic course for the churches, but there were precedents for it and any other course threatened disaster. The 'disaster' would in fact have amounted to no more than the loss of some properties in Jerusalem and perhaps some thinning-out of the clerical ranks if the Israeli authorities chose to join battle with the Christian establishment.

At all events, where the churches were concerned, the victory had evidently gone to those who counselled prudence, whatever the consequences might be for the Palestinians, both Muslim and Christian.

Those consequences were becoming steadily clearer and more intolerable, as the Israelis grew more confident of their position. In the autumn of 1969 General Dayan, who as Minister of Defence held overall responsibility for Israel's occupied territories, proclaimed the policy of "neighbourhood punishment" as Israel's chosen means of controlling the Palestinian population under its rule. Retaliation against those who resisted the occupation would not henceforth be directed only against those who bore arms or planned actions against the occupying forces; it would embrace their families, their neighbours, and if necessary the whole Palestinian community which they represented and which would have to choose, said Dayan, "between terrorism and normality"— "normality" meaning, in this context, submission to Israeli military rule in the Palestinians' own homeland.

One day towards the end of October 1969 the meaning of "neighbourhood punishment" was made plain to the Palestinians of the West Bank and, inadvertently, to the world. Inadvertently, because it was only by chance that there happened to be a visiting correspondent of *The Times* in Jerusalem on the day when Israeli forces moved into the nearby village of Halhul and destroyed the homes of some seventy Palestinian families. At this distance of time, the details of the incident need not concern us. What is of interest now is that, because *The Times* correspondent, Patrick Brogan, was not Jewish and was only visiting the area, he found himself subject to none of the restraints which inhibited the resident "foreign" correspondents in Israel.[89] He reported what he saw without hesitation and with a good deal of feeling. His report, published in *The Times* on 26 October 1969, prompted one more appeal on behalf of the Palestinians, this time to the Archbishop of Canterbury.

As Director of Information of the Council for the Advancement of Arab-British Understanding, I at once wrote a letter to the Archbishop, drawing his attention to the eye-witness account in *The Times* and telling him that it confirmed reports which we in the Council had been receiving for some time of the various oppressive measures to which the Palestinians in the occupied territories were being subjected, in contravention of the Fourth Geneva Convention and of the Universal Declaration of Human Rights. The letter referred briefly to some of the measures which the Israelis were taking against the Palestinians, without any pretence of legal justification, and reminded His Grace that collective punishments of any kind were specifically banned by the Geneva Convention. It told him that many of the unfortunate inhabitants of the occupied territories were asking

The Failure of the Churches

why the church did not speak out in their defence against the brutality of the Israeli army of occupation and urged him to try to use his influence to stop it.[90]

I wish I could say that the response had been swift and sympathetic. Unhappily, and despite the fact that our letter and the cutting from *The Times* must have reached the Archbishop's desk within a day or two of the appeal I described earlier from the meeting in Cyprus of the World Council of Churches—of which at the time we knew nothing—there was no response at all, beyond a polite acknowledgement from the Archbishop's chaplain. And with the honourable exception of the Quakers, who by this time were already preparing their own exhaustive and scrupulously fair report and recommendations on the Middle East,[91] the studied inactivity of the Church of England appeared to be characteristic of the reaction of all the Western churches towards the worsening situation in Palestine. Again there were individual churchmen here and there, though very seldom in positions of authority, who voiced their concern both at the injustice suffered by the Palestinians and at the churches' unwillingness to become involved in the Middle East. Because such dissidents were isolated, they were the more easily attacked and discredited, and it took rare courage for one of them to stand his ground against the Zionists and their fellow-travellers in such organisations as the Council for Christians and Jews. Nor was the situation any better in other western countries; the damaging accusation of anti-Semitism was held like a sword over the head of anyone rash enough to criticise Israel, from a moral or a spiritual standpoint, as from a political one. The experience of an exceptional Canadian journalist, Al Forrest, editor of the *United Church Observer* in Toronto, recorded in a book which the attacks on it turned into a best seller,[92] provides for anyone who still needs it a startling insight into the techniques which the Zionists will use to destroy anyone whom they regard as an enemy.

What made the silence of the churches the more remarkable was the fact that, in one context where the various Christian communions had always declared an interest, even to the point of fighting each other to assert their primacy, they now had nothing to say, even though various secular authorities had given the lead which one might have looked for from the churches. This was over the question of Jerusalem, which the Israelis had tried to resolve by swift unilateral action immediately after the June War of 1967, but around which a sharp controversy had subsequently developed at the United Nations. Eventually, and after infinite soul-searching, the churches were to find it impossible to avoid involvement too; but it was not until 1971 that the Catholics, and not for another year after that that the Protestants, came cautiously out into the open to challenge the Israelis' stand. By that time the unblushing policy of the *fait accompli* had brought the Israelis so close to total victory over Jerusalem that they treated the tentative interventions of the Christian churches with almost as much contempt as they had shown for those of the politicians at the United Nations. For a time it looked as though they had nothing to fear; and in the end it was not the churches, or the governments of the United Nations either, which reopened the question of the future of Jerusalem. It was the Arabs themselves who made the restoration of Arab Jerusalem one of their conditions for a peaceful settlement after the October War in 1973.

At the time of writing, the future of Jerusalem remains uncertain; despite the Arabs' insistence on their withdrawal, the Israelis, who occupied the Arab sector of the city in June 1967 and annexed it to the State of Israel three weeks later, remain in occupation. They find themselves, over this one central point of conflict, in confrontation not with the Arabs alone, but with the whole of the international community. By a series of resolutions adopted in the Security Council, as well as in the General Assembly, of the United Nations, the first of them within a week of the Israeli annexation, the nations of the world have, with rare unanimity, condemned the annexation and the measures which the Israelis have taken to change the face and the demographic structure of the Holy City. By a unanimous vote, the Security Council has ruled that such measures are invalid: and the Council's resolution explicitly applied this term to the expropriations carried out by the Israeli authorities of Arab lands and of the Arab

The Failure of the Churches

properties situated on them. In short, the Israeli Government's position where the Arab sector of Jerusalem is concerned is without any legal justification whatever; lacking obviously the consent of the population, it is opposed also, and in the most categorical terms, by the highest international authority; not even the government of the United States, Israel's constant protector, has cared to go on record against such an overwhelming weight of international opinion.

All this was true by 1970, when the determination of the Israelis to defy the world over Jerusalem was already plain, as well as the damage that they were likely to do in the process to the physical aspect of the city. On land which they had expropriated from its Arab owners, the Israelis had embarked on an enormous building programme which was eventually to encircle the Arab part of the city with housing blocks filled with Jewish immigrants. The aim of this programme was self-evident, nor did the Israelis attempt to disguise it: it was to clamp on the city a Jewish character which its authors hoped would be irreversible. And as the new apartment buildings rose on the city's northern skyline, something else became apparent: that no aesthetic considerations were to be allowed to stand in the way of this political objective. Throughout 1968 and 1969 the building programme went ahead at breakneck speed, and by the end of 1970 the desecration of Jerusalem was far advanced. During all this time, it is depressing to record, there was no public word of criticism from the Christian churches of a programme of action so devastating in its physical consequences and so dangerous in its implications for the future peace of the area.

The point was noted in a striking letter from Professor Arnold Toynbee and Sir Geoffrey Furlonge which was published in *The Times* on 15 March 1971. Expressing the view that "the present policies of the Israeli Government not only threaten the beauty and the character of Jerusalem, but must seriously jeopardise the chances of achieving a lasting peace in the Middle East," the writers pointed out that Israel's expropriation of Arab land in the city was a defiance of a unanimous Security Council resolution. They quoted the warning of an Israeli leader-writer, that in its haste to stake a Jewish claim to Arab Jerusalem

133

the Israeli Government might well turn Jerusalem into "a kind of Los Angeles," and remarked that they found it hard to conceive of such vandalism in the context of the Holy City. Finally they expressed their astonishment that, where the Israelis had put themselves so clearly in the wrong on political, humanitarian and aesthetic grounds alike, "there should be so little protest in the Christian world at a policy of desecration so deliberately undertaken and on such a scale."

It is arguable that it was their behaviour over Jerusalem which, more than any other aspect of their post-1967 policies, was in the end to undo the Israelis. Their massive building programme, which disfigured the skyline of Jerusalem and destroyed the city's proportions, antagonised even the most well-disposed among a group of international architects and town planners whom the Israelis made the mistake of inviting, at the end of 1970, to observe and pronounce upon their plans. The experts' criticisms, brutal in their frankness, startled the Israelis and focused attention on the havoc which their own government was creating in the Holy City; the ensuing uproar encouraged outsiders to voice the objections which they had long felt, but had been keeping to themselves out of an exaggerated regard for the feelings of Jewish supporters of Israel throughout the world. In the spring of 1971 a movement of reaction began to appear against the mood of tolerance for whatever action the Israeli government chose to take, at the expense of others, in pursuit of their own "security". The Israeli authorities now found that, by showing such an open disregard for international opinion where Jerusalem was concerned, they had expended a great deal of the capital of sympathy which they had formerly accumulated in the West.

A relatively minor incident was to provide the turning point. In April 1971, shortly after that convention of town planners in Jerusalem had condemned what the Israeli planners had already done in the city, Israeli troops set up a roadblock one night between Jerusalem and the nearby Arab village of Nebi Samwil. This village, many of whose inhabitants had fled during the fighting in 1967, occupied a hill with a splendid view of the city—tradition said that it was from Nebi Samwil that the crusaders had first set eyes on

The Failure of the Churches

Jerusalem—and for this reason the property developers of modern Israel had their eye on it. A few hours after the troops had cordoned it off, demolition squads moved in, ejected most of the remaining Arab inhabitants and demolished the whole of the upper part of the village, including the cemetery, leaving only the mosque, which had once been a crusader church, and a small group of houses lower down the hillside. It was an action in the classic Israeli tradition of "creating facts", and the excuses later offered by the Israeli authorities that some of the houses were already empty and in bad repair and constituted "a danger to tourists", deceived no one, particularly after the announcement that Nebi Samwil was to be "developed" to provide housing for more Jewish settlers—but not, of course, for the Palestinians who had been displaced.

Hardly a word of the affair found its way into the Western press, but it was reported through diplomatic channels (by chance the British Consul-General in Jerusalem had been one of the first to be turned back at the roadblock, and it is greatly to his credit that he at once took pains to establish the full facts and make them known to his government) and within a few days the destruction of Nebi Samwil was common knowledge in Jerusalem. The incident provoked no public reaction from the Anglican Archbishopric, which must have received the knowledge as soon as anyone in Jerusalem, but for the Catholics it proved the last straw. From that moment on the Vatican used the powerful publicity instruments at its disposal to voice more and more openly its concern at the course of events in occupied Jerusalem.

In June, for instance, a detailed and strongly worded article in the authoritative review *La Civiltà Cattolica*, published in Rome, reviewed the whole history of the Israeli occupation in Jerusalem and in particular the pattern of Israeli housing developments on expropriated Arab land. Noting the actions of the Israeli authorities and especially the public declarations of members of the Israeli government who sought to justify them, the writer said that "the Israeli Government's decision to press on hurriedly with its building programme in the Arab sector of Jerusalem, without thought for the injury this programme is doing to the rights of minorities, appears to have one indisputable motivation: the Judaisation of the Holy City." He took note also of "a growing movement of opinion in Israel, especially among the young," in favour of recognising the rights of the Palestinians and against the policy of creating facts by planting Jewish colonies all over the occupied territories; but suggested that it was precisely in order to forestall this humane tendency within Israeli society that the government was in such a hurry to impose its will, and its building programme, on land belonging to the Palestinian Arabs. What the consequences of all this would be, the writer indicated in a sombre concluding paragraph:

> "The expropriation of land and the destruction of houses represent the initial acts of oppression by the occupying power. Once the building programme is complete—and there is nothing to delay it, since it is given absolute priority and an appeal has been launched for help from the great Jewish industries in America—Jerusalem will be surrounded by a new wall, a wall this time composed of Jewish inhabitants; while the cause of peace will have taken one more step backwards, if indeed it has not disappeared altogether from the horizon of Jerusalem, which for centuries and in the visions of its pilgrims has been regarded as the 'city of peace'."[93]

From then on, the pace of protest quickened. On 14 July 1971 *The Times* published an editorial challenging "the Israeli assumption that Jerusalem is essentially and for ever the capital city of the state—the symbol of Zionist achievement as well as the focus of the Jewish religion." The rest of the world, said *The Times*, "believes that the city should not be the exclusive property of one state, seeing it rather as a shrine which is part of all mankind's inheritance." And a letter signed by all the Arab ambassadors in London took up this last phrase to urge that "if these words have any meaning for your readers, we hope and pray—and dare we say, trust—that they will do everything in their power to ensure that Britain, which is not without responsibility in this matter, insists on effective action to end the desecration of Jerusalem."

Still there had been no open expression of Anglican misgivings over the fate of Jerusalem, no intercession on behalf of those Christian Arabs whose rights as well as their property were threatened, along with those of their Muslim compatriots, by what that Catholic writer in *La Civiltà Cattolica* had had no hesitation in describing as the "Judaisation" of Jerusalem. Both Catholics and Protestants in Jerusalem itself, as I found when I visited the city in June 1971, were by now sadly and openly conscious of the failure of the Christian world to do anything to demonstrate its concern for Jerusalem and for the welfare of its community. And the members of that community, the Arabs of Jerusalem, who saw only that the Western Christians apparently accepted the Israelis as the *de facto* if not the legal rulers of the city—how could one be surprised to learn that they had lost all respect for churchmen who found it so hard to stand up for what they knew to be right? I remember a sobering letter I received at this time from a young Christian Arab who had been born in Jerusalem and whose home the Israelis had seized in 1948. Before the war of 1967, in which the Israelis occupied the rest of the city, this Arab boy used to go every year, he told me, from the refugee camp in the Lebanon where his family had found themselves, to visit relations in Jerusalem:

> ". . . and from the humped roofs of the Old City I used to look to where I was born, feeling sad but with no emotion, perhaps because I was brought up to accept the idea that beyond the walls was a prohibited area. Now the Old City is gone, and in a way I'm glad it did, at least for a short while, because it has awakened and aroused our people and made us realise that Israel is a military camp, heavily armed by the Christian world. I feel that I am drifting away from Christianity towards Communism, due to the completely one-sided attitude of the Christian world, who supported them, regardless of the suffering that we Arabs are feeling."

Convinced by this and other personal contacts of the crucial importance of Jerusalem for any durable peace settlement in the Middle East, the Council for the Advancement of Arab-British

Understanding pursued throughout 1971 an energetic campaign to jolt the West out of its passive acceptance of the Israeli *fait accompli*. In January we wrote once more to the Archbishop of Canterbury, reminding him of the juridical position in terms of international law and urging that, "where the law seems powerless to help them, the Church has the right—and surely the obligation—to come to the defence of the inhabitants of the Holy City of Jerusalem." We lobbied the government, members of parliament and the Foreign Office. We saw to it that the newspapers were at least in possession of the facts about Jerusalem (since these were only very sparingly reported by the correspondents on the spot), even if they remained very reluctant, with the honourable exception of *The Times*, to adopt a firm position in the matter. We made a film which was widely shown to audiences in Britain and the United States including those who attended a crowded meeting at the House of Commons in July 1971. With a slowness which contrasted sadly with the urgent haste of the Israelis in pressing ahead with their controversial building programme in Jerusalem, opinion in the Christian world began to move.

In August 1971 the long silence of the Church of England was broken when Canon Herbert Waddams preached in Canterbury Cathedral a long overdue sermon on the text: "O pray for the peace of Jerusalem: may they prosper that love thee." Christians, he said, did not have the answer to the Middle East problem; but they did have the obligation to think hard about a problem for whose creation they must share the responsibility. Now that the situation had become so highly charged, it was no good for Christians to imitate Pontius Pilate and "try to wash their hands of the whole affair." The United Nations had ruled without opposition that the annexation of Jerusalem was invalid and the Israeli building programme had been "universally condemned by international authority." It was up to Christians, acting as Christians, said Canon Waddams, "to support the only international authority which can maintain peace, and therefore they must press for the United Nations resolution to be upheld."

For another four months Canon Waddams' voice remained an isolated one in the Church of England; and when at last the

The Failure of the Churches

Archbishop of Canterbury himself took a public initiative over the Jerusalem question, his intervention came too late for it to have any practical effect either in preventing the desecration of Jerusalem or in persuading the Israelis that by holding onto the city they were lessening the chances of peace in the Middle East. The years of acquiescence in the Israeli *fait accompli* had cost the church any moral standing it might have had in the matter; what it now chose to say or not to say was of academic interest, and the countdown to the war that eventually broke out in October 1973 had already begun. The objectives of the governments which launched that war were the recovery of the Arab territories occupied since 1967 and the implementation of the Security Council's resolutions concerning the Middle East in general and Jerusalem in particular. Both could have been achieved without war; but only if the international community, including the churches, had been prepared to take a clear stand on issues of principle, even where these could be expected to be unpopular with the powerful Jewish communities in the Western world. More than any other single factor, it was the general unwillingness to face this unpopularity that rendered the Western world impotent to prevent the drift to war in the Middle East. The churches alone could not have altered this picture; but they could have provided an example of moral courage for others to follow. Because they conspicuously failed to do so, they share the responsibility for the fate of Jerusalem and for the October War.

PART TWO

CHAPTER SEVEN

The October War and its Consequences

Michael Adams

The news that broke soon after two o'clock on that afternoon of 6 October 1973 was greeted everywhere with incredulity. Egyptian troops crossing the Suez Canal and storming through the defences of the Bar-Lev line; Egyptian engineers methodically laying pontoon bridges under surprisingly ineffective Israeli fire; Syrian tanks in their hundreds driving across the Golan plateau and overrunning the settlements established there since 1967—these were not the familiar stereotypes of war in the Middle East. It would need some time before a sceptical world came to accept at anything like face value communiqués coming out of Cairo or Damascus which reported such improbable goings on.

The British press found it hard to adjust itself to the novel situation. Next morning the *Sunday Times* carried on its front page a picture of smiling Israeli troops making the victory sign as they rode towards the Syrian front; alongside was the headline: "Egypt across Canal but Dayan says not for long." On Monday both *The Times* and *The Guardian* led with the news that the Israelis claimed to have destroyed the Egyptian pontoon bridges, trapping four hundred Egyptian tanks east of the Canal. During the succeeding days all the newspapers continued to report prominently the claims of General Dayan and the Israeli Chief of Staff, General Elazar, that it was all over bar the shouting and that "we shall break their bones"; but gradually, as the number of Egyptian tanks east of the Canal grew to five hundred and then to a thousand and it became apparent that, whatever General Dayan might be saying, the bridges were intact, the conviction grew that not only had the Arab armies gained an important initial advantage but their accounts of the progress of the fighting were substantially more accurate than those of the Israelis.[94] This last discovery did as much as anything to persuade the outside world that something really new was happening in the Middle East.

It was not surprising that both press and public should have found the readjustment difficult. The impression created by Israel's blitzkrieg victory in 1967 had been reinforced in the years that followed by the ruthless efficiency with which the Israelis had maintained their occupation of territories three times as large as Israel itself. Even the ruthlessness, though it horrified those, including a few thoughtful Israelis, who had any close knowledge of what was going on, was played down by the Western press, from whom the public in Europe and the United States received the impression that the Israelis were a peace-loving nation who happened also to be the world's best fighters, but who really wanted nothing better than to be left in peace to cultivate their own (or somebody else's) garden. The Arabs, by contrast, had been presented to the same public as a mixture of clowns and villains, at once vicious, because they would go on trying to get back the lands of which Israel had robbed them, and incompetent, because they always failed to do so. In many ways the Arabs had contributed to their own poor image in the world; but making every allowance for the effect of their own mistakes, it is difficult not to feel critical of the way in which, between 1967 and 1971, the bulk of the press, including radio and television services, in Britain and in other countries, abandoned their normal standards of objectivity when they came to discuss the questions at issue between Arabs and Israelis.

The role of the press has been discussed in earlier chapters. Here what concerns us is the fact that the initial successes achieved by the Egyptians and Syrians in October 1973 had a disproportionate effect because the Western public had been so conditioned to expect only the worst from the Arabs and to look on the Israelis as almost superhuman. It is ironical that the friends of Israel, who had devoted much effort to cultivating this distortion of the truth, should thereby have done Israel a substantial disservice. For the truth, when it revealed itself in October, came as a devastating shock. Quite apart from the improved image of the Arabs which emerged from the events in Sinai and on the plateau beyond the Golan Heights, the image of Israel underwent a drastic reappraisal, whose effects were felt not least inside Israel itself and were to lead in the end to the fall of Mrs Meir and General Dayan and so to the end of a whole era in which Israeli political life had been dominated by the rigid concepts of primitive Zionism.

But this is to anticipate. All that was immediately apparent by the end of that Saturday in October was that the Egyptians, with well coordinated Syrian support, had achieved an unexpected success in crossing the Suez Canal and breaching the elaborate defences of the Bar-Lev line. It was a remarkable achievement by any standard to put a mechanised army across a water barrier like the Canal, a hundred yards wide and protected by a rampart of sand thirty to fifty feet in height, to say nothing of the complex of fortifications beyond, on whose construction the Israelis had expended some £40 million. For any army, to have accomplished this within the space of a few hours and in broad daylight would have represented a major success. For the Egyptians, dogged by the disastrous memories of 1956 and 1967, it was more than a success; it was a turning-point.

This was no less true, in an inverse sense, for the Israelis. Their past record of unbroken successes over the Arabs in general and the Egyptians in particular, which a sympathetic Western press had enshrined as a legend, now exaggerated the effect of the losses they suffered. Every position overrun, every Phantom shot down, counted for double in the eyes of a world that had never before seen the Israelis caught at a disadvantage. The process had begun whereby a whole complex of assumptions had started to shiver and break up under the impact of unforeseen realities.

It was this psychological imbalance which lent to the campaign its real significance. Had the two sides started the war as equals in the sight of the world, and in each other's estimation, then a fortnight's inconclusive fighting in Sinai and on the Golan Heights would have had little influence on the course of the political struggle between Israel and its neighbours. As it was, a campaign which, in a purely military sense, each could claim as a partial victory left the Arabs with an enormous political advantage; or, to be more accurate, it enormously reduced the political disadvantage under which they had been labouring before 6 October 1973.

The political implications of the Arab success will be discussed presently. But the war marked also a significant alteration in the military balance of power, one which invalidated much of the strategic thinking on which successive Israeli governments had based their stand towards the Arabs. Fundamental to this thinking was the concept that Israel enjoyed a military superiority vis-à-vis the Arabs which would not be altered or reduced for at least a generation. It was argued that the Six Day War in 1967 had shown that superiority to be absolute; this in itself was open to dispute, since the victory in 1967 had been effectively won by a devastating pre-emptive air attack, after which the Arab ground forces had had no chance. But it was further argued that after 1967 the technological gap between the two sides had actually widened, and that this was a natural reflection of the differences between Israeli and Arab societies, the one drawing on a reservoir of technologically advanced manpower while the other was handicapped by the social and economic shortcomings characteristic of an under-developed community. Despite their essentially racialist character, these arguments had not been seriously questioned, and their acceptance was encouraged by the preference shown throughout Western society, and especially in the information media, for whatever favoured the interests (as they were perceived) of Israel, and by the corresponding disregard, amounting often to open contempt, for the interests, and even the values, of Arab society. Once again the sense of shock with which the reports of Arab successes were received was heightened by the distorted view of the Middle East which had been propagated by years of one-sided reporting in the press, on radio and on television.

Now that the picture has had to be so drastically revised, it is easy to forget the unanimity with which the experts agreed, before

October 1973, that if there were to be a further outbreak of fighting between Israel and the Arabs, Israel would inevitably win. Such a conviction seemed to be soundly based, and it was certainly shared by the Israelis, whose confidence in their own ability to control their neighbours formed the basis of their policy of settlement and consolidation in the territories they had occupied in 1967. As an example of the kind of thing that prominent Israelis were saying in the months leading up to the October War, it is interesting to recall a statement by General Ariel Sharon, who was shortly to emerge as the controversial "hero" of the war, to an Israeli newspaper a few weeks before the war began. "Israel is now a military superpower," said this soldier turned politician. "All the forces of European countries are weaker than we are. We can conquer in one week the area from Khartoum to Baghdad and Algeria."[95] Such a pronouncement might be dismissed as a piece of unrepresentative braggadocio, but for the fact that the man who made it was at the time in transition between one of the senior commands in the Israeli army and an equally high position in the leadership of the principal opposition party in the Knesset. Moreover, offensive as they might have found General Sharon's mode of expression, not all of the foreign military experts, perhaps not even most of them, would have disagreed with his opinion. So commanding was the advantage of the Israelis thought to be in leadership, morale and weaponry that an Arab attack was considered to be out of the question because of the retribution it would bring. Israel's superiority in the air, in particular, was known to be as clear-cut as in 1967, when it had settled the issue of the Six Day War within a matter of hours, and this alone was thought to be a sufficient deterrent.

In these circumstances, the fact that the Egyptians and the Syrians were able to launch an attack at all constituted at once a victory of sorts. The demonstration that the Israeli position was not impregnable, either in military or in political terms, had highly important implications; it radically altered the data on the basis of which both sides, and their respective backers, had worked out their strategy for the continuing confrontation. But of course the effect of the attack

The October War and its Consequences

would be negated, and the previous positions and conceptions of all the parties confirmed and reinforced, if the attack were to be swiftly repulsed. If the Arabs were now unable to stand their ground, they would not merely have failed to break the chains with which the Israelis had held them prisoner since 1967; they would have persuaded everyone, above all themselves, that not only victory but even escape was beyond them. They would have lost hope in themselves and credibility in the eyes of others. They would in fact have tightened those chains about them for years, perhaps for generations to come.

For both sides, therefore, the immediate outcome was crucial; and for the first time in a conflict which had continued intermittently for more than a quarter of a century the Arabs, having seized the initiative, were able to retain it for long enough to derive from it a substantial advantage. In strictly military terms, it could not be called a victory, since the Israelis, after absorbing the force of the Arab attack, gradually turned the tide of the battle on both fronts in their own favour. But before that happened, the October War and the Arabs' showing in it had brought about a change in the political and psychological balance of power in the Middle East which would not easily be reversed.

In military terms, three factors contributed to the undoubted success of the Arabs in forcing the world, including, especially, the Israelis, to revise its estimate of the power-relationship between Israel and its Arab neighbours. First, it became apparent that there was little difference, if any, between the soldiers of the two sides when it came to considerations of morale and motivation. Second, the Arabs showed that, far from allowing the technological gap between themselves and the Israelis to widen, they had made significant advances in the expert use of sophisticated weapons. Third, the quality of Arab leadership at all levels was shown to be very much higher than anyone, including the public in all parts of the Arab World, had expected it to be. In addition, the fact that the Israelis allowed themselves to be taken by surprise, just as they had taken the Arabs by surprise in 1967, drew critical attention to their failure in intelligence evaluation and presently to weaknesses in their much-vaunted mobilisation system.

These failures were to prove extremely costly, and they threw into still sharper relief the central element in the Arabs' achievement: their success in maintaining complete secrecy about their intentions until the very last moment.

To this day there is a good deal of mystery about this opening phase of the war and the extent to which the Israelis were caught napping. The official commission of enquiry which later investigated the question of responsibility for Israel's unpreparedness put the blame on the Chief of Staff, General David Elazar. In submitting his immediate resignation, General Elazar angrily protested that the responsibility was as much that of his political superiors, among whom the Minister of Defence, General Moshe Dayan, was already the target for angry recriminations from the Israeli public and, in particular, from the soldiers who had had to bear the brunt of the unexpected attack. It was the publication of the commission of enquiry's preliminary report early in April 1974 that focused criticism on General Dayan and, when he refused to resign, provoked the resignation of Mrs Meir as prime minister.

Before the report was published, it was clearly established that on the eve of the war the Israeli intelligence service, in close co-operation with the American CIA and the Defense Intelligence Agency of the Pentagon, was in possession of a mass of information indicating that an Egyptian attack was imminent on the Canal front. Ten days before the attack came, after a tour of inspection on the Syrian front, General Dayan had noted the preparations on that front as well and had then placed the Israeli army on alert on both fronts. On Friday 5 October, when Soviet advisers in Cairo and Damascus had begun to leave in what seemed to be a hastily improvised airlift and when hundreds of Syrian tanks were being re-deployed into offensive formations behind the Golan Heights, where their every movement was open to inspection by Israeli units on Mount Hermon, General Elazar stepped up the alert to one indicating a state of emergency, and a number of reservists were called up in Israel. Yet, when the attack was launched more than twenty-four hours later, Israeli troops in forward positions on both fronts were caught entirely unprepared. Whoever else was by then expecting an attack had not thought to warn the men in the fortifications of the Bar-Lev line or in the paramilitary settlements which the Israelis had established beyond the Golan Heights since 1967.

It is interesting to speculate on the possible outcome if the Israelis had acted on the evidence they had of an impending Arab attack. Given the overall superiority which, by common consent, the Israelis enjoyed over their opponents, it would have seemed foolhardy for the Egyptians, even with a second front planned by the Syrians, to have undertaken so hazardous an operation as the crossing of the Suez Canal against an enemy fully prepared and forewarned. Yet how could the Egyptians feel confident that they would be able to maintain the element of surprise? And if they did not feel confident of doing so, would they still have pressed on with their attack, presumably in the conviction that they had a reasonable chance of success?

Shortly after the war, I had the opportunity in Cairo of meeting General Abdel-Ghani el-Gamasi, who had by then been appointed Chief of Staff of the Egyptian Army, but who, during the critical period leading up to the October War, was Director of Operations and so principally responsible for the planning of the campaign. I asked him whether he and his colleagues had expected to keep the attack a secret. Of course they couldn't be sure, he replied, and he personally had given them a fifty-fifty chance of taking the enemy by surprise. But he said categorically that the Egyptians had worked out a series of contingency plans to allow for every imaginable set of circumstances, including a pre-emptive strike by the Israelis, like the one in 1967, and that they had no intention of backing down, whatever happened. When one remembers that the Egyptians were having to take these decisions before the successes of the October War and against the background of their previous defeats at the hands of the Israelis in 1967 and 1956, one gets a vivid idea of the way in which morale had been restored in the new model Egyptian Army of 1973.

For that achievement, as for much else, a good deal of the credit must go to General Gamasi, who would himself make an apt symbol for the new Egypt that emerged from the October War. During the subsequent negotiations for a disengagement agreement in which he acted as the Egyptian representative, General Gamasi appeared on the world's television screens as a man of dignity and a somewhat aloof distinction. Meeting him, I was unprepared for the immediate impression of warmth and humour which his personality conveys. Tall for an Egyptian and slender, with an evident distaste for personal publicity and a suggestion about him of austerity until a ready smile lights up his face, he radiates energy and confidence: just the man, in fact, for whom subordinates would make efforts to which another commander might have urged them in vain. If many of us had wondered how it had been possible to inspire Egyptian soldiers, demoralised by the defeat in 1967 and by the next five years of apparently hopeless inactivity, to embark on the storming of the Bar-Lev line, the conundrum seemed less difficult to resolve after talking to the new Chief of Staff.

With the soldiers themselves, the only way to restore morale was to provide them with the best available arms and to train them in their use to the point where they had complete confidence both in the weapons and in their capacity to use them. But beyond this it was essential, especially at the higher levels of command, to destroy the legend that the Israelis were invincible and to search out the chinks in their admittedly formidable armour.

With this in mind, General Gamasi told me, the Egyptians drew up a list of the strengths and the weaknesses of their opponents. The strengths were well known: an immensely powerful air force, equipped with the latest American aircraft and possessing a devastating strike capacity; a highly mobile mechanised army, well led and with a high morale boosted by previous successes; an up-to-date armoury of American weapons and electronic equipment; elaborately prepared positions behind the daunting obstacle of the Suez Canal. Less obvious at first sight were the potential weaknesses on which the Egyptians concentrated and which they were to exploit with such striking and unexpected success. Israeli strategy was based on seizing and holding the initiative; on fighting on one front at a time, with the maximum concentration of forces; on fighting a short war, to avoid the prolonged mobilisation of Israel's "citizen army"; on minimising the number of casualties. In all these respects, the Egyptians determined that the war should be fought on their own terms, the terms least acceptable to their opponents. And there was one further weakness which the Egyptians identified and from which they were able to derive what was possibly their principal advantage: the over-confidence of the Israelis, rooted in their conviction of racial superiority, which led them to underestimate the capacity of the Egyptians and their Syrian allies to launch an attack in the first place and so enabled the Arabs to retain the vital element of surprise.

The course of the fighting, once the attack had been launched in the early afternoon of 6 October, has been described in a number of publications.[96] What concerns us here is the extent to which, in purely military terms, it altered the balance of power in the Middle East. This is not easy to determine, since the purely military is not easily distinguished from the political and even the psychological balance; for instance, the ability of either side in the Middle East to renew the contest or to maintain it once it has been renewed is ultimately dependent on the support of outside powers. This was for Israel one of the more disturbing lessons of the October War. But, taking the situation of the contestants as it is and confining ourselves for the moment to the military implications, there are certain respects in which it is clear that the situation today is very different from the situation on 5 October 1973.

It can hardly be disputed, I believe, that this fourth round of the conflict saw the gap between the two sides, the gap in military and technical competence, significantly narrowed. It may well be, and, as I have already suggested, I believe it to be true, that the gap was never as large as was widely supposed, nor as it was represented as being, out of ignorance or malice, by those who had the ear of the world. It was not widely reported at the time that both in 1956 and in 1967 Egyptian units fought well at a number of places in Sinai, despite their total lack of air cover and despite the demoralising effect on each occasion of a surprise attack by a much stronger enemy. It is possible that if the Egyptians rather than the Israelis had seized the initiative in 1967, the outcome of that war might have been very different. We have no way of knowing. But, if we compare the two sides as they stood in the estimation of competent judges on 5 October 1973 and as they stand today, there is no doubt that the odds against the Arabs have been considerably shortened.

It remains true, so far as I am able to judge, that the Israelis still retain in military terms a definite superiority. In the air, above all, but also in tactical skill and the ability to manipulate the complex machinery of modern war, in the power to improvise and to react promptly to the unforeseen, they appear still to hold the advantage. If this is true, it is important; but it is less important, less significant for the future, than the fact that their superiority is more in question than it used to be; less important than the fact that, in several respects, that superiority seems to have been challenged and perhaps overtaken; less important than the fact that, where the Arabs this time did so much better, the Israelis in a number of ways did so much worse.

❖ ❖ ❖

Turning now from the military to the political context, it is clear that few wars have lasted so short a time and produced consequences so weighty and far-reaching. Within the Middle East itself, the October War put into a wholly new perspective the relationship between Israel and its Arab neighbours, provoking inside Israel an angry debate about the country's objectives and eventually putting an end, with the fall of Mrs Meir's government, to a whole era of Israeli political life. In the world at large it set in motion a train of events which disrupted the pattern of international trade and produced a decisive shift in the balance of power between the industrialised and the under-developed worlds.

Ironically, these momentous consequences flowed from a war in which the Arab aims were strictly limited. The Egyptian and the Syrian governments, when they launched their forces against the cease-fire lines on 6 October, had no illusions about their ability to win an outright victory over Israel; they knew, too, as the Israelis knew, that the slightest sign that such a victory might be in the making would produce an American intervention against the Arabs. Their formal war-aim was the liberation of the Egyptian and Syrian territory occupied by the Israelis since 1967 and the restoration of the rights of Palestinians, but they did not overestimate their chances of achieving even these limited objectives. Their underlying and more subtle aim was to force the world, and especially the two superpowers, to take action over a problem which had been left in suspense, to the great disadvantage of the Arabs. To achieve this, the Arabs needed to demonstrate to the world that the stability of the Middle East was to the interest of everyone, and that that stability could not rest indefinitely on the assumption that Israel was too strong for the Arabs to attack her. They needed, in fact, to puncture the illusion of Israel's invincibility and to show that, if Israel was vulnerable, so were those who, to a greater or lesser extent, supported her. A precise statement of these war aims was made to Christopher Mayhew by President Sadat in a conversation in January 1973, during which the President declared that he had decided to make a crossing of the Suez Canal.

It is tragic that the Arabs should have had to go to war to make their point. To informed opinion throughout the Western world, the facts of the Arab-Israeli situation, despite all efforts to disguise them, were well enough known. Since 1967, Israel's military superiority and the backing of the United States had enabled the Israeli government to resist every initiative to achieve a settlement in the Middle East. As early as November 1967, the unanimous resolution of the Security Council (Resolution 242) had drawn the outline for such a settlement, proposing a bargain by which Israel would return the territories occupied in the Six Day War in exchange for recognition by the Arab governments, the bargain to be sealed in a peace treaty whose provisions would be guaranteed by the international community. In 1969 the government of the United States, Israel's principal ally, had put forward a series of proposals, personally sponsored by the then Secretary of State, William Rogers, for the implementation of the resolution. In 1971 Dr Gunnar Jarring, entrusted by the UN General Assembly with the task of bringing the two sides in the Middle East to a settlement, had asked the Egyptians and the Israelis for specific undertakings along the lines proposed by the Security Council and the American Government. At the end of the same year a delegation of African Heads of State undertook a special mission of enquiry and came up with similar recommendations, which they put to the governments of Egypt and Israel. To each of these initiatives, despite fierce opposition within the Arab World, the Egyptians gave a positive response; to each the Israelis turned a deaf ear, continuing meanwhile to defy a lengthening list of United Nations resolutions calling for their withdrawal from the occupied territories in exchange for the benefits of peace and Arab recognition. It was only the consciousness of their own power and of the unwavering support of successive American administrations that encouraged the Israelis to maintain their obstinate refusal.

It is curious, at first sight, that their refusal should have provoked so little criticism in the Western world. Israeli armed forces were in occupation all this time of Arab territories three times as large as Israel itself. Their seizure of Arab Jerusalem had led to the annexation of the city, in explicit defiance of repeated United Nations resolutions. Because of this and because of its refusal to make peace on the basis proposed by the UN, the Israeli government was brought into constant conflict both with the General Assembly and with the Security Council. Israel's rejection of every peace initiative threatened the interests of Western countries by endangering their oil supplies and by perpetuating the closure of the Suez Canal. Its intransigence put at risk the West's relations with the whole of the Arab World, which represented one of the fastest-growing export markets for Western goods. Its insistence on territorial expansion raised the constant spectre of a local war in this vital area, a war which might easily widen into the East-West conflict whose avoidance was the overriding preoccupation of the statesmen of the world. And yet, despite the contempt it showed for international authority, and despite the fact that its action so threatened the interests not only of its neighbours but of the world in general and

The October War and its Consequences

of the West in particular, Israel was treated, during these years between 1967 and 1973, with a wholly exceptional indulgence, to the point where the Israeli government enjoyed in the eyes of large sections of public opinion throughout the West an immunity from criticism not extended to any other government or people anywhere in the world.

The reasons for this immunity and this indulgence have been examined in the first part of this book. What is of interest for the moment is the fact that, as a result of them, a situation which was palpably both unjust and dangerous, but which was to Israel's advantage, was allowed to continue, until the Egyptians and Syrians blew it apart in October 1973. That this should have been permitted to happen was principally the fault of the American government, and to a large extent of the American press, both of which were unduly sensitive to the pressures of the powerful Zionist movement in the United States. Only the American government commanded the power which could have forced Israel, before the October War, to make the concessions which are being wrung from it since. But this cannot excuse the failure of other Western governments, our own included, to dissociate themselves sooner and more clearly from the United States and its policy towards the Middle East; nor can it justify the hesitancy of the press in Britain and elsewhere to criticise Israeli actions and policies which it would have condemned outright in any other country in the world.

Among their other objectives in going to war, the Arabs set themselves to breach this wall of uncritical support for Israel; and here too they had some success. The more blinkered pro-Israelis continued their precarious balancing act between the arguments that, on the one hand, Israel was poor, weak and threatened, while, on the other, it was the strongest and most reliable ally for the West in the Middle East. But to any normally clear-sighted observer it became plain that, if the Israelis continued to refuse any settlement which might conceivably be acceptable to the Arabs, then the Arabs would continue to be hostile to Israel and therefore to any government which supported it. And with the energy crisis suddenly in full swing, it was remarkable how many previously myopic observers suddenly developed a much clearer perception of events in the Middle East.

To people such as the authors of this book, who had long been accustomed to being dismissed as "pro-Arabs", this development brought a certain wry satisfaction. For years we had tried to persuade anyone who would listen to us that the Middle East would be rendered more stable, and Western interests be better served, by the restoration of something like justice in the area. Justice in this context meant some redress for the Palestinians who had been deprived of their homes to make way for a Jewish state; and since this could be achieved only by concessions which the Israelis were not prepared to make, we had urged the need for some sort of coercion to bring the Israelis to a more conciliatory frame of mind. We found that our arguments were often accepted, especially by anyone with first-hand experience of the Middle East, but that when it came to taking action, or even recommending action, along lines that were distasteful to the Israelis and their supporters, at that point anyone in a position that carried some responsibility could find half a dozen sound reasons (sound, that is, in his own eyes) for doing nothing. Only when the October War and its aftermath had opened their eyes to the significant change that was coming over the Middle East, did some of these fence-sitters start to scramble down on our side. They were acceptable as allies; but they would have been more welcome if they could have come to their decision sooner and in response to the rights and wrongs of the case, rather than because of the new power situation in the area.

However, a change of heart like this on the part of a politician here, a newspaper editor there, provided visible evidence of the advantage gained by the Arabs as a result of fighting the October War. A notable example is the "Declaration of the Nine", the statement issued in November 1973, within a week or two of the end of the fighting, by the foreign ministers of the nine Common Market partners in Brussels. The declaration in reality contained nothing sensational; it was a restatement of the principles embodied in the Security Council's Resolution 242 of November 1967. But in putting their names to it at this particular time, the nine foreign ministers indicated, not that they had formed any fresh opinion about the Middle East, but that they no longer felt inhibited from stating the opinion they already held. They were widely accused of having submitted to Arab blackmail; but the truth was that they no longer felt compelled to remain silent out of deference for the Israelis and their sympathisers in Europe.

What the Arabs had achieved, in fact, was to give some reality to the phrase "a balance of power in the Middle East". And this was all to the good. The factor which had handicapped all previous attempts to resolve the Arab-Israeli problem, which was in essence an extension of the Palestine problem initiated by the British Government in 1917, had always been the *imbalance* of power between the Arabs and the Israelis, or, to be more accurate, between the Palestinians and their Arab supporters on the one hand and the Zionists on the other. All through the story of the conflict over Palestine, at every crucial moment, the Zionists had been able to marshal support, in London at first and later in New York and Washington, with which to outgun the Palestinians, in a political even more than in a purely military sense. Lacking the Power to make their case prevail, the Palestinians had had to content themselves with United Nations resolutions to which everyone subscribed but which no one implemented; and because he too lacked effective influence in the world, the same held true for President Nasser when he tried to reverse the injustice in Palestine, and for President Sadat after him—until 1973. Before that, every effort by the Arabs to persuade the world to check the ambitions of the Israelis failed, because the Arabs could not command any reservoir of influence comparable to that of the Zionist backers of Israel.

After the October War, all this was changed. The change was a vital one, and its results began at once to show in the very different reception accorded to Arab representatives, and to the views they expressed, at every kind of international gathering and in the Western press. The change, of course, was not only, or even mainly, due to the improved performance of the Egyptian and Syrian armies. As we have seen, the Israelis had reasserted their military superiority before the end of the October fighting. But while the fighting was still going on, the Arabs had marked up a political advantage to which the Israelis had no answer. They had brought into play a weapon whose potential was incalculable and which no one had thought they knew how to use: the oil weapon.

On Tuesday 9 October, the fourth day of the war, the Kuwait Government had called for an urgent meeting of the Arab oil producers to discuss the ways in which the oil weapon might be brought to bear in the crisis. At the same time it was reported that King Feisal of Saudi Arabia had sent to President Nixon a personal message, presumed to be a warning that exports of Arab oil could not be maintained to countries which supported the Israeli war effort. Expert commentators varied in their opinions, but the consensus seemed to be that, even if they wanted to, the Arab producers would be unable to concert an agreed policy on production and export restrictions. King Feisal, in particular, was thought to be against any sort of embargo, and it was recalled that less than a year earlier the Saudi Arabian government had been considering expanding its oil production from 8 million to 20 million barrels a day, expressly to meet the rising American demand.

Ironically, the first serious interruption to the West's oil supplies came as a result not of Arab but of Israeli action. On that same Tuesday, 9 October, the Israelis had made the first air raids of the war on civilian targets, attacking the Syrian capital, Damascus, and extending the range of their attacks next day to include the oil refinery at Homs and the Mediterranean ports of Latakia and Tartous. On 10 October Israeli naval vessels bombarded the port of Banias, setting fire to oil storage tanks. In addition to the casualties caused and the severe damage to Syria's economic potential, one effect of these attacks was to put a stop to the export of oil through Banias, where Iraqi oil arrives by pipeline for shipment through the Mediterranean to Western Europe.

As the war continued, the united front presented by the Arabs showed no sign of breaking, and the world's apprehension grew about the safety of its oil supplies. One of President Sadat's senior advisers was touring the capitals of the Arab oil-producing states, and word spread that he was discussing the possibility of a "selective embargo" which would affect the United States, as Israel's arms supplier, without damaging the interests of other Western countries. When the principal oil producers finally met in Kuwait, ten days after the start of the war, their decisions came partly as a shock and partly as a relief. The price of Middle East oil was raised by 17 per cent and production was cut, but only by 5 per cent every month "until Israel withdraws from the occupied Arab territories and the rights of the Palestinians are restored."

Now that the weapon was in action, it seemed at first sight less alarming than the anxious importers of the West had feared; but during the days that followed its edge became steadily sharper. Saudi Arabia, by far the most important of the Arab producers, decided to increase its own production-cut unilaterally to 10 per cent, which meant straightaway the loss to the West of the better part of a million barrels a day; the decision was followed by Qatar. Then Abu Dhabi broke new ground by announcing a ban on all shipments to the United States, and Libya did the same, setting a trend which produced within a few days a complete stoppage of Arab oil exports to the United States and Holland, in addition to the general cutback in production throughout the Arab World. There was no longer any way of disguising the magnitude of the crisis that had overtaken the world.

What had tipped the scale, it later appeared, was a peculiarly inept piece of political action by the government of the United States. When the representatives of the Arab oil producers had met in Kuwait on 17 October, the pressure for an all-out embargo had been resisted by the Saudi Arabians, who were especially reluctant to break their close relationship with their American friends. King Feisal had sent his foreign minister, Omar Saqqaf, to Washington, where Saqqaf met President Nixon and later made a very conciliatory statement, praising Nixon's role in ending the Vietnam war and suggesting that he might play an equally statesmanlike part in working out a satisfactory settlement in the Middle East. Clearly, Saqqaf felt, and doubtless informed King Feisal, that he had been given certain assurances by Nixon, on the strength of which King Feisal was prepared to persist in exercising his enormous influence on the side of moderation. But on the very day after the meeting with Saqqaf, Nixon proposed to Congress that the United States should provide Israel with the breathtaking sum of $2.2 billion in "emergency military aid". The Americans were in fact already rearming Israel by means of a huge airlift, and the request to Congress was only a formal confirmation of this; but the scale of the rearmament and the President's public announcement at this critical moment appeared to King Feisal to indicate that Nixon had gone back on his assurances and in the most insulting way. The Saudi Arabian cabinet met soon after the news was received in Riadh, and next day, 20 October, it was announced that Saudi Arabia was stopping all exports of oil to the United States.

By any standards, the American miscalculation was an astonishing one. In the course of 1973 the managements of three of the leading American oil companies had publicly warned their stockholders and the American public of the extent to which the United States was becoming dependent on Middle East oil and of the resentment aroused in the Arab World by American policy towards the Middle East. The three companies were at once widely attacked by Zionist supporters all over the United States, and an attempt was even made to organise a boycott of the petrol stations of the Standard Oil Company of California, since Otto Miller, Chairman of Standard Oil, had been a leading spokesman of the warning. This violent reaction was characteristic of the methods of American Zionists, and indeed of Zionist methods anywhere in the Western world. The arguments put forward by the oil companies were not examined; instead, their motives were impugned and an open attempt was made to discredit them with the public whose interests they were trying to protect. Yet they had expressed their anxiety, an anxiety which was so soon to be justified, with studied moderation. Mr Miller, in writing to the 40,000 employees of Standard Oil of California, and to the company's 262,000 stockholders, had not called for the abandonment of Israel by its American protector; indeed, he had not mentioned Israel at all.

What he had done, after pointing out America's need to import larger and larger quantities of oil from the Middle East, was to draw attention to "a growing feeling in much of the Arab World that the United States has turned its back on the Arab people," and to urge that "there must be understanding on our part of the aspirations of the Arab people, and more positive support of their efforts toward peace in the Middle East."[97]

The concerted use of the oil weapon in October 1973 underlined President Sadat's most striking success. It had been a remarkable triumph to rebuild the morale of the Egyptian army to the point where it could launch a successful attack against supposedly impossible odds. It had been a crucial achievement to enlist the co-operation of the Syrians and so force the Israelis to divide their forces between two fronts. By themselves, however, these factors were not sufficient to gain for Sadat his carefully calculated objectives. The remaining and most important task was to persuade the oil producers, and especially King Feisal, at once the most influential and the most moderate among them, to play their part in the overall strategy. It was they and not Sadat or the Syrians who controlled the one weapon in the Arab armoury which could really damage the interests of Israel's supporters in the West. There could be no doubt about the effectiveness of the oil weapon, if it was once brought into play. The questions were: could the oil producers agree among themselves, and with the Egyptians, on the circumstances in which they should act? And, if so, would they be capable of devising and executing a plan of action which would make proper use of the power they had in their hands?

Many people must have given thought to these questions besides the Arabs themselves. It can safely be assumed that the Israelis had, and it would be remarkable indeed if the governments of Western Europe, collectively dependent for almost three quarters of their oil imports on the Arab World, had not deliberated with some care on the answers that could be expected. The Americans, less immediately concerned, in that they were much less dependent on Arab oil, must also have thought long and hard about the implications for themselves, as the sole patron of the enemy of all the Arabs, and for their Western allies. If so, the evidence suggests that they seriously underestimated both the competence and the resolution of the Arab oil producers in general, and of King Feisal and his ministers in particular. That it should have come as a surprise to see the Arabs making such swift and skilful use of the oil weapon indicates an intelligence failure as serious as the one which had allowed Israel to be caught with its guard down on 6 October.[98] There had been plenty of warnings besides those of the American oil companies. A few weeks before the outbreak of the October War, Mr Nadim Pachachi, a former Secretary-General of OPEC (the Organisation of Petroleum Exporting Countries) had addressed an American audience in Beirut and emphasised the delicate balance that already existed between the available supplies of oil and the current demand for it all over the world. In the circumstances, he pointed out, the use of oil as a political weapon need not involve anything as dramatic as a total shutdown or a boycott or an embargo against one or more countries. In a seller's market, all the Arabs would have to do to make their weight felt in the world would be to refrain from expanding their production to meet the steadily rising demand. And Mr Pachachi frankly explained that he had proposed to the Arab oil-producing governments that they should do just this, since there seemed to be no other way of obtaining the implementation of the Security Council's unanimous resolution on the Middle East.

What he was proposing, said Mr Pachachi, was "that all the Arab oil-producing countries should adopt a co-ordinated, unified policy to freeze their crude oil production at present levels and to maintain this no-growth situation until such time as Israel withdraws fully from the Arab territories—including, of course, Arab Jerusalem—occupied since the 1967 war . . ." The warning could hardly have been given more clearly, and the policy which the oil producers adopted during the October War was precisely the policy which Mr Pachachi had recommended, except that, in the circumstances of the war and with the Americans operating their airlift of arms to Israel (giant American transports actually landed their cargoes in Sinai, inside the very occupied territories from which the Egyptians were fighting to oust the Israeli army of occupation), the Arabs were not content with a "no-growth situation" but cut back their production and put into operation their embargo against the United States.

There had been other warnings, which were summed up by David Hirst, Middle East correspondent of *The Guardian*, a month before the outbreak of the October War. Hirst wrote that ". . . economic realities have put the weapon in the Arabs' hands, but political ones—what the Arabs see as America's blindly uncritical support of Israel— have given them the incentive to use it." Why then were all the warnings disregarded, and how could President Nixon and his advisers have been so blind to the dangers that they virtually forced the Arabs to put their threats into execution? The answer is in a sense the theme of this book. America's "blindly uncritical support" for Israel had become a habit, a tradition imposed on successive American administrations by the temptations of office and the power of the Jewish lobby. Where the interests of Israel were involved (or Israel's *supposed* interests, for it can be argued that America's unfailing indulgence was actually damaging to the real interests of Israel), President Nixon, like President Johnson before him, was ready to disregard the interests of the Arabs and the advice of America's European allies. Indeed, it often seemed, during the years between the Six Day War of 1967 and the October War of 1973 that there was no advice which the American administration was not prepared to reject, no ally it would not endanger, no principle it would not throw overboard, to retain the friendship of Mrs Meir and General Dayan and the campaign contributions of the American Jews. It was President Sadat's most far-reaching achievement that he was able, by winning the co-operation of King Feisal, to break this stranglehold. It must afterwards have given him a certain quiet satisfaction that when he sent his army across the Suez Canal in October he set in motion a train of events which was to topple the government of Mrs Meir just six months later. And no image can more vividly convey the change of status which President Sadat had achieved for the Arabs than the pictures of Richard Nixon, the saviour of Israel in October 1973, paying a state visit to Cairo in June 1974 and assuring his host of America's new-found sympathy and friendship for the Arab World.

CHAPTER EIGHT

Can Israel Change Direction?

Michael Adams

While we were writing this book, I met a Russian Jew, one of those who had succeeded after much tribulation in emigrating to Israel. At first, he said, it had been a dream come true, and for a few months he was full of grateful enthusiasm. But disillusionment set in when he took a closer look, along with other Jews from the Soviet Union, at this new environment, for whose sake they had burned all their bridges with the old. They found themselves repelled especially by the internal feuds which, he said, put Jews in Israel more at odds with their fellow-Jews than they had ever been with the gentiles in the Soviet Union. This was the first of a string of complaints, which he expressed with forceful candour; and he went on to criticise the lack of idealism in Israel, the unwillingness of most Israelis to do a proper day's work, either because there were Arabs to do the hard work or because they had become accustomed to living on charity, assuming that whatever happened "the Americans will pay." Above all, he said, he couldn't stand Israel because "it's all a big bluff," a confidence trick where nobody believed the lies that were told to win sympathy abroad, but where everybody went on telling them just the same because they needed the arms and the money into which the sympathy could be converted. He hadn't lived in Israel long; but it had been long enough for him to come to the conclusion that, quite apart from the growing Arab threat, and simply on account of its own inner tensions, Israel was, in his words, "a country without a future."

It was a comprehensive indictment, especially interesting because it came from someone to whom Israel had indeed been the promised land, but whom first-hand experience had transformed in a couple of years from a grateful admirer into a critic who couldn't wait to shake the dust of the place off his feet. The Israeli authorities, who are especially sensitive about the whole question of immigration from the Soviet Union, would probably try to discount his criticisms by saying that there are bound to be misfits in any group of immigrants and their views are not representative of the majority. My informant insisted that most of the other immigrants felt as he did. Many of them left Israel as soon as they could raise the money to do so; for the Israelis, like the Russians, won't let them go until they have repaid what the state has spent on them. Some were even undergoing conversion to Christianity as a means of escape. And there is enough information coming out of Israel these days, even if very little of it finds its way into the press in the West, to confirm that the kind of criticisms he was making are not confined to the Soviet Jewish immigrants.[99]

What, then, has happened to the Zionist dream? What in fact was the original Zionist objective, and how far has it been achieved in practice? This is by no means an academic question and the answer to it has a close bearing on our theme. It is a question which more and more Israelis are asking themselves, but which few of Israel's apologists in the outside world have been prepared to consider at any stage in the movement's history. If it had received more attention, the world, and especially the Palestinians, would have been spared much of the misery that has accompanied the birth and development of the State of Israel.

About the original objective there is not much room for argument. It was the establishment in Palestine of a Jewish community which could live in freedom from the disabilities and sometimes the persecution to which Jews had found themselves subject in many parts of the world. This was an objective which aroused the sympathy of most liberal-minded people in the West, conscious that it was in Europe that the persecution of the Jews had been most severe and discreditable. This was true even before the Nazis made anti-Semitism a matter of state policy; and the sympathy and the support for Zionism were immensely reinforced when the secrets of the concentration camps were revealed after the Second World War. Horror and revulsion gave an added impetus to the movement to provide a secure home for the surviving Jews; there is a dreadful irony in the fact that Hitler did as much as anyone to bring about the establishment of the State of Israel.

But was it a Jewish *state* in Palestine that the early Zionists envisaged; and, if so, was this a reasonable ambition? Did they take into account that there was already in Palestine a settled population, whose consent to such a scheme could hardly be expected since it must mean for them a choice between exile and submission to the alien rule of the newcomers? This is an awkward line of enquiry for the apologists of political Zionism, for if it is pursued with sincerity it calls into question the legitimacy of the whole Zionist undertaking. Either those who planned and carried out the undertaking did not realise that there would be strong and justified opposition on the part of the Arabs of Palestine, or else they anticipated this opposition but were determined to overrule it, if necessary by force. In neither case can their attitude escape criticism. Those Israelis who are prepared to face the facts now acknowledge that the failure of the early Zionists to give proper consideration to the Arab problem was the fatal flaw in all their calculations. The failure was a moral as well as a practical one. It reflected a degree of egoism which cannot altogether be excused by the past sufferings of the Jews; and its result was to make of Israel not a refuge but rather a super-ghetto, the one place in the modern world where, for all the Israelis' frenzied pursuit of "security", the Jews today remain wholly insecure.

Things began to go wrong long before a Jewish state became even a remote possibility, and the first to see it were the true visionaries among the Zionists themselves. As early as 1891 one of the foremost Jewish thinkers of his day, for whom Zionism could only be part of a national revival in which the spiritual and moral aspects were all-important, went from his home in Russia to assess for himself the prospects in Palestine. This was Asher Ginzberg, who wrote under the name of Ahad Ha'am (in Hebrew "One of the People") and who published on his return a report, under the title of *The Truth from Palestine*. In it he drew attention to the central problem to which the Zionists must find an answer. Palestine, he emphasised, was not an empty land, nor could it accommodate more than a small proportion of the Jews scattered throughout the world. Those who did go to settle there must be careful to win the friendship of the Palestinians, treating them with courtesy and respect.

> "Yet what do our brethren do in Palestine?" he asked. "Just the very opposite! Serfs they were in the lands of the diaspora and suddenly they find themselves in freedom, and this change has awakened in them an inclination to despotism. They treat the Arabs with hostility and cruelty, deprive them of their rights, offend them without cause, and even boast of these deeds; and nobody among us opposes this despicable and dangerous inclination."[100]

Ginzberg, or Ahad Ha'am, was the first in a line of splendid Jewish nationalists whose concept of Zionism was firmly based on the traditional values of Judaism. He saw from the outset the dangers, as well as the immorality, of an approach which would make of the Jewish settlers an élite and condemn the Palestinians to servitude. He protested against the racialism inherent in so much of the Zionist programme in Palestine, writing for instance in 1913 to a colleague to denounce the boycott proclaimed by the Zionist labour movement in Palestine against the employment of Arab labour:

> "Apart from the political danger, I can't put up with the idea that our brethren are morally capable of behaving in such a way to men of another people; and unwittingly the thought comes to my mind: If it is so now, what will be our relation to the others if in truth we shall achieve 'at the end of time' power in *Eretz Israel*?"

Prophetic words, which went largely unheeded then and were still disregarded half a century later by those who had in the meantime achieved power in *Eretz Israel*. That the leadership of the Zionist movement should have fallen into the hands of men unrestrained by Ahad Ha'am's scruples is not surprising; what does seem strange, though, is the fact that, as its fundamental selfishness and lack of humanity became apparent, Zionism as a political movement should have encountered so little opposition among the gentiles to whom it now turned for support. These international allies were, first, the British government in the persons of Lloyd George and Arthur Balfour, and then, when Britain had served its turn and appeared to be the obstacle to further headway, the government of the United States under successive presidents, of whom Harry Truman earned the largest debt of Zionist gratitude until Richard Nixon stole the crown between 1970 and 1973. Throughout the half century from the Balfour Declaration in 1917 to the Six Day War in 1967, the two Anglo-Saxon powers in turn held in their hands the power to approve or deny the growing demands of Zionist ambition. Although they were aware that every advance by the Zionists was made at the expense of the rights of the Palestinians, rights which the British government had expressly guaranteed in the terms of the Balfour Declaration and which the Arabs, until they were disillusioned, looked to the Americans to protect, neither the British nor the Americans, whatever the shifts and turns of their policies in the Middle East, could ever bring themselves to stand for long in opposition to the Zionists. The Zionists were powerful, rich, influential, and above all persistent, as President Truman in particular was to find in 1947 and 1948, when they scored their most signal successes in Washington, and through Washington at the infant United Nations.

Yet throughout all this time there had been voices on the other side—Jewish voices—offering a constant reminder that what was being allowed and even encouraged in Palestine conflicted with all the principles which the Western governments professed. To Ahad Ha'am, the Balfour Declaration, while it recognised the historical right of the Jews in Palestine,

> "does not affect the right of the other inhabitants, who are entitled to invoke the right of actual dwelling, and their work in the country for

many generations. For them too, the country is a national home, and they have a right to develop national forces to the extent of their ability . . ."

Hugo Bergmann, philosopher and writer, wrote shortly before he left Prague to settle in Palestine that:

"Any agreement with the inhabitants of the land is much more important to us than declarations of all the governments in the world could be. Unfortunately, Zionist public opinion has not yet become conscious of it. What happened in Palestine before the War (the First World War) was almost totally of a kind to turn the Arabs into our enemies. A peaceful confrontation and understanding with them, however, is for us the question of life."[101]

It was during the 1920s and '30s that the fatal pattern of the future was stamped on Palestine, and during those years the chances of reaching the right decision were lessened by a persistent and generally successful campaign to confuse the issue and disguise the true nature of the Zionist objective. It was of course a part of this design to deceive the Arabs, both in Palestine and outside it, and to persuade them that no infringement was intended of the self-evident rights of the Palestinians. It was also important for the Zionists, if they were to maintain Britain's support for their endeavour, to disguise from the British public the full extent of their ambition. Recent research has established that Lloyd George and Mr Balfour knew, when they persuaded the Cabinet in 1917 to accept the terms of the Balfour Declaration, that the innocuous-sounding phrase "a National Home in Palestine" was in fact a euphemism for a future Jewish state.[102] Others were unaware of this, though Lord Curzon suspected it, remarking to Balfour just over a year after the publication of the Declaration that

"while Weizmann[103] may say one thing to you, or while you may mean one thing by a National Home, he is out for something quite different. He contemplates a Jewish state, a Jewish nation, a subordinate population of Arabs, etc., ruled by Jews; the Jews in possession of the fat of the land and directing the Administration."[104]

But at the beginning of 1921 the affairs of Palestine were removed from the jurisdiction of the Foreign Office and Curzon and handed over to the Colonial Office. A few months later Sir Herbert Samuel, an ardent Zionist who had been appointed as the first High Commissioner in Palestine, showed how successful the deception had been. Answering charges that the British Government was prepared to allow the Arabs of Palestine to be deprived of their country, their holy places, and their lands, Samuel gave on Britain's behalf a solemn undertaking that

> "the British Government . . . has never consented and will never consent to such a policy . . . If any measures are needed to convince the Muslim and Christian population . . . that their rights are really safe, such measures will be taken. For the British Government, the trustee under the Mandate for the happiness of the people of Palestine, would never impose upon them a policy which that people had reason to think was contrary to their religious, their political and their economic interests."[105]

This statement was confirmed in the House of Commons on 14 June 1921 by Winston Churchill, then Colonial Secretary. For anyone who cares about Britain's reputation it is humiliating to recall that only fifteen years later British troops had to be used to put down a rebellion in Palestine by that same Muslim and Christian population, who saw their rights as well as their interests being sacrificed in deference to the wishes of the Zionists; and that less than thirty years later a Jewish state was proclaimed in four fifths of the whole area of Palestine, the bulk of whose Arab population had fled into exile.

All this time the warnings of what was likely to happen had continued; and among the voices raised against accepting the demands of the extreme Zionists, the strongest and the most eloquent were those which came from within the Zionist movement itself. Dr Judah Magnes, the founder and first president of the Hebrew University in Jerusalem, consistently urged that by establishing a political dominion in Palestine against the wishes and without the consent of the Palestinians, ". . . we shall be sowing the seed of an eternal hatred of such dimensions that Jews will not be able to live in that part of the world for centuries to come. That is something that you had better try to avoid." If things turned out badly, Dr Magnes warned the hotheads, it would be their own fault, for:

> "We seem to have thought of everything—except the Arabs. We have issued this and that publication and done other commendable things. But as to a consistent, clearly worked-out, realistic, generous policy of political, social, economic, educational co-operation with the Arabs—the time has never seemed to be propitious.
>
> "But the time has come for the Jews to take into account the Arab factor as the most important facing us. If we have a just cause, so have they. If promises were made to us, so were they to the Arabs. If we love the land and have a historical connection with it, so too the Arabs. Even more realistic than the ugly realities of imperialism is the fact that the Arabs live here and in this part of the world, and will probably be here long after the collapse of one imperialism and the rise of another. If we too wish to live in this living space, we must live with the Arabs . . ."[106]

It seems inconceivable, and it is certainly tragic, that such warnings, coming as they did from men of such outstanding calibre within the Zionist movement, should have been disregarded. What made it easier to ignore men like Judah Magnes was the uncertainty that persisted in the outside world about the real objective of the Zionists; of those, that is, who were winning control of the Zionist movement. From the beginning this uncertainty had been deliberately cultivated, and where necessary the Zionists had been prepared to lie to gentile audiences about the aims which they discussed quite frankly among themselves. When the Balfour Declaration first aroused misgivings among those who foresaw that it might lead to the imposition of Jewish rule on the native Palestinian population, Nahum Sokolov, who had been Weizmann's closest collaborator in negotiating the Declaration, protested indignantly:

> "It has been said and is still being obstinately repeated by anti-Zionists again and again, that Zionism aims at the creation of an independent 'Jewish State'. But this is wholly fallacious. The 'Jewish State' was never a part of the Zionist programme."[107]

This was quite simply untrue. Theodor Herzl, the founder of political Zionism, had expounded his idea in a book to which he gave the unequivocal title *Der Judenstaat*, The Jewish State. It was only afterwards that his friend Max Nordau advised against giving currency to this term. When the question came up at the first Zionist Congress in Basle, wrote Nordau, "I did my best to persuade the claimants of the Jewish state in Palestine that we might find a circumlocution that would express all we meant." Instead of *Judenstaat*, he proposed the word 'Heimstätte' (which in English became 'national home'), remarking afterwards that "It was equivocal, but we all understood what it meant. To us it signified '*Judenstaat*' then and it signifies the same now."[108]

Thus the element of deception, of dissimulation, was there from the start. The early Zionists could not afford to be honest about their objective, since it was one which, if openly acknowledged, must repel those whose sympathy they had to win. Only the liberals like Ahad Ha'am and Judah Magnes could be frank with the world, because their aim was a shared Palestine, in which the rights of the indigenous population would be respected. And the liberals, alas, were to lose out to the extremists, those who wanted nothing less than a Jewish state in Palestine and who saw that this could only be achieved at the expense of the Palestinian Arabs. Accepting this brutal fact, but shielding it as long as possible from the eyes of the world, they pursued their aim in the knowledge that only force could bring them success.

It was the Nazi persecutions which finally cut the ground from under the feet of the moderates. By 1945 the pressure for the establishment of a Jewish state was so strong that the arguments against it were almost completely ignored. President Roosevelt saw the dangers, warning shortly before his death that such a state ". . . can only be installed and maintained by force and we should not be a party to it"; but his successor, President Truman, found the influence of the Zionist lobby more than he could withstand, and the authority of the White House, despite the opposition of the State Department, was put at the disposal of the Zionists.

The capture of the White House made the victory of the Zionists a certainty; but it was still necessary to go through the motions of international authorisation. The Israelis today, despite their open contempt for the United Nations, rest their case on the fact that the decision to divide Palestine, and to establish in the greater part of it a state for the Jewish minority, was taken in 1947 by the United Nations General Assembly. Is this not proof that, however questionable the concept of a Zionist state may have been originally, it had attained by 1947 a sufficient legitimacy in the eyes of world opinion? The argument is superficially appealing, until we recall that the crucial majority for partition in the General Assembly was only achieved by shameless gerrymandering on the part of the American delegation,[109] and that the United Nations in 1947 included only about one third of the nations represented there today, and more than half of these were in Europe and North America. If the establishment of a Jewish state in Palestine had not been authorised by the Assembly in 1947, it would have had no chance of approval once the United Nations had been expanded to include the new nations of Asia and Africa, whose experience of colonialism would have ensured their opposition to so openly colonialist a design.

The political victory, however, was won in 1947 and the establishment of the Jewish state in the following year was enormously facilitated by the flight of the Palestinian refugees, whose homes, farms, shops, factories, plantations and all their personal belongings were simply appropriated by the victorious Israelis. Here again, one must pause in wonderment at the way in which this act of

Can Israel Change Direction?

plunder on a vast scale was permitted, even encouraged, by the Western world. Where it would have been reasonable to expect a concerted international movement to obtain the return of the refugees to their homes once the fighting was over, or at the very least to ensure that they received compensation for the material losses they had sustained, what we have seen has been the exact opposite. The plunderers have been rewarded by international acceptance and by aid, principally but not only, from the United States, on a scale unparalleled anywhere else in the world; while those who had lost everything and found themselves condemned to exile and near-starvation have been kept alive, but sternly repressed whenever they presumed to remind the world of their claim to any redress.

Here was the logical conclusion of all that had gone before. The hard-liners among the Zionists, those against whom Ahad Ha'am and Judah Magnes and others like them had warned for half a century, had their way and the Jewish state was achieved: at the price of total disaster for the Palestinians. Given the approach of the men who had come to dominate the Zionist movement, this conclusion was inevitable; even so, it seems in retrospect almost incredible that, in robbing the Palestinians, the Zionists could not see that they were fastening an albatross about the neck of their infant state. What most outsiders must find even harder to understand is the unconcern of ordinary Israelis, of the men and women who streamed into the Jewish state after 1948 and took the places of the exiled Palestinians, ploughing their fields, living in their houses, or else destroying them and building instead dwellings in a style as alien as were their new inhabitants to the Palestinian environment, with no apparent thought for those they had displaced. A later generation was to see things differently, although by then it was too late to put right the injustice. In a book whose title focuses precisely on this change in attitude between those who built Israel and those who merely inherited it, a young Israeli has written:

> "Every revolution has its price, of course, and the Zionist revolution was no exception. By a brutal twist of fate, unexpected, undesired,

unconsidered by the early pioneers, this price was partly paid by the Arab inhabitants of Palestine. The Arabs bore no responsibility for the centuries-long suffering of the Jews in Europe; yet, in the end, the Arabs were punished because of it. The price extracted was heavy; it is impossible to measure it in terms of human bitterness and suffering. Whatever their subsequent follies and outrages might be, the punishment of the Arabs for the sins of Europe must burden the conscience of Israelis for a long time to come."[110]

Even this relatively liberal interpretation of events rests on an assumption which it is difficult to accept. To speak of what happened in Palestine in 1948 as "the Zionist revolution" is essentially to distort its character. A revolution implies a struggle against oppression. But the Zionists were not oppressed in Palestine; they were privileged immigrants, seeking to overthrow an authority whose function it was to judge fairly between their claims and those of the native Palestinians. By their successful use of a combination of violence and political influence, the Zionists succeeded in perverting justice and fastening their own oppression on the Palestinians. And by approving their success, the world subscribed to the fundamentally unjust proposition that "it was right for the Jews to fight to acquire; wrong for the Arabs to fight to hold."[111]

To their political success in capturing first the American administration and then a majority vote in the General Assembly of the United Nations, the Zionists thus added in 1948 a military success on the battlefield. The greater part of Palestine was theirs and the fate of the Palestinians was in their hands. At this critical moment it was more evidently true than ever that, as Weizmann had said, "the world will judge us by the way we treat the Arabs of Palestine." Had they made at the outset of their national existence a generous settlement with the Palestinians, recognising the injury they had done to them (even if, to some extent, they might claim that it had been done inadvertently) and undertaking as far as possible to make redress, the Zionists might have averted the retribution which must sooner or later overtake them. Instead, they compounded the injury by

Can Israel Change Direction?

preventing the return of the refugees, initiating by this brutal decision the train of events which was to lead, twenty years later, to the excesses of a Palestinian resistance movement driven beyond the limits of endurance.

Again the voices of the liberal minority inside the Zionist movement were raised in favour of an approach to the Palestinians which would be wise as well as humane; but by now the triumph of the hard-liners had reduced the liberals to a tiny and powerless fraction in the composition of the new state. When Count Bernadotte, speaking for the United Nations and with the backing of the American Government, pressed for the return of the refugees, it was the voice of Ben Gurion, then the all-powerful prime minister of Israel, that answered. And Ben Gurion was unequivocal about the refugees. "We must do everything," he said when the state was only a few weeks old, "to ensure that they never do return."[112] Apart from a single proposal, initiated in 1949 by Moshe Sharett and almost unanimously opposed by Israeli public opinion, to repatriate 100,000 of the refugees, who by this time numbered more than 800,000, successive Israeli governments over the next quarter of a century never modified this stern refusal.

A question which is relevant here has often been asked and never satisfactorily answered. Was the dispossession and spoliation of the Palestinians deliberate and premeditated; was it an inherent part of the Zionist design? Or did it come about accidentally, as the result of unforeseen developments in the way the design unfolded? The evidence here is difficult to get at; this crucial part of the story has been camouflaged with especial care by the apologists for Zionism, who needed the sympathy of the world as much after the creation of the State of Israel as they had done during the period of its conception and preparation. Here and there, as in that revealing outburst by Ben Gurion, we can gain insights into the attitude of mind of the dominant figures in the Zionist movement on this all-important question. Long before Ben Gurion was in a position to influence the fate of the Palestinians, Herzl had confided to his diary that it should be possible to "spirit them across the frontier" when the time was ripe for the establishment of his *Judenstaat*.[113] Between the first and second world wars, an openly colonialist and militarist approach to the problem of the Arabs in Palestine had been advocated by Vladimir Jabotinsky, a Russian immigrant whose ideas gained support from those who were impressed by the early successes of Hitler and Mussolini in Europe. As Weizmann's influence among the Zionists declined and Ben Gurion's increased, such ideas made headway and they were reflected in the Biltmore Programme, in which the Zionist goal of a state in Palestine was clearly set out in 1942. Soon afterwards (it seems beyond belief, but it is true) the British Labour Party, in a policy statement issued in 1944 and affirming the party's support for the creation of a Jewish state in Palestine, advocated openly that "the Arabs should be encouraged to move out as the Jews move in."[114]

It was ill-considered support of this kind from people with no knowledge of the situation in Palestine which encouraged the more unprincipled elements among the Zionists. Ben Gurion, like Weizmann a generation earlier, spoke with one voice to his supporters in the outside world, but used a quite different tone with those inside Palestine to whom he looked to carry through his design; such as a young soldier, Moshe Dayan, who shared his views about the future role of the Palestinians. Ben Gurion, says his biographer, was

> ". . . sceptical about any possibility of co-existence with the (Palestinian) Arabs. The fewer there were living within the frontiers of the new Jewish state, the better he would like it. He did not say this in so many words, but the impression which emerged from his interventions and remarks was clear enough—a major offensive against the Arabs would not only break up their attacks but would also greatly reduce the percentage of Arabs in the population of the new State. This might be called racialism, but the whole Zionist movement was based on the principle of a purely Jewish community in Palestine . . ."[115]

So the idea that the Palestinians would have to be displaced in order to permit the establishment of a Zionist state in Palestine (which would, by definition, be a state for Jews) was current long before the state became a reality. And if there is insufficient evidence for a categorical statement that the removal of the Palestinians was an integral part of the Zionist design, there is clear evidence that before and immediately after the establishment of the State in 1948 and while the fighting with the neighbouring Arab states was going on, the Israelis took action both to provoke the flight of the Palestinians and to prevent the return of those who had already left the country. The extent to which the Zionists (whom it now becomes proper to call the Israelis) contributed to the Arab exodus from Palestine in 1948 is well documented.[116] The actions of Moshe Dayan, for instance at Lydda, and Yigael Allon in Galilee, both of whom were to become prominent figures in the political life of Israel, are only less well known than the part played by the *Irgun Zvai Leumi* under Menachem Beigin at Deir Yassin. But the debate about how many Palestinians were driven out by the Israelis and how many fled of their own accord out of fear for their lives and those of their families is essentially irrelevant. What matters is that, once they had fled, the Israelis decided not to allow them to return, despite the urging of Bernadotte, whose insistence on the refugees' right of return undoubtedly contributed to his murder by Jewish terrorists in Jerusalem in September 1948; despite requests by the United Nations and the governments of Britain and the United States; and despite the simple claims of humanity on behalf of an innocent and defenceless civilian population.

The decision was a fateful one, in the short term for the Palestinians who suffered by it, in the long term for the Israelis themselves, who thus perpetuated an enmity which wiser counsels could have dissipated at the start. What prompted them to adopt a policy which the history of their own people should have condemned as sterile and ultimately counter-productive? There was first of all the dangerous ideal of a *Jewish* state: a state which should be, by its very nature, exclusive, and in which only Jews (whom the Israelis were to find it very hard to define) might enjoy to the full the privileges and the prerogatives of citizenship. And there was the intoxication of victory on the part of a people which had known more than its share of suffering and oppression, and which now accepted with sadly little hesitation the idea that others must suffer and be oppressed in order that it might live. As Ahad Ha'am had noted half a century before, "Serfs they were in the lands of the diaspora and suddenly they find themselves in freedom, and this change has awakened in them an inclination to despotism." With all the allowances that can and should be made for the sufferings of the Jews in Hitler's Europe, the new attitude was not a pretty one; nor can one overlook the fact that in their dealings with the Palestinians the Israelis took their stand without apology on the same principle of racialism which had been used with such dreadful effect against their own kin by the Nazis.

Even Chaim Weizmann, who had tried to hold the balance for thirty years between the liberals and the activists within the Zionist movement, fell in with the disastrous policy adopted in 1948 towards the Palestinian refugees. A document available until now only in Hebrew makes plain the swiftness with which the Israelis decided that, as Ben Gurion had said, "we must do everything to see that they never do return." This document shows both the techniques adopted to achieve this result and the unanimity with which the leaders of the new state approved its planning and execution. Anyone who still finds it hard to believe that the Israelis, in their moment of triumph, could have acted with such inhumanity, should read the account of what is called the "postfactum transfer" (of the Palestinians) in the diary kept by one Yossef Weitz in 1948.

Yossef Weitz was a Zionist who had been since 1932 Director of the Land and Afforestation Division of the Jewish National Fund in Palestine. As soon as David Ben Gurion had proclaimed the state of Israel in May 1948 and war had broken out with the Arabs, Weitz became aware of something which he immediately realised was of crucial importance for the future of the state. The Arabs were fleeing from Palestine in large numbers and the question arose of whether they should be allowed to return when the fighting was over. Weitz had no doubt whatever of what should be the answer; and because he confided his thoughts to a diary which was later published, we are able to get from him a clear insight into the way in which the fate of the Palestinian exiles was decided.[117]

We have been refused permission to quote directly from the diary, but we hope that it may one day be translated from the Hebrew into English and published in this country. It shows that in May 1948, just after the withdrawal from Palestine of the British mandatory power, Moshe Shertok (who later changed his name to Sharett), whom Ben Gurion had appointed foreign minister of the new-born state, was ready to agree to plans which would ensure that those Arabs who, for whatever reason, left their country during the fighting should not be permitted to return.

Acting on plans carefully prepared in advance, Israeli troops, within a few weeks of the outbreak of the war, had overrun a considerable area of territory beyond the boundaries drawn by the UN partition plan, and several hundred thousand Palestinian Arabs had left their homes. To them, it probably never occurred that they would not be permitted to return as soon as the fighting was over. Indeed, negotiations were announced to allow 20,000 refugees to return to Haifa, which had fallen to the Israelis in the earliest days of the war. Such negotiations were resisted by Weitz, among others, and Ben Gurion himself was prepared to accept the creation of an organisation which should become responsible for the conversion of Arab lands into Israeli lands in such a way that the Palestinians could have no hope of returning.

Ben Gurion appears to have agreed to such a "solution of the Arab problem in Israel". While there were those in Israel who considered it impracticable to exclude the Palestinians altogether, virtually none of them opposed the destruction of Arab villages. It is clear from the Weitz diary that many villages were destroyed not during the fighting, as an act of war, but by deliberate design, in order that there should be no homes for the Arabs to return to, and that new Israeli settlements should take their place.

The United Nations Mediator, Count Bernadotte, was working hard to stop the fighting, and on 11 June 1948 a truce came into effect. Naturally enough, Palestinians began to reappear in their villages and on their lands, to retrieve such belongings as remained and to attempt to harvest their crops. Weitz certainly hoped that such a reflux of Arabs could be stopped. He proposed the creation of a chain of settlements to consolidate the Israeli gains and to prevent the return of the dispossessed Palestinians. While the truce was still in force, tractors were being used to demolish the villages; and, although doubts of the legality of the procedure were felt by some of the Israeli leaders, who may have been disturbed by the possibility of protests from external sources, the great majority of those taking part in the demolitions seem to have acted without scruple and were willing to sacrifice any moral considerations to those of expediency in the service of the new state.

At the beginning of July the truce broke down. Israeli organisations, which by then included officers of the army and of the intelligence services, continued to tour the country marking out the sites for settlements to replace the Arab villages. Where existing buildings could be put to use by the settlements, they were preserved, but always with the aim of their occupation by Israelis, not by returning Arabs. The operation was put into the hands of the significantly named "Transfer Committee", of which Weitz was the moving spirit, and whose activities were expressly approved by Ben Gurion and other leaders.

Months later, Weitz claims to have talked on the matter to Chaim Weizmann, President of Israel, and to have received his agreement that the Arabs need not return. It is well known that Weizmann and others believed, and stated, that the Palestinians could readily be absorbed and accepted by other Arab countries. Proposals were made for compensation by Israel for those deprived of their property, but twenty-six years later no payment had been made.

The immediate fate of the dispossessed Arabs seems not to have concerned the Israelis in the least. On the contrary, when the Security Council had ordered a second truce, which came into force on 18 July 1948, and charged Count Bernadotte with supervising its observance until a peaceful settlement could be reached, Weitz was apprehensive. Bernadotte was insisting on the right of the refugees to return to their homes, many of which, as we have seen, the Israelis had by this time destroyed; when the Israelis refused this for reasons of security, Bernadotte reported to the Security Council that "notwithstanding the views expressed by the Provisional Government of Israel, it was my firm view that the right of the refugees to return to their homes at the earliest practicable date should be affirmed,"[118] adding that any of the refugees who did not wish to return should receive adequate compensation for the property they had lost. Bernadotte had no doubt that the great majority did wish to return, and in his diary he described a visit in that summer of 1948 to Ramallah, where thousands of refugees from Lydda and Ramleh were assembled:

> "I have made the acquaintance of a great many refugee camps," he wrote, "but never have I seen a more ghastly sight than that which met my eyes here at Ramallah. The car was literally stormed by excited masses shouting with oriental fervour that they wanted food and wanted to return to their homes."

Bernadotte touched on the danger that the refugee encampment at Ramallah might become a breeding-ground for an epidemic that might sweep through Palestine, and he wondered what would happen when the winter rains set in, ". . . a thought that one preferred not to follow to its conclusion."[119] But this was not the way the Israelis looked at this vast human problem. When Bernadotte wrote his last report to the United Nations, completing it the day before his murder in Jerusalem, and urged once again that no settlement of the Arab-Israeli problem could be "just and complete" if the refugees were not allowed to return to their homes, Weitz and his friends were deeply concerned. If Bernadotte's solution were accepted and enforced, a vast number of the Arab refugees would come flooding back to resume possession of their homes and lands, which had already been settled, or prepared for settlement, by the Israeli occupiers. Weitz saw this, not as the legitimate repossession of their lands by those temporarily dispossessed by war, but as a direct threat to the well-being of the new State of Israel.

To circumvent this threat, Weitz drew up a programme, which he discussed with Ben Gurion in September of 1948. Ben Gurion, it seems, accepted the proposal for direct and deliberate harassment of the refugees, with the declared purpose of preventing their return. No details were made clear, but there is no doubt that the Prime Minister himself gave his support to the organisation which was proposing to undertake the task. It may be that the details were left to the organisation itself; when one considers what action they may have involved, it is understandable that a Prime Minister might be reluctant to associate himself at all openly with them. It must be stressed again that the aim was to prohibit the return to their homes of people who had fled from a war, leaving their houses and their goods and, in many cases, the stock and the land of farms from which they and their ancestors had drawn their living for many generations. The United Nations had not, then, nor at any time thereafter, any doubt that the return of the refugees must be seen as an essential element in any settlement.

Israeli leaders, however, were equally free from doubt. They had no hesitation about taking any action they felt necessary to prevent the return of the refugees, whatever anyone else might say. Ben Gurion and his cabinet, the Jewish Agency, the Jewish National Fund, and the army all appear to have given their support to the proposal; certainly there is no record in Weitz's diary of any dissentient voice from any of these.

From Weitz's diary, one feature is appallingly evident: for him, the Palestinian Arabs were the enemy, to be treated as an enemy. The Israelis, he most firmly believed, had a perfect title to the land of Palestine—to whatever lands they could conquer in addition to the lands allotted to them by the UN partition plan. As far as he was concerned, the Arabs had no rights whatever. Weitz conceived himself and his companions to be fighting a holy war. It seems never to have entered his head that the crimes of the Arabs were, first, to be in possession of land which the Israelis wanted, and, second, to have

Can Israel Change Direction?

resisted attempts to dispossess them. It seems never to have entered his head to think of the Palestinians as anything more than human obstacles, to be removed without mercy and as expeditiously as possible.

❖   ❖   ❖

The dispossession of the Palestinians was a tragic and a discreditable story, which stained for ever the idealism of the original Zionist conception. For the troubled Jewish conscience there is some relief in the thought that throughout the stormy history of political Zionism there has been a persistent current of intellectual resistance against the movement's illiberal tendencies. The mantle of Ahad Ha'am, of Judah Magnes, of Martin Buber, has fallen more recently on the shoulders of Isaac Deutscher, of Elmer Berger, of I. F. Stone and Michael Seltzer and Israel Shahak. This resistance movement, like the resistance movement against the Nazis in Germany, has been pitifully small and so far ineffectual; but like its German counterpart it has salvaged something from the shipwreck of an ideology that has run out of control.

Born as it was in violence and dissimulation, it was inevitable that the Zionist state should continue on the same lines, at least initially. The pattern of fraud, for it was nothing else, which won Israel admission to the United Nations in exchange for assurances that its government would respect the rulings of the United Nations on Palestine, was bound to persist so long as acceptance of the UN resolutions conflicted absolutely with Israel's proclaimed policy. On Macbeth's principle that, having "stepped so far in blood, returning were as tedious as go o'er", the Israeli authorities after 1948 not merely maintained their refusal to accept the return of the refugees, but set about dispossessing of their land even those Palestinians who had refused to flee and who were now technically Israeli citizens. Partly by force—simply driving Arab villagers off their land and sometimes across the frontier altogether—and partly by devising a special series of laws designed to authorise and regularise the expropriation of Arab property inside Israel, the Israelis took possession, within ten years from the establishment of the state, of about one million dunams of land belonging to Palestinian Arabs who had remained in Israel.[120] When the Arabs resisted, or when those who were already across the border "infiltrated" to try to recover their property and sometimes to kill those who had usurped it, the Israeli policy was to mount reprisals on such a scale as to terrorise their opponents into submission. As year succeeded year in this way, the possibility of reconciliation grew steadily more remote.

Yet still the critics from within Israel and among its supporters continued to denounce what they saw as distortions of the Zionist purpose. When the Israeli parliament passed in 1953 a Land Requisition Law, with the express aim of legalising the expropriation of Arab lands, an old man who has been described as "one of the pilgrim fathers of Zionism," Moshe Smilansky, wrote an article attacking this cynical measure. It was published shortly before his death, when he was close to despair over the abandonment in Israel of the human values he had spent his life defending. Remarking that it was strange for Jews to complain, who had returned to Palestine after an absence of two thousand years, if Arabs too felt an attachment to the land from which they were now evicted, and where they would be shot in cold blood if they tried to return, he asked;

> "Where are you, Jews? Why do we not at least, with a generous hand, pay compensation to these miserable people? Where to take the money from? But we build palaces . . . instead of paying a debt that cries unto us from earth and heaven . . . And do we sin only against the refugees? Do we not treat the Arabs who remain with us as second-class citizens? . . . Did a single Jewish farmer raise his hand in the parliament in opposition to a law that deprived Arab peasants of their land?. . . How solitary, in the city of Jerusalem, sits the Jewish conscience!"[121]

It is extraordinary how little echo of all this reached the outside world. Israel, until 1967, was very much a closed society, its internal debates carried out in something approaching secrecy, its newspapers published in Hebrew, which not all Israelis could read and hardly any foreigners. But even so, there were journalists reporting from Israel; there were churchmen by the score from every Western country living and working among the Israelis; there were consuls and international civil servants, and scholars working in the admirable Israeli universities and research institutes, and doctors and engineers and social scientists sharing in the technical advances of which the Israelis were justly proud. Without subscribing to the theory of an international conspiracy to hide the truth about Israel and its treatment of the Arabs inside and outside its borders, one yet must wonder with anxiety and disillusionment at the measure of tolerance these foreign observers showed for faults which would have been unhesitatingly condemned had they appeared in other societies less shielded from criticism than the Jewish state.

In December 1973 there appeared in the British press an English translation of an article which had been first published in Hebrew just twenty years earlier, on Christmas Day of 1953, in the Israeli newspaper *Ma'ariv*. In it an old man is pictured leading his granddaughter through Galilee, which had then been in Israeli hands for five years. He explains to the child the ways in which the former Arab inhabitants have been despoiled of their land, acknowledging the unfairness and hoping that when she comes of age her generation will not be called upon to pay for the sins of their fathers. For, says the old man, you can judge the quality of a state by the way it treats its weakest citizens—and he says mournfully:

> "But if we are asked: 'Did you, in all this wide country, with her many deserts and her few Jewish farmers, did you have to make a mockery of all your oaths before yourselves and before the council of nations? Did you have to betray all the prophecies of your prophets who foresaw the return of the people to the land? Did you have to desecrate all law and all justice—in order to steal a few thousand dunams from a handful of miserable Arab villagers ...?' When we are asked that, we shall not be able to lift our heads."[122]

It was seldom that such voices were raised; and when they were, they were not heard beyond the frontiers of Israel. It was indeed easier for an Israeli to draw attention to this kind of inhumanity in Israel than it was for a European or an American. For Westerners in the twentieth century, objectivity, which is never an easy ideal, has become particularly difficult in any context involving the Jewish people. Because of the appalling crimes perpetrated by Europeans against Jews within living memory, the temptation always presents itself to anyone of liberal tendencies to relieve his conscience by extending a particular tolerance to any Jewish cause. To support, to glorify, to idealise Israel has been for many decent-minded Europeans a way of wiping out past horrors, of cleansing the mind by a vicarious generosity, in the same way that the Germans tried to make amends for the crimes of the Nazis by paying reparations to Israel. Behind this support and this idealisation there was a wholesome instinct; but a moment's thought will show that its expression was perverted as soon as it encouraged the Jews to seek redress, not from the Europeans who had so deeply injured them, but instead from the unoffending Arabs, who had no connection with the original crime.

Riding this wave of sympathy, the leaders of Israel in the 1950s and '60s saw no need to modify their dismissive attitude towards the rights of the Palestinians. On the contrary, as their position became more secure they became even less willing to entertain any suggestion that they should settle for anything less than a Palestine "as Jewish as England is English." What this implied for the remaining non-Jewish inhabitants of Palestine could always be obscured by sophistries when the matter was brought up by tiresome humanitarians like Arnold Toynbee or Bertrand Russell; but when it came to actions, the Israelis left no doubt of their will to win, no matter how much suffering they might cause to others who stood in their way. In 1953, for instance, the notorious Unit 101 was formed within the Israeli army, whose express responsibility it was to mount reprisals against "infiltrators" and others threatening the armistice lines which separated Israel from its neighbours. Unit 101, under its forthright leader Ariel Sharon (later to achieve prominence in the October War of 1973) showed what it was capable of at the West Bank village of Qibya in October 1953, when a uniformed Israeli task force attacked without warning and blew up thirty houses over the heads of their inhabitants, killing more than fifty Palestinian men, women and children. This time there was a brief outcry abroad and Israel was censured by the Security Council of the United Nations; but since no action followed the vote of censure, the price was a negligible one for Israel, whose clear purpose it was to announce to the Palestinians that no considerations of mercy would be allowed to temper the severity of Israel's retaliation policy.

Qibya represented one strand in the old Zionist tradition, the one against which Ahad Ha'am and others had protested, but which had been fostered by Jabotinsky and the militarists, for whom Ben Gurion became the father figure and Moshe Dayan the standard-bearer. It harked back to Deir Yassin in 1948[123] and the spirit behind it found expression again at Kafr Qasim in 1956;[124] in each case the Israeli authorities tried to make out that these atrocities were the work of individuals or organisations unauthorised by the machinery of the Zionist state, despite the fact that, whoever did authorise them (and in the case of Qibya it was the Israeli army, acting under the orders of the Minister of Security, who at that time was Pinchas Lavon), they had become, more and more clearly as time went on, the expression of an official policy which saw violence of an extreme kind as its necessary instrument. In the West such incidents were played down, or else justified as the response of a beleaguered Israel to the attacks of Arab "terrorists". But who were the terrorists, and why? Jews were more clear-sighted on this point than most gentiles, inhibited as the latter were by their collective sense of guilt and their unwillingness to be tarred with the brush of anti-Semitism. It was a Palestinian Jew who wrote in 1959, in answer to an apologist for Israel's treatment of the Palestinians:

> "If Rabbi Kaplan really wanted to know what happened, we old Jewish settlers in Palestine who witnessed the fight could tell him how and in what manner we Jews forced the Arabs to leave cities and villages . . . some of them were driven out by force of arms; others

were made to leave by deceit, lying and false promises . . . We came and turned the native Arabs into tragic refugees. And still we dare to slander and malign them, to besmirch their name. Instead of being deeply ashamed of what we did and trying to undo some of the evil we committed . . . we justify our terrible acts and even attempt to glorify them."[125]

Israel's overwhelming victory in 1967 seemed to mark the final triumph of the "activists", those who saw in the pre-emptive strike and the *fait accompli* the appropriate techniques for Israel's mission of colonisation in Palestine. Yet, paradoxically, it was that victory which, besides stimulating Palestinian nationalism, was to give new strength to the resistance movement within Zionism. Israel's occupation in 1967 of the West Bank, the Golan Heights, the Gaza Strip, the Sinai peninsula, and Old Jerusalem encouraged in the old generation in Israel, who still dominated the Zionist establishment, the mood of grandiose expansionism which was to lead to a renewal of the war six years later; but long before that happened, Israeli society was divided as it had never been before over the nature of the Zionist goal. Under the anachronistic leadership of Golda Meir, Israelis found themselves invited to behave in the newly conquered territories as their grandfathers had behaved in the Palestine of the 1920s and as though nothing had happened in between: no United Nations, no process of decolonisation, no Universal Declaration of Human Rights, no recognition by the international community of the reality of the Palestinian national consciousness. The result was that 1967, while it fostered among some Israelis the delusion that the frontiers of the Jewish state could be established wherever the Israelis themselves chose to draw them, awakened others to the way in which the original Zionist ideal had been distorted.

These dissenters included men who had played prominent roles in the struggle to establish and maintain the state of Israel. Natan Yalin-Mor, a former leader of the Stern Gang, the most violent of the Jewish terrorist groups in Palestine in the 1940s, came out after 1967 in opposition to the Israeli government's plans for territorial expansion at the expense of the Palestinian Arabs. Contributing to a seminar organised in Tel Aviv by the magazine *New Outlook*, he remarked that he had repeatedly risked his life for the freedom and political sovereignty of the Jewish people, which he would defend to his last breath. But he added:

> "I fought against an oppressor—but not in order that my own people should in turn oppress another people; I fought to establish the roots of my people in its homeland, but not so as to uproot another nation from its land. I am convinced that the struggle against chauvinism in Israel (which is driving my nation beyond reason), and for the rights of the Palestinian people, is the real struggle for the good of the state of Israel and its future."

Nahum Goldmann, the President of the World Jewish Congress, and one of the most respected figures in the Zionist movement, crossed swords with Mrs Meir's government over her refusal to acknowledge the rights of the Palestinians, observing that other Zionist leaders had made the same mistake of counting on military force and the intervention of foreign powers to attain their goals. Dr Israel Shahak, a former inmate of Belsen concentration camp and now President of the Israeli League for Human and Civil Rights, publicly and insistently denounced the discrimination practised against non-Jews in Israel and the ill-treatment by the Israeli Military Government of the Palestinians in the occupied territories. Professor Jacob Talmon of the Hebrew University in Jerusalem, one of the leading figures in a protest movement which developed among Israeli intellectuals, took issue publicly with the then Minister of Information over the same question of the rights of the Palestinians. In an open letter to the Minister (Yisrael Galili), he denounced the attitude on the part of the Israeli government after 1967 according to which "power has become our absolute aim and we consider the neighbouring people (the Palestinians) as instruments to fulfil our divine interests." Dr Talmon warned the Minister of the effect that illiberal policies in Israel would have on Jews outside Israel, recalling the words of a friend of his whom he described as "an educated Jew, a genius of this generation and a spokesman for the American Left":

> "Don't put us in a position where we are forced to choose between our loyalty to the human ideals we are fighting for and our loyalty to Israel. Remember always that everything has a limit and don't alienate us from you—don't force us to disintegrate."

Of all the warnings and admonitions addressed to Israel since 1967, Dr Talmon's is perhaps the one most likely to be heeded; for Israel without the diaspora, and especially without American Jewry and its powerful economic and political support, has no future. In adopting the Zionist ideal and politicising it, those who built the state of Israel risked cutting themselves adrift from the mainstream of Jewish life and thought. As things turned out, they proved stronger than those who disagreed with their approach and they were able to persuade most Jews to ignore, though they could never silence, those who spoke with the authentic tones of the Judaic tradition. This was true especially after the triumph of 1967, when their success, in material terms at least, appeared to be crowned with success beyond all imagining. But there was another war to come; and the war of October 1973, with its far more doubtful outcome and the blow it gave to the political and strategic concepts of the Israeli establishment, revealed also the doubts and reservations at work in the minds of many Israelis.

Visiting Israel three months after the October War, a particularly sympathetic British journalist wrote in *The Times*:

> "All of a sudden it seems blindingly clear, not to all, but to many, who had somehow looked the other way, that the permanent relegation of large numbers of people as second-class citizens will bring the Zionist mission to an end and may threaten the state itself. According to some religious thinkers, far from the political arena, a policy based on occupation will ultimately corrupt the essential value of Judaism itself . . ."[126]

Can Israel Change Direction?

Unless doubts such as these can be resolved—and they can be resolved only by a fundamental reappraisal of the relationship between the Israelis and their closest neighbours—the impression is likely to gain ground in the world that Israel in its present form is indeed a country without a future.

CHAPTER NINE

A New Look at the Future

Christopher Mayhew and Michael Adams

As the previous pages show, we reject entirely the moral, legal and historical arguments for Zionism, and would never argue for the continued existence of Israel on these grounds. Nobody who reviews the last half-century of Middle Eastern history with sympathy for the Arabs as well as for the Jews can avoid the conclusion that Zionism has so far caused more misery to mankind than it has alleviated. While a large number of Jewish immigrants have found new homes in Israel, large numbers of Arabs who used to live in Palestine have become refugees. Within twenty-five years, both sides have suffered grievous loss of life and property in four major wars, and the scale and frequency of acts of violence and terror seem to be increasing rather than diminishing. Since the foundation of the State of Israel there has been no increase at all— possibly a diminution—in the sense of security felt by Jewish people either inside Israel or in the Diaspora.

Year by year, the Zionists' case has been steadily eroded. For a long period they based their claims largely on the Balfour Declaration. But, as we have seen, the Declaration promised only a "home" and not a "state" in Palestine, and laid down safeguards for the Arabs which ever since have been neglected. Today we have access to the British Cabinet papers of the time, and can see for ourselves the shameless pressures, intrigues and deceptions which led to the publication of the Declaration in the first place.

Nor do the historical arguments for Zionism carry weight with world opinion today. God's promise to Abraham, as described in the

A New Look at the Future

Old Testament, has no validity outside the religious consciousness of Jewish people themselves;[127] indeed, the belief that most, or even many, Israelis are descended from the Jews who were dispersed from Jerusalem by the Romans is increasingly recognised as a myth. No doubt some Israelis are so descended; but many others are descended from Jewish people living at that time in Babylon or Alexandria, or in some other place outside Palestine, or, in many instances, from people who became Jews long after the dispersion and had no connection with the Middle East at all; for example, people living in Russia, Poland or the Yemen who were converted by Jewish missionaries. The fact that a Jew adheres to Judaism and speaks Hebrew does not necessarily mean that his ancestors lived in Palestine, any more than the fact that an African adheres to Christianity and speaks English means that his ancestors lived in Britain. The Jews, like the British, are a racial mixture. Despite age-old popular beliefs to the contrary, they cannot be distinguished from other peoples, such as Arabs, Greeks, or Italians, by physical features such as noses, hair or skin colour, as anyone can see who visits Israel today.

And what of the moral argument for Zionism: its promise of salvation from racial oppression? The Zionists themselves have destroyed this argument by their ruthless exercise of racial discrimination against others. Striving to create a state which would be, in Weizmann's phrase, "as Jewish as England is English", they have been led to condone the forcible dispossession of the non-Jewish Palestinians, and have applied rigorously the Israeli "law of return", which grants or withholds the right to live in Israel on a strictly racialist basis, actually excluding among would-be immigrants those who have the closest family and residential ties with Palestine.

In short, it is impossible to justify the continuance of the State of Israel on legal, historical or moral grounds. There is, however, a strong argument in favour of its continuance on grounds of expediency. For what are the alternatives? It would be neither practicable nor humane to require the immigrant Jews to return to their countries of origin. Nor is it possible, in the circumstances of today, to put into practice the Palestinian formula of an independent, democratic, non-sectarian state in all of Palestine. According to this idea, the "legitimate inhabitants" of Palestine would share equal rights, irrespective of religion or language. The term "legitimate inhabitants" would include all Jews now living in Israel who were prepared to renounce Zionism and live in a liberated Palestine, alongside and on equal terms with their Arab neighbours.

This conception of a united, multi-racial Palestine, in which Arabs and Jews coexist peacefully, is attractive in principle and has a wide appeal for that part of world opinion—perhaps the largest part—which does not understand, or which rejects, Zionist ideas. There is no reason to suppose that the Palestinian Arabs will ever abandon this deeply-felt aspiration, even if they have no early prospect of realising it. Their claim that Palestine belongs to the Arabs is at least as deeply felt as the Zionist claim that it belongs to the Jews, and by any objective criteria the Arab claim has a far greater validity in terms of history and natural justice. If it is not satisfied, it can be expected to persist and to retain its hold on the Arab mind for decades and probably for centuries to come.

But we still have to face the fact that, however attractive it may be in principle, this objective of the Palestinian Arabs is plainly not practicable for the time being. It may offer the best eventual solution, the ideal to which men should work by degrees, but for the moment the difficulties are insuperable. For example, it would imply joint control, by Arabs and Jews working together, of Palestine's defence and security—something which will plainly remain no more than a daydream for many years to come. There is no set of circumstances in which, in the foreseeable future, one can imagine the Israelis agreeing voluntarily to the dismantling of the Israeli defence forces. It is only possible to envisage a bi-national state coming into being after some sort of collapse of the power of the Israeli state, either through internal dissension or as the result of a successful external attack. While this certainly cannot be ruled out (if Israel's leaders are not wise enough to come to terms with their neighbours while the chance is there), it would be unrealistic to plan for the next stage in the Middle East on the assumption that such a collapse is an immediate possibility.

A New Look at the Future

For one thing, and leaving aside the question of Israel's ability to defend itself, the United States is pledged to prevent the forcible destruction of the State of Israel and, in the circumstances we are imagining, the pressures that would be brought to bear on the American administration to intervene directly and with military force on the side of Israel would probably prove irresistible. Nor would the rest of the international community, despite the provocation that Israel has given by its consistent attitude of contempt for the United Nations, accept without protest the suppression of the Jewish state. Not even the Russians, who have always insisted on Israel's right to survive within her proper frontiers, could be expected to take the Arab side on this issue. We have to conclude therefore that, however just and reasonable may be the case for a multiracial state in partnership in Palestine, as proposed by the Palestinians, it is not for the moment a practical proposition; and that there is no immediate alternative to the continued existence, in one form or another, of the State of Israel.

What that form should be and how long Israel can be expected to endure are of course very different questions. Indeed, when we turn our attention to the long term, Israel's capacity to survive without making far-reaching concessions, concessions which would severely modify the nature and potential of the Jewish state, seems very doubtful. So far, Israel has established herself, and expanded her territories, on the basis of her dominant military power. But since October 1973 the balance of power has shifted significantly against Israel and the shift seems likely to continue in the same direction.

The Arabs did not win the October War; indeed, they might well have lost it if the ceasefire had not come when it did. But long before that they had demonstrated their capacity to learn from experience, to fight bravely and to use modern weapons with coolness and skill. Even more strikingly, they had proved that they could combine in sophisticated military operations. If a settlement is not reached now, Israel's prospects are very bleak. She is likely to have to face another war, perhaps quite soon; and this war may not be a lightning war of conquest as in 1967, exploiting Israel's air superiority and strategic mobility, but a war of attrition in which the Arabs would have all the advantages arising from their enormous financial resources and their vastly greater manpower. In addition, the world-wide diplomatic and political influence which the Arabs now command would be a new and immensely important factor in the balance of power.

Even if Israel were able to win such a war, or to forestall it by another pre-emptive strike, what good would it do her in the long run? After all, Israel represents, in terms of territory and population, a mere two per cent of the Middle East. The idea that the Jewish two per cent can indefinitely dominate the non-Jewish ninety-eight per cent is manifestly absurd—almost as absurd as it would be to envisage Hong Kong extending its power over the whole of mainland China.

Could the possession of nuclear weapons save Israel? It seems certain that she has the capacity to produce them, and very likely that she has already done so. But these weapons, while increasing the danger of catastrophe, could not be of decisive use to her. In the first place, the nuclear threat would not be effective against Israel's most relentless opponents, the Palestinians. Of all peoples in the world, the Palestinians are the least vulnerable to nuclear attack, and the least likely to be deterred from violent policies by a nuclear threat. Moreover, if Israel does develop nuclear weapons, the Arabs will certainly do their utmost to develop or acquire them as well; and they could reasonably expect the Russians to place a nuclear umbrella over them, threatening retaliation against Israel. Even the United States could hardly be expected to condone the offensive use of nuclear weapons by the Israelis.

In spite of these considerations, if war did break out and if the Israelis did find themselves threatened with total military defeat, they might, with the same spirit of suicidal desperation as their ancestors showed before the Romans at Masada, launch nuclear weapons in despair. From everyone's point of view the prospect is an appalling one, not least for the Israelis themselves.

At present the Israelis have a technological advantage over the Arabs, which they can expect to retain for some time to come. But there is no reason to suppose that this differential will last indefinitely. As *The Times* commented in an editorial on the first anniversary of the October War, "Israel is dependent as never before on American support and time is not on Israel's side. The Arabs grow richer and stronger and better educated with almost every day that passes."[128] As long ago as 1971 the Arab World had some 600,000 university graduates, and there were 400,000 students in Arab universities with a further 40,000 studying abroad. These numbers are increasing rapidly, along with the spectacular growth in Arab population, wealth and educational facilities.

Israel must also expect a continuing decline in political and diplomatic support from countries outside the Middle East. Already she is extremely isolated, and has been condemned more often, and more unanimously, by both the Security Council and the General Assembly of the UN than any other member state. It is hard to see why this trend should be reversed: on the contrary, the continued improvement in Arab diplomacy and propaganda, and the increasing deployment of Arab oil and financial power, seem likely to intensify Israel's isolation from the rest of the world and in particular to weaken her strong but brittle ties with the United States.

These factors should also ensure a growing partnership between the Arab World and Western Europe, where the possibilities seem limitless. The Arabs are in urgent need of technological support of all kinds for their rapid development, and they will look for it to developed countries which pose no threat to their independence. Western Europe provides the obvious answer: an area linked to the Arab World by history and geography, more powerful than the Arab World but posing no threat to it, dependent on it and eager in return to offer the technical assistance which the Arab World requires.

In other regions—Africa, Asia, the communist world—the pattern of increasing Israeli isolation seems likely to continue. The links which Israel so painstakingly developed during the 1960s with the countries of Black Africa have all been broken. Only with South Africa and Rhodesia does it seem likely that Israel will be able to develop any further her existing friendly relations.

There is, moreover, another factor in the power balance which seems likely to weigh against Israel in the future. Hitherto, she has gained immensely from the divisions in the Arab World, by contrast with which Israel has appeared firmly united. In future, this factor seems likely to be less important. On the one hand, the Arabs show an increasing capacity to work together. Though there is still tension in varying degree between some Arab states, disunity is born of failure rather than success, and since October 1973 there has been significantly less internal conflict than before in the Arab World.

On the other hand, internal strife seems to have increased in Israel. There is growing tension between the dominant Ashkenazi, coming from Eastern Europe, and the Oriental Jews, who rank as second class citizens; and also between Israeli Jews and Israeli Arabs, who are at the bottom of the pile.

To sum up so far: the case for Israel's survival as a state rests on considerations of expediency and not on any legal, historical or moral right. Her survival even within her 1948 borders, let alone as an occupying power in the territories seized in 1967, cannot be taken for granted in the light of the change that is already taking place in the balance of power in the Middle East.

What options, then, are open to Israel and to the Arabs in the future? And what role, if any, should outside powers seek to play in the conflict?

On any realistic assessment, the options appear to be extremely limited for both sides. In the short term at least, for reasons which have been explained, the elimination of the State of Israel is not a practicable option for the Arabs. The threat of it would almost certainly provoke military intervention by the United States, and might goad the Israelis to resort to a pre-emptive attack with nuclear weapons. Even if there were no such pre-emptive attack by the Israelis and no intervention by the Americans, an all-out attempt to destroy the State of Israel would require from the Arabs a military effort well beyond their capabilities in the near future. And even if, against these odds, the Arabs were to achieve a total victory over Israel, they would still find themselves saddled with political and humanitarian problems which they would be hard put to it to solve. It has been clear for some years now that the leaders of the Arab "confrontation states" appreciate the strength of these arguments and that they have in fact abandoned any idea of eliminating Israel and have set their sights on a negotiated settlement.

At the other extreme it has to be clearly understood that the continuance of a *status quo* which allowed Israel to occupy territory beyond her frontiers and to deny the rights of the Palestinians offers no practical solution either. It would impose intolerable strains within the Arab World, since any government which accepted it (and with it the explicit violation of both the rights and the vital interests of the Arabs in general and the Palestinians in particular) would find itself at odds with its own subjects, with the Palestinians and with other Arab governments. The continuance of the *status quo* could thus lead to internal conflict within the Arab World, maintaining the dangerous instability along the borders between Israel and her Arab neighbours and threatening the continuity of the supply of Middle East oil to both the developed and the developing countries. These would be sufficiently grave dangers; even more acute would be the danger that such a solution (or non-solution) would lead to a renewal of the Arab-Israeli war, either out of frustration on the part of the Arabs or out of nervousness, leading to a pre-emptive attack, on the part of the Israelis.

For Israel, apart from the perils inherent in such a prospect, the continuance of the *status quo* would also greatly increase the difficulties the Israelis are already experiencing in maintaining their control over the Palestinians in the occupied territories, and even inside Israel itself. The improved showing of the Arab armies in the war of October 1973, with the transformation in the political balance of power which that war brought about, has already done much to revive Palestinian hopes of liberation and to strengthen support for the resistance movement. If these hopes are disappointed and there is no agreed settlement, a bitter reaction can be expected among the Palestinians, with the likelihood of sabotage and perhaps open revolt imposing on the Israelis the need to resort to even sterner methods of repression. The Israelis themselves might not shrink from these consequences, but they would do well to remember that already only American support stands between them and total isolation, and that somewhere there must be a limit to the degree of tolerance which the Americans are prepared to show to the methods employed by their Middle Eastern protégé.

Looking back now with the wisdom of hindsight, we can see that it was a mistake to attempt to impose a Jewish state on the Arab Middle East. We cannot tell yet whether the experiment is doomed to eventual failure, but clearly the possibility exists that sooner or later, unless the Israelis seek acceptance from their neighbours rather than domination over them, their state will go the way of the Crusader kingdom in the Middle Ages, whose history was in some ways so similar. But for the immediate future one thing, surely, is plain: that it is in the interests of both parties to the dispute to reach an accommodation with each other, an accommodation which would avoid the two extremes of, on the one hand, the elimination of Israel and, on the other, its maintenance as a Jewish empire carved out of territory belonging to its Arab neighbours.

The proper way to achieve this seems obvious enough: through a settlement based on the implementation of the resolutions of the United Nations, and in particular of the Security Council's Resolution 242 of November 1967. Such a settlement would restore to the Arabs the territories appropriated by the Israelis in 1967 and would make it possible to grant at least a measure of justice to the Palestinians: self-determination in the liberated territories, with repatriation to Israel for those Palestinians (probably not many) who chose to exercise this right, and generous compensation for the loss of their lands and property in Israel for those Palestinian refugees who did not wish to return.

The major objection to the idea of establishing in the liberated territories an independent, sovereign Palestine state is that these territories are small in area and have strictly limited economic resources;[129] moreover, there would have to be a corridor, with extra-territorial rights, to link the Gaza Strip to the main area of the West Bank. The state thus formed would certainly not undo the historic injustice that has been done to the Palestinians; nor of course could it provide a home for anything like the whole of the dispossessed Palestinian people. But it would go some way towards removing the central grievance which has kept the Palestine problem inflamed for more than a quarter of a century, and it is at least possible that it might provide the starting-point for an eventual co-existence of Arabs and Jews in the whole of Palestine. In any case, it is no more logical to deny the Palestinians the right to a state of their own, on the grounds that such a state could not accommodate all the Palestinians, than it would be to deny Israel the right to exist because it cannot contain more than a fraction of the Jewish people. As to the argument that a "mini-Palestine" state would not be economically viable, it should be remembered that the new state would be able to rely on receiving massive quantities of development aid from both Arab and non-Arab countries. It would also be open to its citizens, if they saw advantage in doing so, to join in a federation with the Kingdom of Jordan or, conceivably, with Syria—or even, in some not impossibly remote future, with Israel.

It is not in the least surprising that ideas of this kind should be distasteful to many Palestinians. Their unwillingness to accept them is understandable and logical. After keeping alive through a quarter of a century the concept of Palestinian nationalism, they are naturally reluctant to engage now in political bargaining which implies the modification, if not the total abandonment, of the Palestinian Arab claim to the whole of Palestine. Nevertheless, in the circumstances of an Israeli withdrawal, opposition among the Palestinians to such a compromise solution could be expected to weaken. Although few Palestinian Arabs will ever abandon completely their hope of a united Palestine—which could come about in any case, evolving peaceably from a long-term process of de-Zionisation within Israel—this half-way solution might be acceptable to enough of them to make a peaceful settlement viable.

Nevertheless, the establishment of a new Palestinian state would not be enough. A long overdue act of restitution also needs to be made to the Arabs who became refugees in 1948. According to UN

General Assembly Resolution 198 (III) of December 1948, they are entitled to a choice between repatriation to Israel or resettlement elsewhere with full compensation for their lost property. It seems likely that only a very small minority will choose now to return to their former homeland, to live under Israeli rule within a specifically Jewish state; almost certainly too few to constitute either a political or a security problem for the Israelis. Even so, to allay Israeli fears, the terms of the settlement might include an agreed annual quota which would set a limit to the number of refugees returning in any one year and so spread the repatriation process over a period of several years from the date of the agreement.

For those Palestinian refugees who fled from the area which became the State of Israel and who do not now wish to return, compensation and resettlement should be made available. The three nations most responsible—Britain, the United States and Israel herself—should be important contributors to the required resettlement fund.

After a settlement on these lines had been agreed and implemented, there would be several further ways in which the surrounding Arab countries could help towards peace and understanding in the region. They could, for example, accept willingly within their own frontiers, and treat generously, those Palestinian refugees who chose not to return to Israel and for whom there was no room in Arab Palestine. They could allow the new Palestine state to develop as independently of themselves as it wished, without trying to interfere in its internal development or international alignment. They could turn aside from their preoccupation with Zionism and concentrate on the positive side of the Arab renaissance. They could move towards unity not by feeble gestures and declarations, but by slow, secure stages, based on a growing habit of day-by-day co-operation. They could aim at a relationship with the Arabs in Israel which was neither more nor less intimate than the relationship they would wish to see Israelis maintain with Jews in Arab countries.

And what options are open to the Israelis? It will be seen already that they are few and narrow. The Israelis cannot hope to dominate their Arab neighbours, who are already on the way to becoming more powerful than themselves. It may well be that for the moment Israel has the capacity to defeat her neighbours in a sudden all-out war on the 1967 pattern. She may still be able to destroy a large part of their economic potential and to occupy Damascus, Amman and Cairo. But the pursuit of objectives such as these would impose a probably fatal strain on Israel's vital ties with the United States, and might also involve unacceptable losses in manpower and materials. Moreover, after winning their new "victories" the Israelis would find themselves saddled with a score of urgent new problems to solve, in addition to old problems which would remain.

And if a policy of all-out war is unrealistic for Israel, even more so would be a policy of limited war, offering the bleak prospect of permanent semi-mobilisation and continuing casualties over an indefinite period on a scale which the Arabs could afford but which the Israelis themselves could not.

And yet, as we have seen, the Israelis can only hope to maintain the *status quo* at the expense of all hope of a lasting peace. It follows that their best immediate hope lies in a policy of reconciliation, of purposeful negotiations for the best security guarantees they can get, in return for withdrawal from the occupied territories and acceptance of a Palestinian state in the liberated area.

The question is, can the Israelis make the necessary adjustment to their thinking? And can they make it in time? Can they be brought to see that the risks inherent in such a conciliatory policy are less than the dangers of a continued attempt at domination and occupation?

Unfortunately, the Israelis' judgment of their own security requirements is often extremely short-sighted. On several occasions since 1948 they could, with courage and statesmanship, have established a *modus vivendi* with their Arab neighbours, especially perhaps in 1954/5 and again after their overwhelming victory in 1967.[130] By tragic misjudgment, however, they have acted throughout on the assumption that their best chance of safety lay in imposing military domination on their neighbours, seizing and holding tactically advantageous territory far beyond their own frontiers. Yet it is obvious that a country which occupies tens of thousands of square miles of its neighbours' territory, imposing itself as a conqueror on more than a million people, cannot expect to live in peace and does not deserve to do so.

It is a sad feature of human nature that insecurity breeds aggressiveness. For historical reasons which every civilised person understands and respects, the Jewish people are haunted by an almost pathological sense of insecurity. It is almost universally believed in Israel, for example, that President Nasser stated that his aim was "to drive the Jews into the sea"—to destroy the Jewish people. There is in fact no evidence whatever that President Nasser ever made such a threat, even during the heady days of 1967. Yet the myth is still fostered in Israel, is very widely believed, and is of course very damaging to the prospects of a peaceful settlement.

The fact is that their pathological sense of insecurity has led the Israelis to seek power over their opponents in ways which, by tragic paradox, create the very dangers they are so anxious to avoid. It is possible to say at the same time that Israel's over-riding demand is for security, and that the actions which she takes are aggressive and likely in the end to prove self-destructive. In the past, for instance, Israel has opposed schemes for a settlement involving the substitution of an international force for Israeli troops in such strategically important parts of the occupied territories as Sharm El Sheikh and the Golan Heights. Instead she insists on retaining her conquests, so that her demand to be allowed to live in peace sounds increasingly hollow: like the plea of a burglar to be left alone with his loot.

What is tragic is that, in their search for security, the Israelis have behaved towards their neighbours with a ruthlessness which constituted a complete departure from the ethical basis of Judaism. Their treatment of the Palestinians has been inexcusable, and until they make amends for it the Israelis have no right to complain about the bitter resentment they have provoked in the whole of the Arab World. When they have driven so many innocent Palestinians out of their homeland and into the desert, there is something curiously insensitive about the Israelis' shrill protest that the Arabs only want to "drive the Israelis into the sea." Nor has the world ever given an adequate answer to the Palestinian who asked why it was so much worse to hijack an aeroplane than to hijack someone else's country.

Least justified of all, since it is not even prompted by a desire for security, is Israel's insistence on maintaining physical control over the whole of Jerusalem, which arouses particularly wide opposition among both Muslims and Christians throughout the world. Israel's attitude over Jerusalem has been condemned with remarkable frequency and unanimity by the General Assembly and by the Security Council of the United Nations. It has no basis in law, in history, or in natural justice, and by their refusal to modify it in any way in deference to Arab or international opinion the Israelis have put the most substantial roadblock of all in the way of the search for a peaceful settlement.

If the Israelis have proved poor judges of their own security interests, an equally dangerous misjudgment on their part has been their failure to recognise the reality of Palestinian nationalism. This has been from the beginning the fatal weakness of the entire Zionist concept. If Palestine had been uninhabited at the time of the Balfour Declaration, few people would have opposed its settlement by the Jews. The fact that the land was already occupied by large numbers of people, each one of whom had a better title to live there than had any Jew of the diaspora, constituted a fatal moral and political flaw in the Zionist idea. The Zionists, rather than face this crucial fact, have tried to wish away the reality of Palestinian nationalism by engaging in a series of rationalisations. They have tried to present the problem of the Palestinian Arabs as a refugee problem, and not a political problem. They have argued, against all the evidence, that the problem was created by the Arab states, who urged the Palestinians to flee and then deliberately maintained them in misery to be used as a political weapon against Israel. These are empty arguments, whose hollowness only underlines the fact that, with few and honourable exceptions, the Zionists have never dared to face up to the central problem confronting them: the old problem, now more acute than ever, of their relationship with the Palestinians.

The same thinking underlay Israeli reactions to the Palestinian resistance movement. Since it could not be a manifestation of genuine Palestinian nationalism, it must be something fostered and controlled by neighbouring Arab states; and therefore the best way of stopping it must be by punitive action against these states. In the event, since the diagnosis was faulty, because the motive behind the resistance was Palestinian nationalism and not the state interests of Israel's neighbours, the counter-measures were generally ineffective. The true remedy, granting justice to the Palestinians, involved a course of action that seemed distasteful to some Israelis and simply never occurred to many others. Now, however, faced with the reality of Palestinian nationalism and urged to permit the establishment of a Palestinian state on the West Bank, the Israelis ask what guarantee they would have, after such a state had been established, that the Palestinians would not use it as a springboard for further attacks on Israel.

They ask this question with good reason. It can hardly be denied that virtually all Palestinian Arabs would *like* to see the disappearance of the State of Israel, and it is natural enough that they should, since the creation of Israel meant the destruction of Palestine. There is no way of avoiding the possibility—or probability—that some Palestinians will remain ready to use violence against Israel even after a settlement, much as some Irishmen remained ready to use violence against Ulster after the Anglo-Irish Treaty. What is more important is that the mainstream of Palestinian opinion has come, after much heart-searching, to accept the idea of Arab-Jewish co-existence in Palestine; and the question now is not whether there will be Arab opposition to the settlement after it has been made, but whether that opposition will be sufficiently powerful and united to upset the settlement. This, fortunately, seems extremely unlikely.

In the first place the settlement would decisively reduce the intense feeling of frustration and resentment among the Palestinians, who would gain the right of self-determination in the West Bank, Gaza and Jerusalem. A settlement would see the emergence of a new Palestinian state, internationally recognised, welcoming back the 1967 refugees to their old homes. Most probably it would also see the

A New Look at the Future

majority of the 1948 refugees accepting the offer of compensation for their lost land and property in Israel, and thus, in effect, renouncing their claim to Israeli territory. Though the Israelis themselves seem unable to appreciate it, these events, while not giving the Palestinians all that justice would demand, would remove the deepest long-term threat to Israel's security.

And even if, in spite of all this, an irreconcilable section of Palestinians continued to work for the destruction of Israel, who would back them up? Would Egypt or Syria tear up the settlement, brush aside the UN forces in the demilitarised zone, breach the great-power guarantee of the frontier, and engage in a bloody war with Israel on their behalf? It is inconceivable.

It follows that the Israelis' best course is a complete reversal of their disastrous post-1948 policies, which, as their critics predicted, have gradually alienated them from world opinion and brought them to the edge of catastrophe. They should now negotiate purposefully and at reasonable speed for the best guarantees they can get. They should then withdraw to their proper frontiers, perhaps with minor rectifications, and contribute generously towards compensating the 1948 Palestinian refugees for the precious land and property they seized from them more than a quarter of a century ago.

However, to achieve a lasting reconciliation, other profound changes in Israeli attitudes and policies will be needed. Israelis should cultivate and show greater respect for the Arabs, especially the Palestinians, and for their history and culture. They should discard the Zionist myths about Israel's legitimacy and accept the harder, more realistic truths about the violence and injustice which their fathers used to establish their state. And they should accept limitations on Jewish immigration into Israel, at least until all Palestinians wishing to return have had an opportunity to do so; in this way they could demonstrate that they have no further ideas of territorial expansion and get rid of one of the major sources of Arab-Jewish bitterness in the Middle East, the notorious "Law of Return".

In general, the Israelis should abandon their grandiose dreams of domination and expansion, and seek instead to win acceptance from their neighbours. They should face the fact that their destiny lies in the Middle East and that they cannot maintain themselves there indefinitely by force of arms and by relying on foreign aid.

In the interests of Jewry as a whole, the Israelis should also show greater discretion in their relations with the Jews in the diaspora. It can be argued that the support of diaspora Jews will be a powerful help to Israel for decades to come, but this cannot be taken for granted. During the wars of 1967 and 1973, it is true, Jews throughout the world rallied strongly to Israel's support. But the idea that Israel is "the homeland of the Jewish people" at once raises an insoluble problem of divided loyalties for those Jews who prefer to go on living outside Israel. British Jews, for example, are British nationals; they have been born in Britain, to British parents, or else have been naturalised. They have no right to dual nationality, nor have most of them any wish to acquire it. To suggest that a particular section of the British people has rights and duties in respect of a foreign government, which the rest of the people do not share, is both distasteful and dangerous. To foster political differences between British citizens on the grounds that they are Jews or gentiles is objectionable in principle and likely in practice to foment anti-Semitism.

The dangers of divided loyalties are well appreciated by many Jews outside Israel. They see clearly that the claim of Israel to be the homeland of the Jewish people everywhere must prove untenable in the long run. For one thing, without territorial expansion there can never be room in Israel for more than a fraction of the Jewish people. And, quite apart from the problem of divided loyalties, assimilation and intermarriage are on the increase among Jews in the Western world, few of whom (from the United States fewer than two per cent) have emigrated to Israel. Religious faith, the bond that held the Jews together during the dispersion, is declining.

At the same time, within Israel itself new generations are growing up with no personal experience of anti-Semitism, or of exile, or of Jewish life in the dispersion, and without any deeply held religious faith. These people may increasingly lack the wish or the ability to act as torchbearers for the millions of Jews outside Israel. Indeed, insistence on the Jewishness of the Israeli state may increasingly seem to them irrelevant and provocative.

Any weakening of the "Jewishness" of Israel and of its ties to the Jews in the diaspora seems at first sight to be a source of danger to the state. But in the longer view it may point the way to Israel's ultimate security, through identification with its Arab neighbours and with non-Jews abroad, and through sharing of power with the Arabs in Palestine.

In writing this book, our main concern has been to obtain for the Palestinians some redress for the terrible wrong that has been done to them. But we believe also that those who genuinely have Israel's interests at heart should urge the Israelis to set themselves this new objective of reconciliation. Only in this way, it seems to us, can Israel's survival into the twenty-first century be assured.

APPENDIX A

The Guardian, 15 June 1967

The Foundations of Peace

Michael Adams

In the awful aftermath of defeat the situation of the Arabs looks desperate indeed. Their armies destroyed and much of their territory occupied, their economies in ruins, the bluster of Arab nationalism ruthlessly deflated, their morale subjected to a surely intolerable strain—what hope can there be of recovery from such a bottomless pit?

It is sad, but not surprising, that the jubilant Israelis, as startled as the rest of us by the completeness of their victory, should see no limit to the fruits it should bring them—in the immediate future. When the fighting started, Mr Eshkol's government disclaimed the intention to annex even one foot of Arab territory. A week later, General Dayan was talking casually of absorbing the Gaza strip, the old city of Jerusalem, the whole west bank of the Jordan, and the heights beyond the Syrian frontiers. I have no wish to argue about these claims, only to state as forcefully as I can that they will destroy any chance of creating in the Middle East an environment in which Israel will be able to live at peace.

It is realistic to say that Israel's lightning victory proves one thing, and one thing only. It proves that the Israelis are more adept than the Arabs in the manipulation of the sophisticated instruments of modern war. What it does not do is alter in any particular the moral balance of forces (and the Israelis are surely too realistic to deny that such a balance exists) in the Middle East. Putting this in more practical terms, the Israeli victory will not and cannot convince the Arabs that their cause is not a just one or that they do not have grievances which should be recognised. It follows that this victory, unless it becomes the prelude to a genuine attempt to refashion, not just the map of the Middle East but rather its pattern of realities, can only sharpen the resentments which have made life intolerable for Jews and Arabs alike, for 20 years.

A Sure Guarantee
The State of Israel was founded on force and so far it has been able to find no surer guarantee of its own survival. This is not for want of trying, but it is arguable that the efforts the Israelis have made to find an alternative guarantee have lacked conviction. However they have looked to the rest of the world, they have not reassured the Arabs that territorial expansion is not the true aim of Israeli policy. If Israel now seizes the first opportunity since 1949 to expand its boundaries (other than in removing minor inconsistencies), it will only confirm this deep-rooted Arab suspicion, and persuade the Arabs that not merely their best hope but their only one lies in rebuilding their shattered strength and waiting for the next round—when perhaps it will be they who will adopt the Pearl Harbor technique, with what may be deadlier weapons and in a suicidal mood of disregard for the consequences to themselves or to the rest of the world.

If this seems at the moment to be a possibility so remote that it can be disregarded, the Jewish people would do well to reflect on their own not so distant history. In 1943 or 1944 amid their unspeakable sufferings in Europe, and with little more than an uncertain bridgehead established under the British mandate in Palestine, who but the most romantic visionary could have looked forward a mere five years and envisaged the existence of an independent Jewish State triumphant over all the obstacles that beset it ? The Arabs too have their visionaries, less practical perhaps, less hardened by experience, but no less resolute than their Jewish counterparts. Is it certain that they are mad, after last week's debacle, to look forward five or ten or even fifty years to their revenge?

What, after all, is irretrievably lost? An army, some reputations (though not those that count), perhaps a few scraps of territory—a minuscule Alsace-Lorraine. And what remains? A physical presence in all the Arab lands that surround Israel, a rapidly growing population unversed in but no longer wholly ignorant of modern techniques and practices; tremendous economic resources in the shape of three quarters of the world's oil reserves and the Suez Canal (worth £80 millions a year to its owners); the backing of the whole Eastern bloc, so long as Israel tries to impose a settlement by force rather than seek one by international agreement; and, most potent and incalculable of all, the terrible frustration of a people that feels itself victimised, humiliated, ground down. The Jews indeed should understand.

And if they don't, what then?

If the Israelis want a peace as savage as the war, what freedom of choice does this leave the Arabs? They can submit, come submissively to General Dayan's negotiating table (for it is Dayan rather than Prime Minister Eshkol who seems to be the spokesman and the embodiment of Israel triumphant), and nurse in silence their grievance and their hate. Or they can maintain their refusal, which looks so unreasonable to those who live comfortably behind their own frontiers, to discuss or accept their own dismemberment, and can work and plan, with Russian help, for the next round in a battle which (on the time scale of history) has only just begun.

There should be no doubt anywhere in the world that if this is the choice which Israel offers them, they will adopt the latter course. It will condemn them to instability and extremism, to sufferings as pointless as those of an earlier generation of Jews, to revolutions and a recurrence of the bitter internal rivalries which have distracted them ever since the original Palestine tragedy. We in the West, and Israel too, and possibly the whole world, will live in the shadow of these consequences—and it is at least conceivable that out of them all will emerge a people as tempered by adversity, as hard and determined as the present generation of Israelis.

But there is an alternative. It too demands vision, but of a different kind. It too is beset by difficulties, but they are no greater. It too could provide a solution to Israel's terrible dilemma of how to find the means, other than war, by which to live in peace. Its starting point would be a disposition on the part of the Israelis to conciliate rather than any further to antagonise and humiliate the Arabs. Its essential condition would be the willingness to acknowledge, with no lessened emphasis on Israel's rights, that the Arabs have rights too. Its intention would be to right wrongs and remove grievances, rather than create more of both.

Its conclusion would be a settlement, rather than a "solution", a bargain, if you like, since nothing else can reconcile claims so conflicting and where each side is so much in the right.

Nothing Impossible
To those who object that such a settlement between Jews and Arabs is impossible, one can only reply first that nothing is impossible (and the Jews themselves have proved this) provided men want it badly enough; and secondly, that recent history suggests not only that it is possible, but that it could with unbelievable swiftness transform the pattern of the Middle East. After Nazi Germany had terrorised Europe and then been battered into snarling submission, how long was it before a generous peace had restored the German people to full European citizenship? How long did it take the new Germany to win the confidence even of Israel?

No one who knows the problems and the mental attitudes of the Arab world, who has sat, as I have, by the hour and been instructed in the dismal catalogue of Arab woes, would suggest that a reconciliation could be easy. But I believe that it is possible—and I am certain that in the present circumstances no other course offers even the smallest chance of a solution that can be permanent. At the very least, to attempt it now would put Israel incontestably in the right. It would be tragic indeed if she were to throw away the opportunity, when she has everything to gain, and nothing to lose but the world's respect.

APPENDIX B

Notices of Motions, 25 March 1970
17 Arms Delivery to the Middle East

Mr Christopher Mayhew, Mr Colin Jackson, Mr Frank Hooley, Mr Will Griffiths, Sir Dingle Foot, Mr William Wilson
That this House welcomes the refusal of Her Majesty's Government and of the United States Government to make further arms deliveries to the Middle East, likely to upset the balance of power; and urges Her Majesty's Government to work for a Four-Power arms embargo against any Middle Eastern country which rejects a peaceful settlement on the lines of Security Council Resolution No. 242.

As Amendments to Mr Christopher Mayhew's proposed Motion (Arms Delivery to the Middle East):

Mr Ian Mikardo, Mr David Weitzman
> Line 1, leave out from 'House' to first 'to' in line 2 and insert 'deplores the frantic, if dubiously successful, attempts of Her Majesty's Government to sell tanks to Libya, which is merely a front organisation for Egypt, a process which is'.

Dr Miller, Mr Paul B. Rose, Mr Stanley Henig
> Line 1, leave out from 'House' to 'urges' in line 3.

Mr Shinwell, Mr Julian Snow, Mr David Weitzman
> Line 1, leave out from 'House' to end and add 'deplores the persistent propaganda by an insignificant minority in the Parliamentary Labour Party on behalf of the Arab States and their hatred of the State of Israel, including their failure to recognise the persecution to which millions of Jews have been subjected which has made the creation of

the State of Israel and the need for its people to live in peace and security essential.'

Mr Arnold Shaw

Line 1, leave out from 'House' to end and add 'urges Her Majesty's Government to supply arms to such countries in the Middle East whose security is threatened by the imperialist intervention of the Union of Soviet Socialist Republics in that area.'

Mr Raymond Fletcher

Line 1, leave out 'welcomes' and insert 'notes'.

Mr Ian Mikardo, Mr David Weitzman

Line 3, after 'power', insert 'in the Middle East; notes that the honourable Gentlemen who have signed this Motion express no disapproval of Soviet deliveries of arms which have the same effect;'.

Mr Eric Moonman

Line 3, leave out from 'power' to end and add 'in the expectation that Her Majesty's Government will use every means at its disposal to urge the Government of the Union of Soviet Socialist Republics to similarly withhold not only arms but the movement of several thousand troops to Egypt, to be used, not only as advisers and technicians but as operators of weapons systems.'

Mr Edwin Brooks

Line 3, leave out from 'power' to end and add 'but hopes they will quickly remedy any imbalance due to the Brezhnev doctrine of preferring despotism to Socialism in the Middle East or elsewhere.'

Mr Raymond Fletcher

Line 3, leave out from 'power' to end and add 'but draws attention to the shift in the global balance of power being accomplished by massive Soviet arms deliveries to Arab states committed to a war involving, in President Nasser's words, "rivers of blood and horizons of fire" and the concomitant Soviet naval build up in the Eastern Mediterranean; and in the light of this shift in the global balance urges Her Majesty's Government to base its policy on arms supplies to any state in the Middle East only on cold calculations of the strategic interests of Great Britain and her allies, always bearing in mind Her Majesty's Government's wider policyof seeking four-power agreement on a timetabled implementation of Security Council Resolution No. 242 that safeguards the frontiers of all states in the area.'

Dr Miller, Mr Paul B. Rose, Mr Stanley Henig
Line 5, at end add 'namely Syria, Iraq and Palestinian terrorist organisations; and deplores the attempts of some great Powers to inflame the Middle East situation for self-interest at the expense of the legitimate claims of Israeli and Palestinian national aspirations.'

APPENDIX C

To the Editor of *The Times*, 27 June 1969

Sir,

As contributors to the supplement on Palestine which you publish today, we would like to make the following points:
1. You introduce the supplement by stating, with exceptional emphasis, that it constitutes a political advertisement sponsored by The Arab League and that *The Times* disclaims any responsibility for the facts or opinions expressed.
2. In a leading article you go further, describing the supplement as "extremely partisan" and categorising the contributors to it as "people in Britain who strongly sympathise with the Arab cause". The supplement, you add (in terms which Pontius Pilate would surely have approved), "is certainly not the sort of publication that is helpful."
3. The ethics of this procedure are interesting. You have accepted money in return for the publication of a series of articles which you are at pains to denigrate—on the ground that their authors express a point of view, and ignoring the fact that these authors are accepted authorities on the subject under discussion.
4. It is also interesting that you recently published a comparable supplement on Israel on your own initiative. The contributors to it were equally "partisan", although few of them could be described as authorities on the politics of the Middle East. Yet you saw no reason to comment in any way on their right to express their views or on the "helpfulness" of their contributions.

The fact is that if newspapers like *The Times* were willing to give equal weight to the arguments of both sides to the Middle East controversy, it would not be necessary for the Arab League or anyone else to pay to advertise the views of acknowledged experts in this field.

You also publish on the front page of today's issue a dispatch from your correspondent in Israel. This correspondent is, we understand, an Israeli citizen. Is he then less "extremely partisan" than ourselves, and do you consider the publication of his opinions to be necessarily more "helpful" than ours? If so, why?

Yours faithfully,

Ian Gilmour
Christopher Mayhew
Basil Aql
Geoffrey Furlonge
Michael Adams
Anthony Nutting

APPENDIX D

To His Grace the Archbishop of Canterbury,
Lambeth Palace   27/28 Oct. 1969.

Your Grace,

Members of this Council have watched with growing dismay the deteriorating situation in the Arab territories occupied by Israel since June 1967. Many reports have reached us, besides those published in the press, of the various ways in which Arab citizens of Jerusalem and the West Bank are being deprived of the rights guaranteed to them by the Charter of the United Nations, the Declaration of Human Rights and the Geneva Convention for the treatment of civilians.

Many have been detained without trial, some have been tortured, while others have seen their houses destroyed—all this by administrative action, without any legal process or justification. All of these contravene specific clauses of one or other of the international agreements I have referred to.

A particularly terrible example of this kind of victimisation is reported on the front page of today's *Times*. Here, according to the correspondent of *The Times*, 60 or 70 Arab families have had their homes destroyed in the village of Halhul, not far from Jerusalem, because one villager resisted arrest by an Israeli patrol which surrounded the village in the small hours of last Friday morning.

What this means, in human terms, is that some 350 to 400 people are now homeless and destitute, because *one* of their number dared, in his own homeland, to offer resistance to the soldiers of a foreign army of occupation. Collective punishments of any kind are specifically banned by the Geneva Convention, as is the destruction of domestic or public property except where it is made necessary by military operations. In this case, not only was there no such necessity but the villager who had at first offered resistance had already been persuaded by the Arab mukhtar to surrender. The mukhtar was rewarded for his intervention two hours later when (in the words of *The Times* correspondent) "the Israelis destroyed virtually the whole village."

The Arabs in the occupied territories are entirely at the mercy of the Israeli occupation forces. In theory they enjoy the protection of the international community, as expressed in the Geneva Convention—but the story in today's *Times* illustrates the gap between theory and practice. When I visited the occupied territories last year, many Palestinian Arabs (both Christian and Muslim) asked me why the Churches at least did not speak out in their defence and in condemnation of practices by the occupation forces which contravened all the canons of civilised behaviour.

May I ask Your Grace to give this matter your consideration and to see whether there is any way in which you could bring your influence to bear to prevent this kind of brutality on the part of the Israeli army of occupation? When the Germans engaged in similar actions in France or in Czechoslovakia, the world expressed its abhorrence. Can such actions be tolerated in the Holy Land?

Yours most respectfully,

Michael Adams
Director of Information,
Council for the Advancement of
Arab-British Understanding

APPENDIX E

Marion Woolfson's Testimony

After being suddenly widowed while in my thirties, I moved from Glasgow (a city I disliked, having been born in Edinburgh) to London because I thought I could earn more money there. My husband had a large number of relatives living in London and one of them, a cousin, invited me and my two young daughters to dinner. During the meal, the cousin's wife began talking about Christopher Mayhew, a Labour member of parliament (he later joined the Liberal Party and then received a peerage). I was astounded at the things being said about Christopher Mayhew who, I was told, was "evil, murderous, a Nazi and a terrible Jew-hater".

What, I asked, had he done to deserve such opprobrium? "He supports the Arabs," was the reply. Before the State of Israel was established (the Zionists always refer to it having "gained independence" which is completely inaccurate), Jews who lived in Palestine were always referred to as "Palestinian Jews" but then, suddenly, the word "Palestine" was forbidden and was never used. The indigenous Palestinian Christians and Muslims, whose ancestors had lived in the country for centuries, and who had been cruelly evicted by Jewish settlers, were called the "Arab refugees", the "Arab enemy" and then "the Arab terrorists".

In 1968, I was commissioned by Michael Christiansen, the editor of the *Sunday Mirror,* to go to India to interview the Prime Minister, Mrs Indira Gandhi, and also to write a series of articles on the status of women in that country. Then, Sandy Webster, the editor of the *Mirror*'s Scottish stable-mate, the *Sunday Mail,* suggested that I should visit Israel en route and write a series of articles about the aftermath of the 1967 war.

I stayed at a lovely two-storey Palestinian-run hotel in East Jerusalem, and I was fortunate enough to meet a group of non-Jewish American academics who were staying there. They put me in touch with some of their Palestinian friends, and I was appalled to learn about the savage treatment they had received at the hands of the Israeli authorities. Seeing a family group walking along the street, I remarked on the beautiful hand-embroidered dresses of the women, and a Jewish immigrant from London growled, "There's nothing 'beautiful' about them. They are filthy, treacherous Arabs."

Visiting Jerusalem a few years later, I did not stay at the same hotel. Above it, a number of Israeli flags were flying. It had been redecorated and the interior was garish and ostentatious. There was a "dairy restaurant" and a "meat restaurant" which indicated that the Jewish dietary laws, according to Leviticus, were being observed.

My series on Israel was not published because, I was told, it was "too critical". "But I have been just as 'critical' about other countries," I protested. The reply was "One doesn't criticise Israel." This was the first time in my journalistic career that something that I had written was rejected. No other newspaper would publish the series. John Knight, the features editor of the *Sunday Mirror*, said to me, on one occasion, "We are a pro-Zionist paper."

I noticed an announcement in *The Times* that the Council for the Advancement of Arab-British Understanding was holding a meeting at the House of Commons when there would be a talk on Palestine by an expert on the subject. I applied to join CAABU and was asked to go along to their offices to meet the two directors, Michael Adams and John Reddaway, who had formerly headed UNRWA (United Nations Relief and Works Agency, which provided assistance to the displaced Palestinians.) I imagined that all prospective members of CAABU were vetted until Leila Ingrams, who worked for the organisation and later became a close friend, told me that I had been summoned because I am Jewish. My credentials seemed to be satisfactory, and so I joined CAABU.

My views on Palestine had become known, and so I was ostracised by my former Jewish friends and all my husband's relatives.

One of them decided to give me a "last chance" and organised a "confrontation" during which I was to be harangued by a number of Jewish people who wanted to point out the error of my ways. I declined the invitation because I did, genuinely, have another engagement at the appointed time, but no one believed that, and so I was a coward in addition to being "a traitor".

Christopher Mayhew, "the rabid Jew-hater", and I became good friends, and we worked together on gathering material for a brochure on the activities of the Jewish National Fund and the way in which it purported to be a charity when it clearly was not one. Those who ran it in Britain seemed to have little intelligence because their gift to the Queen, on her silver wedding anniversary, was a forest of a million trees planted on Palestinian land in Galilee.

Christopher also wrote in *Publish it not* about the treatment I received from Jewish supporters of Israel. After the book was published, the situation became much worse with shoals of anonymous, highly emotional, abusive and threatening letters. One letter declared, "You have had sex (sic) intercourse with the Arab gangsters." My telephone rang throughout the night with voices screaming that I was "a treacherous, lying bitch" who was being paid vast sums of money by the "filthy Arabs" or, alternatively, that I was sleeping with the "filthy Arabs" and ought to be ashamed of myself.

Why, I often wondered, did there have to be some disreputable reason for my stance? Did it not occur to any of these brainless morons that I was telling the truth? And did it not occur to them that my life would have been much easier if I had been pro-Zionist? Perhaps savagery towards non-Jews simply did not matter.

I had visited women whose husbands, fathers, brothers and sons had been in prison for years, without charge or trial. Young people, who attended universities in Arab countries, were automatically enrolled in Palestinian student unions and on their return home they were, just as automatically, imprisoned by the Israelis for "membership of enemy organisations."

I had watched families being evicted from their homes without time to remove their possessions, and had seen their houses being demolished on various flimsy pretexts. I had seen the suffering caused by "collective punishments"—identical to those inflicted on the Jews by the Nazis—such as lengthy curfews lasting for days, weeks or months when a daily hour was allowed for food shopping but with no time to tend crops or feed animals, and those who were on the streets during curfew being shot dead. The sick and dying could not get to hospital, and women about to give birth often lost their babies or their own lives because of the cynical delays.

The telephone calls continued and so I had my number changed and made ex-directory, but someone had got hold of the new number, and several times during each night, a voice would say, "Are you still alive? That's a pity, but you will soon be dead."

A report from Tel Aviv in *Le Monde* on 15 July 1972 stated that: "Gangs of Keren Keyemeth (Jewish National Fund) workmen have begun systematically to destroy all buildings and houses in the town of Kuneitra, administrative capital of the Golan Heights area, in Syrian territory, occupied since the Six Day War." According to the Hebrew newspaper *Ma'ariv* on 13 July "the town will be entirely razed to the ground, and the territory upon which the buildings once stood will be *improved* (my italics) by being put at the disposal of the kibbutzim and Israeli villages now installed upon the Golan Heights. Only religious buildings and cemeteries will be preserved."

However, the Israelis did not evacuate Kuneitra until after the Kissinger-brokered disengagement agreement of 1974. I was one of the first journalists to enter the town where I learned, from UN observers, that the Israelis had brought bulldozers and built ramps to destroy the upper storeys of the remaining buildings. They had used the hospital for target practice and they had put diesel in the drinking water supply. They had also desecrated the Christian cemetery where the custom had been to bury corpses with their jewellery. This had been stolen, and even the gold fillings from teeth had been removed.

In addition to the destruction of every building in the town, all moveable objects had been looted. I was accompanied round Kuneitra by the former Medical Officer of Health. He showed me what had once been his house and the house of his parents-in-law. Both were in ruins, and none of the former occupants' possessions remained.

Although my report on Kuneitra was published (I was, of course, attacked for this in the *Jewish Chronicle*), as were those of other journalists who had visited the town, the British media declined to reveal details of other gross Zionist violations of human rights, and so I sent letters to the papers, and all of these were published.

On 11 October 1973 Eric Silver, the *Guardian*'s correspondent in Israel, wrote that during the recent war there was "no straggle of boots left behind by fleeing fellahin." The following day, the late Peter Niesewand also wrote in the *Guardian* about "The Arabs of the Six-Day War in 1967 who took off their shoes and ran away." I replied, quoting an Egyptian army officer (whom I had met on a train from Cairo to Alexandria in 1972). Apparently, the Arabs had been forced at gunpoint by the Israelis to take off their boots before being chased across the desert. "Do you think any Arab would be mad enough to walk without shoes on burning sand in the heat of June?" he asked. Many of the men sustained severe injuries. Michael Adams said to me, "I'm so glad you wrote that letter. I have been meaning to nail that lie for years."

Among the barrage of Zionist hate mail were some lovely letters from Akiva Orr, an Israeli living in London who became a good friend (he eventually returned to Israel to look after his elderly father), Jim Muir (he is now Middle East correspondent of the BBC), who later left London and moved to Beirut with his first wife and two young sons. They were living in Einab, in the mountains above Beirut, during the civil war, and we used to sit on the terrace outside a small, local restaurant and eat fried eggs (there was very little food available) and listen to the explosion of bombs, mortars and gunfire and watch the sky being lit up, as if by fireworks.

I also received a warm, complimentary letter from Soraya Antonius, a Palestinian writer who entertained me to lunch at her lovely flat near the harbour in Beirut, two years before the fighting (triggered by an Israeli attack) had begun. Soraya's father, the late George Antonius, was the author of the splendid book, *The Arab*

Awakening. Another of my correspondents was the late Dr Mohammed Mehdi, an Iraqi-born senior mathematics lecturer and an expert on the subject of Palestine. In fact, before I started reading massively on the subject, much of my information came from Akiva and Mohammed.

The late Fergus McKenzie also wrote to me. He was a journalist with the BBC whose life was ruined after he entered a competition in the *New Statesman*. He wrote, under a pseudonym, a very funny polemic addressed to Israel's Prime Minister Mrs Golda Meir (formerly Myerson, who was Russian-born, and had lived in America for many years) about the people squatting on her land. The Zionists discovered who had written the piece and denounced him as a "subversive". They reported him to the security services, and he was interrogated by members of the Special Branch. A number of very prominent Zionists demanded that he be dismissed, and the BBC meekly obeyed. The National Union of Journalists intervened, and he was reinstated, but he was told that he would never receive promotion. He eventually left the Corporation, and his life went to pieces after that.

David M. Jacobs, who wrote from his home address, accused me of not checking my facts "before rushing into print." He added that what I had written was "totally untrue", although I was able to prove that every word (about the fact that Palestinian passports were different from those of Jews) was absolutely true. What he did not reveal was that he was employed in the public relations department of the Zionist Federation. (I pointed out this fact in my reply.) He also wrote that the Arabs who had given me this information "found your Jewish surname useful" although, in fact, I had not received any information from Arabs.

Eric Silver, the *Guardian*'s correspondent in Israel, also attacked me in the readers' letters columns of the paper. I wrote, in reply, that "Eric Silver has been a Zionist long enough" to know the facts. I wrote this deliberately because CAABU had been trying for years to persuade the media not to employ Zionist Jewish journalists in Israel. Eric Silver did not deny the fact that he was a Zionist.

Appendices

After the Israelis shot down a Libyan airliner, which had strayed over Israeli-occupied Egyptian territory, killing all those on board, a group of Arab students decided to hold a silent protest outside the El Al (Israeli airline) office in Regent Street. Erich Fried and I joined them, holding placards stating that we were Jews. Then John Reddaway arrived, in black jacket, striped trousers and bowler hat, carrying a rolled umbrella.

A Jewish man, on a bus travelling along Regent Street, jumped off the bus when he saw us and came rushing over. He spat in Erich's face and then in mine. "Have you no shame, you treacherous bastards?" he yelled. We asked one of the numerous policemen there to arrest him, but he refused so we threatened to take his number and report him. He took the man's details and then arrested a Palestinian student for "obstruction". When the case came to court, the student was fined. The magistrate did not find the Jewish man guilty of any offence. He said, "I am sorry that you were so provoked. It must have been very upsetting for you."

In the succeeding years, my situation deteriorated. No newspaper would employ me, and the harassment increased. Arriving home one evening, I found two Special Branch officers waiting at my front door. They had been told that I was "a member of a pro-Arab terrorist organisation". I invited them in and offered them a drink. "The only pro-Arab organisation I belong to is CAABU," I said.

They laughed because CAABU, with its eminently respectable membership of retired British ambassadors to various Middle Eastern countries, members of parliament and academics specialising in the subject of the Middle East, was far from being a "terrorist organisation".

The *Jewish Chronicle* referred to me as "a nice Jewish girl gone wrong", and it occasionally questioned my sanity, calling me "confused" and "a self-hater". The only Jewish individuals in Britain who not only shared my views but were prepared to express them publicly were the late Mick Ashley and the late Erich Fried, who had lost most of his family in Hitler's gas-chambers. He was a well-known, award-winning poet and writer and translator of Shakespeare.

In an article entitled "At Odds With Their People" in the *Jewish Chronicle* on 25 October 1972, the late Richard Grunberger described Jewish critics of Zionism as practising "antisemitism" and suffering from "self-hatred". He referred to Erich and me as "two self-proclaimed Jewish pro-Arabists whose letters receive automatic publication in the British press." I was described as "a China traveller" (I had been sent to China by the *Sunday Times* to report on the Cultural Revolution in 1967, but he made it appear that I was some sort of "fellow-traveller" like those who supported the Soviet Union) "and journalist, writer of letters to the Editor and of independent means. She inherited some of her family's wealth, but seemingly little of their Jewish attachment." (This was one of many examples of the pretence that there was no difference between the words "Jewish" and "Zionist".) He had obviously assumed that I was a member of the millionaire, extremely pro-Zionist Wolfson family.

CAABU had organised a seminar, to be held at the Liberal Club. The day before the appointed date, a large notice, obviously emanating from a Zionist source, appeared in *The Times* and other newspapers which declared that the event had been cancelled. A meeting at Kensington Town Hall, at which I was to be among the speakers, had to be postponed and the hall evacuated because of bomb threats.

As I entered my house after returning from a visit to Damascus, I could hear the telephone ringing. The caller was John Dingle, London editor of the *Eastern Daily Press* and a member of CAABU. He told me that the paper had published a letter which stated: "Left-wingers and communists like Marion Woolfson support terrorism." It was signed "Frank Savage".

My solicitor immediately raised a libel action. While he was out, Mr John Levy (although he only gave his name, we knew that he was head of public relations of the Zionist Federation), telephoned my solicitor's office and said he would call back, but he did not. The letter gave an address in Regent Street. The headquarters of the Zionist Federation were at that time at 4-12 Regent Street.

The paper published a grovelling apology which stated that the letter had been written "under an assumed name by a political organisation." I received damages (which I donated to a Palestinian charity) and costs.

Each evening (and this was while my telephone number was ex-directory) salesmen from a number of double-glazing firms would call and then throughout the night there would be a procession of taxis "to take me to the airport". The trouble was that whenever the front-door bell rang my dog would bark and I got very little sleep. The taxi-drivers told me that, when they asked for a telephone number, the caller would say that I had just moved in and had no telephone. When the number from which he (or she) was calling was requested, the excuse was that the caller was at work and was not allowed to receive personal calls.

Then lorries began arriving from early morning, laden with cement mixers, sand or gravel so that the narrow mews in which I lived was totally jammed, and the lorry-drivers (who had all come from Kent or Surrey or somewhere else outside London) would be cursing. I tried to explain matters to them and to the double-glazing salesmen and the taxi-drivers but, not surprisingly, they found it difficult to understand what I was talking about.

Eventually, I had to move out of my house until the harassment stopped. Not long after my return, I found a large swastika painted on my front gate. I was about to take my dog for a walk one Sunday morning when I saw a car parked outside my house. One of the two men in it got out and took some pictures of me. I looked at the number-plate of the car but it was covered up.

Each year, the late Said Hammami (who was murdered in 1977), the first PLO representative in Britain, Mohammed Mehdi and I sent a notice to *The Times* in memory of the inhabitants of Deir Yassin who had been massacred on 9 April 1948, an atrocity that caused many of the panic-stricken Palestinians to leave their country because the Zionists threatened them with the same fate as the people of Deir Yassin.

In 1974 we sent our notice to the newspaper but it was not published. Instead, there appeared an announcement which said, "In loving memory of the brave soldiers of Israel who died in the battle of Deir Yassin."

I wrote to *The Times* pointing out that United Nations observers had testified that the houses had been sealed, hand-grenades had been thrown and guns fired through the windows, and the bodies of the people of Deir Yassin were found near the doors because they had tried, unsuccessfully, to get out. Furthermore, not even the Zionists pretended that there had been a "battle" and, besides, there was no "State of Israel" on 9 April as it did not come into being until 15 May. My letter was ignored.

My relationship with *The Times* was a strange one because, some years later, the paper published a number of articles I had written. My writings on countries such as Morocco and Iraq received no complaints, but then the paper published on 9 August 1978 a long article I had written concerning a report in the widely-circulated Israeli Hebrew newspaper *Ha'aretz* entitled "Persecution of Christians in Israel". Every word I wrote came from Israeli Hebrew sources. *The Times* published an angry letter from Dr Abraham Marcus of the Zionist Federation. Referring to me as "a propagandist", Dr Marcus deplored the publication of "an article from a member of CAABU, an organization that has established itself as a maligner of Israel." His letter ended, "The Jewish community of this country is deeply offended." As the letter was dated the day after my article appeared, I wondered how he had had time to consult "the Jewish community of this country".

I replied, denying that I was a "propagandist" and saying that I had joined CAABU nearly ten years previously "because of my interest in the Middle East, and in order that I might, like many other journalists and specialists, attend CAABU's excellent monthly lectures on various countries in, and aspects of, the Middle East. I did not consult nor inform CAABU about the article in question."

John Reddaway also had a letter published in the same issue of the paper in which he pointed out that CAABU had "a more lively concern for the true interests of the Israeli people than some of their so-called friends and supporters." He also referred to "the shortsighted folly, arrogance and injustice of Israeli official policy."

I then told John that I wished to resign from CAABU. He tried very hard to persuade me to stay, but I thought it best not to provide the Zionists with any more pretexts for implying that my membership of CAABU made me "a propagandist". I remained, however, in contact with CAABU. I learned from friends on the paper that leading members of the Jewish community had put enormous pressure on *The Times* not to employ me in the future, even threatening to cancel advertising and, as other national newspapers had succumbed to similar blackmail, that was the end of my journalistic career.

The Zionists, who had begun sending letter-bombs to those opposed to the idea of a Jewish State in the 1940s, renewed these attacks in the 1970s. They were determined to deprive the Palestinian people of any leadership and so they deported or killed doctors, lawyers, teachers and academics living in occupied Palestine, and sent letter-bombs to PLO leaders who were living abroad. The *Daily Mirror* published a cartoon of an Arab man saying to his secretary, "Take a letter-bomb, Miss Mustapha," although it was the Israelis, and not the Palestinians, who were responsible for all the explosive devices which, incidentally, killed a number of my Palestinian friends.

Dr Anis Sayigh, a much-respected Palestinian academic, who had been badly injured by a letter-bomb, was invited to his old college at Cambridge to receive an award. The *Daily Mirror* published a report under a headline "Cambridge to Honour a Terrorist." The paper was then edited by Michael Christiansen and so I wrote to him pointing out that Dr Sayigh had been the victim of terrorists, but received no reply.

After the Israelis invaded Lebanon in 1982, I visited the PLO Research Centre, which I always did on my visits to Beirut. It was run by Dr Sayigh, and I discovered that the Israelis had carted off all the books, documents and equipment so that the place was totally empty.

Although *The Times* had stopped commissioning work from me, to my surprise, a very long letter I had written to the paper was published in its entirety as the lead letter on 16 June 1982. I commented on a report that 5,000 British Jews had "packed the Albert Hall" to protest at the attack on Mr Shlomo Argov (Israeli ambassador in London) "and to demand the closure of the PLO office in London" because they considered the PLO to be "the cruellest, most ruthless, murderous and despicable evil organisation of terror, murder, death and destruction." I asked why those 5,000 British Jews had not considered that the PLO had repeatedly denied all knowledge of, and responsibility for, the attack on Mr Argov before indulging in what the report described as "emotional and highly charged scenes".

My letter ended, "Is there not even one prominent Jew in Britain who has the compassion, wisdom and courage to state publicly that he, or she, condemns *all* terrorism, whether perpetrated by states or individuals?" My plea was, of course, ignored.

Another letter in that issue of *The Times* was from my good friend, the late Peter Mansfield, who had left the Foreign Office because of Suez. From 1961 to 1967 he was the Middle East correspondent of the *Sunday Times* and he wrote many acclaimed books about the Middle East. In his letter he quoted Dr Robert Fisk, another expert on the Middle East, who had reported in *The Times* the suffering caused by the Israeli invasion of Lebanon—14,000 dead and wounded (the number eventually reached 17,000 killed and 30,000 wounded): "almost all of them civilians and most of them women and children... a Red Cross official said that more than 600,000 people had been driven from their homes." (Later reports described how the Israelis dropped napalm and cluster bombs on hospitals and schools.) Peter added that "Mr Yehuda Ben Meir, Deputy Foreign Minister of Israel had been reported in *The Times* on 14 June as saying "there had never been a more just war" (sic). No comment."

Then, a huge rock was thrown through my large, plate-glass, dining-room window with such force that it broke the wall opposite. Fortunately, I was not in the room at the time. (There was a similar incident last year when the missile crashed through my bedroom window, at my present home, at 2 a.m. I tell myself this was merely the action of a local hooligan.)

Soon afterwards, a man called at my house. He said he had come especially from Manchester to see me because he shared my views.

Like a fool, I invited him in. He looked around and said, "This is a lovely house. How much do the Arabs pay you?"

I asked him to leave. He said I deserved "a good beating-up". The first thing that occurred to me was to call for help to an imaginary person upstairs. My visitor said he had decided not to attack me this time, but if anyone followed him, there would be trouble because he had "people outside".

A few days later, I went into the garden to empty some rubbish into a dustbin which was kept in a small outhouse near the front door. Suddenly, I heard a noise and turned round. A man, who had obviously been hiding in a large clump of bushes, and had what looked like a metal cosh in his raised hand hit me on the forehead instead of the back of my head which had obviously been his intention before I turned round. As I ran back into the house, he hit me, with some force, on my back which caused a nasty injury.

Shortly afterwards, an Early Day Motion in the House of Commons stated: "That this House salutes the courage and integrity of Mrs Marion Woolfson, one of the United Kingdom's most distinguished Jewish citizens for her condemnation of terrorism in her letter in *The Times* newspaper of 16 June and her criticism of the terrorism of the present Israeli government: condemns the cowardly terrorist attack on her, on her own doorstep: and awaits condemnation of that attack from one or more prominent British Zionists." There was nothing but a deafening silence from the British Zionists.

Suddenly, I saw a policeman in my garden. What was he doing there? He was, he said, guarding me, having been instructed to do so by the Home Office. It was time, I thought, to leave London.

When President Clinton was invited to Britain in 2001, by the Jewish National Fund, to give talks at fund-raising dinners in Glasgow, London and Manchester (with tickets costing £100 each) to celebrate the Jewish National Fund's centenary, I thought it would be a good idea to write an article about the JNF and its charming regulations, which state that non-Jews may not live nor work on its land (much of it illegally expropriated from its Palestinian owners). The bizarre treatment I received from two national newspapers (which, naturally, refused to publish what I had written) will be detailed elsewhere when I will be happy to reveal many appalling facts about the increasing savagery of the Israeli authorities which would have caused Christopher and Michael much despair had they lived longer.

2005

APPENDIX F

Hidden Hands?

By Shelby Tucker

Such was the noise made about a controlled press in the "police states" under Communist rule in the fifties and sixties that it did not occur to those of us who were young then to question whether the British or American media were controlled.

For me, the first intimation of this possibility came with reports of opinion polls taken in Britain and America during the 1973 war between Israel and Syria, Jordan and Egypt. Half of those interviewed in Britain expressed a preference for Israel, while nine out of ten people interviewed in the United States expressed a preference for Israel. Same war, same antagonists, but such a marked difference in public opinion imputable to the different *reporting* of this war in Britain and America. It was only when I read *Publish it not*, however, that I learned just how pervasive Zionist control of our media was and recognized the extent and effectiveness of its indoctrinating power. That was the moment that I changed my allegiance in this cause. It was the simple response of a man who awakened to the fact that he had been lied to.

"The essence of [*Publish it not*] is to show how some… Zionist deceptions were accomplished in the United Kingdom, how it *was* done, being not so very different from how it *still is* done," Tim Llewellyn writes in his Foreword. He points out that Adams and Mayhew wrote at a time when it appeared that honest coverage of the Middle East was at hand, and adds, alas, "I am afraid I would have to tell the two writers were they able to hear me that the forces they so bravely resisted are stronger than ever."

I have experienced these Adams and Mayhew resisted forces myself. I will mention three instances.

In 1973, Secretary of State William Rogers interviewed live over one of the three American radio networks, stated (more or less verbatim), "We believe that it is increasingly inappropriate, in view of US support for Security Council resolutions 242 and 338, for the Arabs to continue to interpose against us their oil embargo." However, when the interview was broadcast over one of the three national television networks later that day, what transmitted was, "We believe that it is increasingly inappropriate for the Arabs to continue to interpose their oil embargo against us." The reference to US support for two Security Council resolutions mandating Israel to return to its 1967 borders had been excised, lest those hearing it investigate and learn what these resolutions required of Israel.

In 2001, I watched an interview of an Arab scholar on American Broadcasting Company (ABC), a television network in the United States. The subject of the interview was a statement made by an American diplomat working in the Middle East. The scholar praised the diplomat's Arabic and discussed his statement in general, and the interview proceeded in a friendly way, until he said, "The only problem with the ambassador's statement was, it did not mention the central issue." "And what was that?" asked the interviewer? "The Palestine-Israel issue, of course," the scholar replied. "Well, we'll just take a station break!" said the interviewer, and the interview ended.

My final example of these "forces" at work (I could give many more examples) relates to two books that a leading review journal commissioned me to review recently. Aware of the sensitivity of the subject, I read both books carefully, twice, spent a fortnight re-reading various books pertinent to the subject, wrote the review and sent it to a number of people better informed about the subject than I, seeking their suggestions. Then I submitted the review to the review journal. It sent me the proofs. I corrected them and returned the corrected proofs to the review journal. Two months later I rang the review journal to ascertain what had happened to the review. A lady advised me that she would inquire and get back to me, and, later that day, I received the following email from her:

Dear Shelby Tucker

I'm afraid that the editor has decided against using your piece on The Question of Zion. He doesn't feel that the review is right for [us]. I'm sorry to disappoint you. You will however receive a fee, and I'll put forward your details to the relevant department. I'll also let [the editor who commissioned the review] know.

Best wishes

Here is the review. The reader may judge for himself why it was not "right for" this review journal.

Shelby Tucker

Jacqueline Rose
The Question of Zion
202 pp. Princeton University Press. £12.95. 0691 117500

John Rose
The Mythis of Zionism
232 pp. Pluto. Paperback £14.99. 07453 20554

Jacqueline Rose and John Rose represent a swelling tide of "diaspora" Jews who deplore actions by the Zionist state perpetrated in the name of Jewry and Judaism.

In 1917, when the British Government declared its intention to establish "a National Home for the Jewish people" in Palestine, Jews comprised less than eight per cent of Palestine's population; almost all of the remaining 92-plus per cent were *filastiniyyoun* (Philistines, Palestinians). It is true that a small community of Jews had lived there for more than two millennia, just as there have long been Jewish minorities in Europe and America, but this is very different from allowing that Palestine has always been a "common" land "shared" by Jews and Arabs, as Professor Jacqueline Rose suggests. Rose also repeats uncritically the "myth" that Zionist enterprise in Palestine "made the desert bloom". The steep limestone hills and the Negev were bare in biblical times and are bare today, but the coastal plain, Galilee and the Jordan Valley abounded in grains, fruits and vegetables long before Zionist settlement. Laurence Oliphant described the Vale of Esdraelon in 1887 as "a huge green lake of waving wheat" presenting "one of the most striking pictures of luxuriant fertility ... possible to conceive"; and Arthur Ruppin, Zionist settlement leader from 1907, lamented that there was "hardly any land which is worth cultivating that is not already being cultivated". These are my only misgivings about Professor Rose's book, which on the whole is an earnest attempt at explaining the triumph of militant over ideological Zionism and the disastrous implications for Israelis, Palestinians, Jewry and Zionism itself.

David Ben-Gurion, Israel's first prime minister, we learn, imputed the new nation's success to "spiritual superiority", decreeing in his memoir that "it is only an elite nation that can produce an elite army" – which Professor Rose paraphrases as "we kill better because we are better". Such an ethos, the ethos of Zev Jabotinsky, Menachem Begin and Ariel Sharon, she suggests, derives from a communal obsession with Jewish shame and suffering. Tens of thousands of high school students "make pilgrimages to Auschwitz to discover their 'roots'"; Israeli reservists serving in Hebron are sent on a visit to Auschwitz to "strengthen their military resolve"; and, when questioned about the deaths of Palestinian children, the army commander in Gaza replies, "I remember the Holocaust". When the Knesset enacts in August 2003 a law preventing Palestinians who marry Israelis from living in Israel, it is to preclude repetition of Jewish shame by ensuring the survival of a "Jewish" state. When Israeli soldiers compel an elderly Palestinian to kiss his donkey's bottom or "force young Palestinian men to bark like dogs", it is to show them who is master now. Palestinians, described by the Hebrew writer and Labour Zionist

Moshe Smilansky in 1913 as "semi-savage people with extremely primitive concepts" and by Chaim Weizmann in 1930 as "squatters who did nothing except superficially scratch" the land of *Eretz Yisrael*, have become the "symbolic substitutes" of the progenitors of the Holocaust, which excuses all.

"Today, as a matter of policy," Professor Rose states, "the Israeli army breaks the bones of the Palestinians." There was another kinder, more humane Zionism, that of Ahad Ha-'Am, Gershom Scholem, Hannah Arendt, Martin Buber and Hans Kohn, to whom Israel was meant to be "a light unto nations". "How did we get from there to here?" Rose asks. "The Jewish nation is in danger of destroying itself," she concludes – as any nation that is incapable of honest self-examination.

John Rose, self-styled "veteran from the 1968 student revolution", maintains that "Zionism is held together by a series of myths ... that have become part of Zionist folklore". Examples of these "myths" include: the belief that there is racial and ethnic continuity between biblical Israelites and modern Jewry; that Jews endured ubiquitous, unrelieved suffering, ostracism and persecution from the fall of the Second Temple in 70 AD until the establishment of the State of Israel in 1948 and, throughout their long "exile", longed to "return" to the "Promised Land"; that Zionism is not a project of ethnic cleansing to replace the indigenous population of Palestine with "Jewish" immigrants, but a "liberation movement"; that Palestine was an uninhabited land coveted by a landless people before Zionist colonization; that the Bible mandates the establishment of a Jewish state in Palestine; that Israel has always sought, and its Arab neighbours have always rejected peaceful relations. Rose in his broadly encompassing, informative, unforgivingly honest book, ten years in the making, sets himself the task of unravelling this "folklore" and succeeds admirably.

He points out that Israeli archaeologists excavated in Palestine for more than five decades in search of Ancient Israel, the United Monarchy of David and Solomon of the 10th century BC, extending from the Euphrates to Egypt, before "the realisation began to dawn that it just might not be there". Contrary to "the Zionist myth at the core of modern Israeli identity", *Eretz Yisrael* was "at most a small tribal kingdom, if it existed at all", while the god of this "notorious visionary geographical concept", the "God of Israel", was a pagan deity with a female consort named Asherah, who demanded animal and other sacrifices, as Canaanite and all other deities in the region. Of the "myth" that Arab-Jewish relations are inherently adversarial, Rose reminds us that Zionism destroyed a rich, symbiotic Judeo-Mesopotamian-Judeo-Arab-Judeo-Islamic culture that existed for 2600 years with terrorist tactics such as planting bombs in synagogues to promote the "ingathering" of Jews from Arab lands. Indeed, Rose is at his ferocious best when probing the wellsprings of Zionist fanaticism. In 1938, Roosevelt convened the Evian conference to co-ordinate an international solution for the flood of Jewish refugees from Germany. Ben-Gurion opposed the conference and opposed a British plan to allow several thousand Jewish children into the UK. Ben-Gurion: "If I knew that it would be possible to save all the children in Germany by bringing them over to England, and only half of them to *Eretz Yisrael* [Palestine], then I would opt for the second alternative."

Supporting the two Roses are "post-Zionist" Israeli writers and historians such as Simha Flapan, Benjamin Beit-Hallahmi, Ephraim Nimni, Uri Avneri, Ilan Pappé, Tom Segev, the late Israel Shahak, Meron Benvenisti and Avi Shlaim, who are unwilling to perpetuate the "myths" of their predecessors. Perhaps together they will succeed in forcing upon the nation honest self-examination.

NOTES

1. *Jewish Chronicle*, 7 June 1974
2. Maxime Rodinson, *Israel and the Arabs*, Penguin Books, London, 1968
3. This is not the place to pursue the question, but I would refer the reader who is interested in doing so to Doreen Ingrams, *Palestine Papers 1917–1922, Seeds of Conflict*, John Murray, London 1972
4. *The Guardian*, 15 June 1967. The article is reproduced in full in Appendix A.
5. Mr Lever was a senior minister in later Labour governments.
6. *Hansard*, 10 June 1948, columns 2265–7
7. Such as Mr Sidney Goldberg, quoted in Chapter 4, p. 58
8. However, the former Stern Gang leader, Mr Natan Yalin Mor, was shown this letter recently, and denied its authenticity.
9. *The Jewish Chronicle*, 16 October 1969
10. See Chapter 8, pages 152-8
11. "It would be an offence against the principles of elemental justice if these victims of the conflict were denied the right to return to their homes while Jewish immigrants flow into Palestine, and, indeed, offer at least the threat of permanent replacement of the Arab refugees who have been rooted in the land for centuries." Count Folke Bernadotte, Report to UN Secretary General, 16 September 1948
12. "Gordon Walker, appointed Foreign Minister, apparently wanted Mayhew as his deputy. But Mayhew did not get the post. Why?
    "In London there are rumours that the leaders of the Jewish community in Britain, or Israeli friends of Wilson, brought to the Prime Minister's attention the dangerous misunderstandings that might result from such a nomination. How can a pro-Arab be put in charge of Middle East affairs, while Wilson claims to treat Israel with friendship?" *Ma'ariv*, Jerusalem, 14 July 1974
13. *The Times*, 16 September 1970
14. PRO FO371/3058, quoted by Doreen Ingrams, *Palestine Papers 1917–1922*, John Murray, London 1972
15. PRO CAB23/4
16. PRO CAB22/4
17. PRO FO395/202, quoted by Doreen Ingrams, *op. cit.*, page 19

18. PRO FO371/3395
19. For this quotation, which comes from Beatrice Webb's diaries for 1924/1932, edited by Margaret Cole, Longman Green, London 1956—and also for other quotations and information relating to the early influence of Zionism on the Labour Party—I am greatly indebted to Mr David Watkins, MP, who is Chairman of the Labour Middle East Council.
20. Drummond Shiels, "Sidney Webb as a Minister", essay included in *The Webbs and their Work*, edited by Margaret Cole, Muller, London 1949, page 213, footnote
21. A remarkable first-hand account of the 1929 riots is contained in Vincent Sheean's *In Search of History*, Hamish Hamilton, London 1935, pp. 391–407
22. Chaim Weizmann, *Trial and Error*, Harper Brothers, New York 1949, p. 335. See also Alan R. Taylor, *Prelude to Israel* (an analysis of Zionist diplomacy 1897-1947), Darton, Longman & Todd, London 1961
23. Mr Walter Elliott, at that time Secretary of State for Scotland.
24. Professor Sir Lewis Namier, the famous historian.
25. Dr Chaim Weizmann, the Zionist leader

William Ormsby Gore (Lord Harlech), the Colonial Secretary.
27. Moshe Shertok, who later changed his name to Sharett and became the first Foreign Minister of Israel.
28. *Diaries of Blanche Dugdale*, Valentine Mitchell, London 1973
29. Professor Hugh Thomas, *John Strachey*, Eyre Methuen, London 1973, pages 228–229
30. Richard Crossman, later a senior Cabinet Minister in the Labour Government, and a fervent Zionist.
31. Author's italics.
32. *1944 Annual General Conference Report* page 9
33. Chaim Weizmann, *Trial and Error*, page 535
34. This question is discussed in Chapter 8.
35. See for example Chapter 2, page 17
36. Kingsley Martin, *Harold Laski*, Victor Gollancz, London 1953, pages 206/219
37. *Jewish Chronicle*, 18 October 1974
38. *Hansard*, Volume 747, cols. 142/53, 31 May 1967. I am grateful to Mr David Watkins, MP, for this piece of research.
39. *The Guardian*, 7 June 1967
40. Since these amendments convey something of the bitter and emotional nature of Zionist propaganda at the time, they are reproduced in full in Appendix B.
41. *Jewish Chronicle*, 24 November 1972

42. See for example *Socialist Worker*, 30 March 1974, and *Private Eye*, 6 May and 23 May 1974
43. Letter of 15 May 1970
44. *The Times* and *The Guardian*, 28 December 1972
45. 29 December 1972
46. PRO FO371/4153, quoted by Doreen Ingrams, *op. cit.*, pages 47, 48
47. Doreen Ingrams, *op. cit.*, pages 92, 93
48. A. J. Balfour, Memorandum to Lord Curzon, 11 August 1919. PRO FO371/4183
49. Public Record Office File CO733/35 quoted by Doreen Ingrams, *Middle East International*, Volume 12, March 1972
50. Perhaps with the notable exception of Paole Zion, an affiliated organisation, which in practice operates a racial test for membership.
51. In a letter published in the *Jerusalem Post Weekly* on 29 January 1974, the Counsellor for Information at the Israeli Embassy in London, Mr Benad Avital, defended the Israeli information services against the charge that they had failed to put over the Israeli case. Writing specifically about the debate in the House of Commons on 18 October 1973, Mr Avital claimed that "... our Ambassador and I met personally with more than 100 MPs shortly before the debate, and when I entered the House of Commons to listen to the debate, I had to thread my way through an enormous crowd, apparently entirely pro-Israel, who had appointments to see their MPs. According to the Anglo-Jewish press, they were there at the behest of the same Zionist leadership which Mr Driver believes was inactive." Mr Avital added that, because Israel's resources for propaganda work were limited, "inevitably, we concentrate on target-groups which we consider opinion-making, rather than on every man in the street. *This policy has so far paid well.*"(Author's italics)
52. The Israelis, it is worth remembering, have experienced a good deal of difficulty in deciding among themselves just who is a Jew.
53. November 1970
54. Author's italics.
55. Zionist contributions to political leaders, and the consequent influence of the Jewish lobby in the United States, are discussed with singular frankness in an article by Dan Margalit in the weekly supplement of the Israeli newspaper *Haaretz*, 20 September 1974, reprinted in *Israeli Mirror*, Middle East International Publications, No. 34, October 1974
56. Edwin Montagu, "The Anti-Semitism of the Present Government", 1918
57. See Chapter 5
58. *The Middle East: A handbook*. Anthony Blond Ltd, London 1971

59. *Evening Standard*, 14 March 1973. *The Palestine Problem* was eventually published by Martin Brian and O'Keeffe at the end of 1973
60. *Jewish Observer and Middle East Review*, 17 November 1972
61. *Israel and the Arabs* was eventually reviewed, very favourably, by *The Times Literary Supplement*—oddly, in the French edition.
62. My counsel left out my most effective piece of evidence: the fact that my television film about Judaism pleased some members of the Jewish community so much that they actually planted a grove of trees in my honour in Israel: the "Christopher Mayhew Grove".
63. Letter to Christopher Mayhew of 8 May 1970
64. Memorandum to Christopher Mayhew, August 1974
65. Nor, of course, about either the press or television in the United States.
66. See Doreen Ingrains, *Palestine Papers 1917-1922* John Murray, London 1972, p. 58
67. See the article "Seeing for Oneself", by Colin Wilson, in *Middle East International*, November 1974.
68. The Chairman of the Israeli League for Human and Civil Rights, Dr Israel Shahak, has been documenting evidence about the torture of Palestinians since 1967, evidence which is available to the British press, and has three times addressed Public meetings in London on the subject, but his protests have met with little response from the national newspapers and with none at all from the BBC.
69. The situation is not much better today, except that *The Times* now employs as its correspondent in Jerusalem an Englishman, Eric Marsden, who has made a notable effort to give fair coverage to both sides of the argument.
70. Article by Harold Jackson in *The Guardian*, 4 June 1968
71. I am happy to say that he later modified this injunction.
72. The letter is reproduced in full in Appendix C.
73. *The Guardian*, 26 October 1969
74. *International Review of the Red Cross*, Nos. 113 *and* 114, published by the International Committee of the Red Cross, Geneva, August–September, 1970
75. *The Transformation of Palestine*, edited by Professor Ibrahim Abu-Lughod, North-western University Press, Evanston, Illinois 1970
76. See Chapter 7
77. Despite the fact that in John Bulloch the *Telegraph* had a Middle East correspondent notable for his forthrightness and objectivity.
78. *Daily Mail*, 8 October 1973
79. *Daily Telegraph*, 8 November 1973
80. See Chapter 1, pp. 13–14, and Appendix A.
81. Toynbee *op. cit.*

Notes

82. A letter to Mr Michael Adams, Council for the Advancement of Arab-British Understanding, dated 23 January 1974
83. Letter to Michael Adams, 16 October 1973
84. Letter to Christopher Mayhew of 7 March 1974 (my italics)
85. Letter to Michael Adams, 29 April 1971
86. The series was called *The World About Us* and the programme under discussion was shown by the BBC on 17 February 1974
87. The idea that the state of Israel represents the fulfilment of biblical prophecy has been effectively dealt with by Professor Alfred Guillaume, later Professor of Old Testament Studies at the University of London, and by Rabbi Elmer Berger and others. See the collection of essays published under the title of *Christians, Zionism and Palestine* by the Institute for Palestine Studies in Beirut.
88. *Sunday Times*, 15 July 1969
89. See Chapter 5, pp. 73–4
90. The letter to the Archbishop is reproduced in full in Appendix D.
91. *Search for Peace in the Middle East*, American Friends Service Committee, Philadelphia 1970
92. Dr Al Forrest, *The Unholy Land*, McClelland and Stewart, Toronto 1971
93. *La Civiltà Cattolica*, 19 June 1971
94. In his foreword to the book *Information and the Arab Cause* by Abdel-Kader Hatem (Longman 1974) the experienced Middle East correspondent of the *Daily Telegraph*, John Bulloch, wrote after the war: "For it was clear within hours of the outbreak of fighting that this time the communiqués issued in Cairo were telling the truth, and in their factual simplicity were in marked contrast to the rather hysterical commentaries being broadcast from Israel . . ."

    The *New York Times* correspondent in Israel, Terence Smith, wrote that "the credibility of Israeli information in the past was generally regarded as high by most of the newsmen here. But in this war, the feeling is that it has diminished. . . . A significant credibility gap developed on the third night of the war when Lieut. Gen. David Elazar, the Israeli Chief of Staff, spoke at a huge news conference in Tel Aviv and pictured the enemy as being on the run on both fronts." *(New York Times*, 17 October 1973)
95. Yediot Aharanot, Tel Aviv, 26 July 1973
96. The best account is still the first to be published, by a team of journalists from the *Sunday Times* who collaborated in writing *Insight on the Middle East War*, published by Andre Deutsch in February 1974
97. *Middle East International*, September 1973
98. For an analysis of Arab oil policy on the eve of the October War, see "Arab Oil: the Distribution of Power", by David Mitchell, in *Middle East International* (October 1973)

99. See *Israeli Mirror*, published fortnightly by *Middle East International*, in London.
100. For Ahad Ha'am's attitude to Zionism, see the essay by Hans Kohn, "Zion and the Jewish National Idea" in the Menorah Journal, Vol. XVI, 1958, reprinted in *Zionism Reconsidered*, Macmillan, New York 1970
101. Hans Kohn *op. cit.*
102. See Doreen Ingrams, *Palestine Papers 1917-1922*, Murray, London 1972, p. 146
103. Chaim Weizmann, President of the World Zionist Organisation and later first President of Israel
104. Doreen Ingrams, *op. cit.*, p. 58
105. Sir Herbert Samuel was speaking at the celebration of the King's birthday, 3 June 1921. See Desmond Stewart, *The Temple of Janus*, Doubleday, New York 1971, P. 283, and Doreen Ingrams, *op. cit.* p. 128
106. *Palestine: A Search for Truth*, Public Affairs Press, Washington 1970, p. 68
107. Nahum Sokolov, *History of Zionism*, quoted by Desmond Stewart, *op. cit.*
108. Christopher Sykes, *Crossroads to Israel*, London 1965, p. 24
109. For details see Alan Taylor, *Prelude to Israel* (an analysis of Zionist diplomacy 1897–1947) Darton, Longman & Todd, London 1961, pp. 102-107, as well as the *Memoirs* of Harry S. Truman and the *Forrestal Diaries* (James Vincent Forrestal was US Defence Secretary, 1947-49)
110. Amos Elon, *The Israelis: Founders & Sons*, Weidenfeld & Nicolson, London 1971, P. 22
111. Michael Ionides, *Divide and Lose*, Geoffrey Bles, London 1960, p. 79
112. Michael Bar-Zohar, *The Armed Prophet* (a biography of Ben Gurion), Arthur Barker, London 1967, p. 158
113. Entry for 12 June 1895. On the other hand, Herzl pictured in his later novel *Altneuland* a utopia where happy Arabs lived in harmony with the Jewish colonists.
114. See Chapter 3, p. 34
115. Michael Bar-Zohar, *op. cit.* p. 109
116. See G. Kirk, *The Middle East 1945–50*, Oxford University Press, London 1954; and M. Beigin, *The Revolt*, New York 1951
117. Yossef Weitz, *My Diary and Letter to the Children*, Massada Publishers, in five volumes, Tel Aviv 1965
118. UN Document A/648, pp. 14-18
119. Folke Bernadotte, *To Jerusalem*, Hodder & Stoughton, London 1951, p. 200
120. One dunam equals approximately a quarter of an acre
121. Hans Kohn, *op. cit.*, p. 206
122. "Cry the Beloved Country", *Ma'ariv* (Tel Aviv), 25 December 1953, reprinted in *Middle East International*, December 1973

123. At Deir Yassin on 9 April 1948, 254 Palestinian villagers, including many women and children, were massacred by the *Irgun* acting in collaboration with the Haganah, the embryonic Israeli army
124. At Kafr Qasim, on the eve of the Sinai campaign in October 1956, 49 Palestinian villagers who were Israeli citizens were shot in cold blood by Israeli border guards enforcing a curfew of which the villagers had been given no previous warning. See Walter Schwartz, *The Arabs in Israel*, Faber & Faber, London 1958
125. Nathan Chofshi, *Jewish Newsletter*, New York, 9 February 1959
126. David Spanier writing in *The Times*, 15 January 1974
127. See William Holladay, *Is the Old Testament Zionist?*, Middle East Newsletter, June-July 1968, published by Americans for Justice in the Middle East
128. *The Times*, 7 October 1974
129. This objection will become much less substantial if reports that the Israelis have discovered oil near Ramallah in the Occupied West Bank are confirmed.
130. See Appendix A

INDEX

Abu Dhabi 159
Abu Haydar, Mrs Nancy Nolan 126
Adams, Michael [sections written under his name and important references to him] 2-16, 60-64, 76-109, 120-1, 142-64, 165-93, 210-13, 219-20
Africa 27, 154, 199
Ahad Ha'am 168-70, 173, 175, 180, 185, 189
Allon, Yigael 179
Amnesty International 102-3
Analysis 123
anti-Semitism 18-19, 40, 65-7, 97, 99-101, 131, 166-7, 189, 210
Antonius, George 225
Any Questions 116-18
Arab League 94-7, 217-18
Arafat, Yasser 123
Argov, Dr Shlomo 231-2

Balfour, Arthur 31-3, 36, 47-8, 169, 170
Balfour Declaration 9, 30-3, 57, 78-9, 169, 170-3, 194, 207
Banias 158
Bar-Lev line 142, 144, 149, 150
BBC 83, 86, 107, 109-23, 225, 226
" World Service 123
Begin, Menachem 179
Beirut 225, 231
Ben Gurion, David 177-8, 180, 181-4, 189, 238, 240
Berger, Elmer 185

Bergmann, Hugo 170
Bernadotte, Count Folke 26, 177, 179, 182-3
Bevin, Ernest 17, 22, 29, 40, 67
Biltmore Programme 178
Board of Deputies of British Jews 82
Brilliant, Moshe 85
Brogan, Patrick 130
Buber, Martin 185
Burnet, Alastair 78

Canterbury, Archbishop of 130, 138-9, 219-20
Catholic Church 132, 135-7
Church of England 129, 138-9
churches 124-39, 219-20
Churchill, Randolph and Winston 64
Churchill, Sir Winston 47, 171
Civiltà Cattolica 135-7
Conservative Party 105
Council for Christians and Jews 131
Council for the Advancement of Arab-British Understanding (CAABU) 12, 59-61, 81, 83, 104, 115, 116, 119, 121, 130, 137, 22, 226, 227, 228, 230-1
Crossman, Richard 37, 77
Curran, Sir Charles 118, 119, 120
Curzon, Lord 170-1

Daily Express 123
Daily Mail 108

249

Daily Mirror 107
Daily Telegraph 107-8, 123
Damascus 158
Dayan, Moshe 14-15, 45, 129-30, 142-4, 148, 178, 179, 189, 210, 212
Deir Yassin 25, 179, 189, 229-30
Deutscher, Isaac 185
Douglas-Home, Sir Alec 105-6
Dugdale, Blanche 36

Easterman, A.L. 23-4
Eastern Daily Press 228
Eban, Abba 110
Economist, The 78
Eden, Sir Anthony 21, 79-80
Egypt 79-81, 94, 109-10, 112, 142-64, 225, 226
Elazar, General David 148
Elkins, Michael 85, 107, 118-20
Eshkol, Levi 210, 212
Europa Year Book 62-3
Evening Standard 61-2, 77

Faulds, Andrew 45, 56
Feisal, King 158-64
Ferguson, Pamela 61-2
Financial Times 106
Fisk, Robert 232
Forrest, Al 131
Fox, Paul 110
Fried, Erich 227-8
Furlonge, Sir Geoffrey 133
future prospects 194-211

Galili, Yisrael 191
Gamasi, General Abdel-Ghani el- 149-51
Gaza, *see also* Occupied Territories 87, 88, 89, 90-91, 93, 94, 202, 208

Geneva Conventions 90, 102-4, 130, 219-20
Germany 166-7, 185, 188, 213
Golan Heights 86, 142, 144, 148-9, 224
Goldberg, Sidney 66-7
Goldman, Nahum 191
Granada Publishing 61-2
Griffiths, Will 41
Grimond, Jo 111
Gross, Walter 85,
Guardian 5-6, 60, 64, 77, 78-80, 85, 87, 90, 107, 108, 163, 210-225

Ha'aretz 230
Haifa 181
Hammami, Said 229
Heath, Edward 70, 72
Herzl, Theodor 173, 177
hijacking of aircraft 16, 94
Hirst, David 163
Histadrut 38
Hodgkin, E.C. 98-101
Holland 159
Howard, Anthony 77
Hussein, King 24

immigration of Jews to Palestine 20, 22, 34, 38, 240
Ingrams, Doreen 64
Irgun Zvai Leumi 179
Isaacs, Anthony 121
Israeli League for Human and Civil Rights 104, 191
ITV 110-12, 116, 122

Jabotinsky, Vladimir 178, 189
Jacobs, David 116-18, 226
Janner, Lord 82
Jenkin, Patrick 72
Jerusalem 11, 26, 33, 78, 86-94, 125-7, 132-9, 207, 208

Index

Jerusalem Committee 102
Jewish Agency 35, 184
Jewish Chronicle 45, 61, 65-6, 68-9, 82, 227-8
Jewish National Fund 70-2, 82, 184, 223, 224, 233-4
Jewish Observer 44-5, 90-92
Johnson, Paul 77, 97
Johnson, President 163
Jordan 16, 24, 78, 203

Kafr Qasim 189
Kimche, John 77
Knightley, Philip 103
Kuneitra 224-5
Kuwait 158, 159

Labour Friends of Israel 38, 43, 66-7
Labour Middle East Council 49-50, 56, 59
Labour Party (Britain) 18, 26-8, 29-30, 33-45, 49-53, 56, 178
Land Requisition Law 1953 186
Laski, Harold 40
Lebanon 231-2
Lever, Harold 17
Liberal Party 38
Libya 159, 226
Lloyd George, David 35, 57, 79, 169, 170

Ma'ariv 187, 224
MacDonald, Ramsay 35-6
Macgregor, Alan 103
Magee, Bryan 121-2
Magnes, Dr Judah 172-3, 175, 185
Mandate over Palestine 32-41, 46-9
Mansfield, Peter 232
Marsden, Eric 107
Martin, Kingsley 40, 77

Mayhew, Christopher [sections written under his name and important references to him] 17-28, 29-57, 58-60, 64-75, 97, 109- 23, 153, 221, 223
McKenzie, Fergus 226
media 76-123, 217-18, 221-34
Mehdi, Mohammed 226
Meir, Golda 26-7, 45, 89, 106, 129, 144, 148, 152, 163, 190, 226
Mellish, Robert 51
Middle East International 68
Mikardo, Ian 29-30
Miller, Otto 160-1
Morris, Claud 68
Muir, Jim 225

Nasser, President 109-10, 157, 206
National Association for Mental Health (MIND) 67, 69
Nazism 118, 166-7, 173, 180, 185, 188, 191, 213, 238
Nebi Samwil 134-5
New Statesman 77
Niesewand, Peter 225
Nixon, President 158-60, 163-4, 169
Nordau, Max 173
Norris, James 113-15
nuclear weapons 198
Nutting, Anthony 10

Observer 85, 106, 107
Occupied Territories 10-11, 14, 84-94, 98, 101-4, 124-6, 129-39, 190, 202-4, 206-7, 219-20, 221-6
October War (1973) 2-3, 50-1, 89, 107-8, 115-16, 139, 142-64, 197, 199, 201
Ofner, Francis 85
oil producers' actions, 1973 158-64

Old Testament 194-5, 112-13, 239-40
OPEC 162

Pachachi, Nadim 162
Palestinian petitions and protests 46-9
Palestinian prisoners 84, 88-9, 102, 223
Panorama 110, 122
Paole Zion 29-30, 38, 43
parliamentary debates and motions 48-9, 56, 214-16, 233
Parliamentary Labour Party 17-18, 40-3, 45, 51, 65, 111
Passfield, Lord (Sidney Webb) 33-5
Passfield White Paper 34-5
Pilger, John 106, 122
pilgrimages 124-5
PLO 229, 231-2
Prittie, Terence 77
Private Eye 106
punitive actions in Occupied Territories 92-3, 98, 129-31, 186, 188-9, 219- 20, 223-4

Qibya 189
Quakers 131

Ramallah 183
Red Cross, International Committee of the (ICRC) 102-4
Reddaway, John 222, 227, 230-1
refugees (Palestinian) 10, 13, 24-8, 39, 86, 95, 124-7, 137, 174-90, 203-4, 207-9
Rodgers, William 71
Rodinson, Maxime 63-4
Rogers, William 236
Roosevelt, President F.D. 174
Rose, Jacqueline 237-40

Rose, John 237-40
Russell, Bertrand 104

Sadat, President 153, 157, 158, 161, 163
Samuel, Sir Herbert 47, 171
Saqqaf, Omar 159-60
Saudi Arabia 158-64
Sayigh, Dr Anis 231
Schwartz, Walter 107
Scott, C.P. 78-9
Scott, Robin 121
Seltzer, Michael 185
settlements in Occupied Territories 70-1, 107, 133, 135-6
Shahak, Dr Israel 104, 185, 191
Sharett, Moshe 177, 181
Sharon, Ariel 146, 188-9
Shiels, Sir Drummond 33-4
Shinwell, Lord (Emmanuel) 82, 99-100
Sieff, Sir Marcus 82
Silkin, John 111
Silver, Eric 77, 107, 225, 226
Silverman, Sydney 22
Sinai 94, 144, 151, 162
Six-Day War (1967) 10-15, 59, 81, 85, 126, 145, 146, 210-13
Smilansky, Moshe 186
Snow, Julian 99, 101
Sokolov, Nahum 173
South Africa 52-3, 199
Spanier, David 77
Standard Oil 160-1
Stern Gang 180
Stone, I.F. 185
Strachey, John 37
Suez Canal 81, 94, 142, 150, 153, 154
Suez War, 1956 10, 26, 79-80
Sunday Mirror 221-2
Sunday Telegraph 64, 107-8

Sunday Times, The 86, 93, 103-4, 106, 129, 232
Syria 84, 86, 142-9, 157-8, 161, 203, 225

Talmon, Jacob 191-2
terrorism 16, 21, 94, 106, 189, 190, 231
Times, The 59, 77, 85, 94-7, 99-101, 104, 107, 130-1, 138, 192, 217-18, 222, 230, 232, 233
Toynbee, Arnold 105, 109, 133
Tribune 106
Truman, President Harry S. 20, 169, 174
Tucker, Shelby 235-40

Unit 101 188-9
United Nations 24-6, 44, 52, 82, 88, 92, 94, 95, 103, 123-4, 132, 153-4, 157, 174, 176, 181-5, 189, 197, 199, 202, 204, 207, 236
Universal Declaration of Human Rights 130
UNRWA (United Nations Relief and Works Agency) 222
USA 20, 128, 133, 138, 148, 153-5, 159- 64, 174-5, 197, 200, 205, 236
USSR 148, 165-6, 197

Vatican 135
Voluntary Service Overseas (VSO) 60-1

Wailing Wall riots, 1929 33
Wallich, Walter 120
Weitz, Yossef 180-5
Weizmann, Chaim 31, 32, 35, 39, 78-9, 170, 173, 176, 178, 180, 195, 239
West Bank, *see also* Occupied Territories 98, 202, 208
Wilson, Harold 28, 29, 97
Woolfson, Marion 73-5, 221-34
World at One, The 113-16, 123
World Council of Churches 127-9, 131
World Jewish Congress 23-4, 191
World Zionist Congress 54-5, 172

Yalin-Mor, Natan 190-1

Zionist Federation 82, 226, 228, 230